FAITH AND ETHICS

FAITH AND ETHICS

RECENT ROMAN CATHOLICISM

Vincent MacNamara

GILL AND MACMILLAN
Dublin
GEORGETOWN UNIVERSITY PRESS
Washington, D.C.

Published in Ireland by
Gill and Macmillan Ltd
Goldenbridge
Dublin 8
with associated companies in
Auckland, Dallas, Delhi, Hong Kong,
Johannesburg, Lagos, London, Manzini,
Melbourne, Nairobi, New York, Singapore,
Tokyo, Washington

©Vincent MacNamara 1985

7171 1403 1

Print orgination in Ireland by Keywrite Ltd
Printed in Great Britain by
Biddles Ltd. Guildford and King's Lynn

First published in the United States of America in 1985 by Georgetown
University Press, Georgetown University, Intercultural Center, Room
III, Washington, D.C. 20057.
ISBN 0-87840-414-7

Library of Congress Cataloging in Publication Data

MacNamara, Vincent.
　Faith and Ethics.

　1. Christian ethics — History — 20th century.
　2. Catholic Church — Doctrines — History — 20th century.
　I. Title.
　BJ1231.M33 1985　　241'.042'09　　85-5539
　ISBN 0-87840-414-7 (Georgetown University Press, paperback)
　ISBN 0-87840-426-4 (Georgetown University Press, hardcover)

Contents

Introduction

The annual meeting of French-speaking Roman Catholic moralists chose as the theme of its 1969 meeting 'The Specificity of Christian Morality'. The moralists had met annually for several years and had discussed a variety of topics. They chose this theme, they said, because they found that behind the particular topics there lurked a general question. That was the question of the bearing of faith on ethics. The findings of that conference were published under the intriguing title, 'Christian Ethics in Search of its Identity'.[1] This book is about the history of that search over a forty-year period — roughly from 1940 to 1980.

The need for such a conference is an indication of the confusion in which Roman Catholic morality has found itself. For the past three or four decades there has been questioning of many traditional positions. Behind the questions and partly the cause of them has been a deeper questioning. That concerns what the French rightly referred to as the identity of Christian ethics. By that they mean the significance of referring to ethics as Christian. In what sense is it to be considered Christian? What is the significance to be given to the words 'Christian', 'theological'/'theology' in the expressions 'Christian ethics', 'theological ethics', 'moral theology'?[2]

The question is far from being of purely speculative interest. It concerns the source, method and justification of moral judgments in the Christian community. One has only to advert to the broad range of issues that are matters of controversy at the present time — life, abortion, marriage, justice, revolution, work, experimentation, sterilisation — to see that questions of method immediately arise. How is the indissolubility of marriage arrived at in Christian ethics? What is the source of the

1

prohibition on taking life? What is the basis of Catholic social teaching? What is one to make of frequent references to the immutable laws of God? Is the appeal to the biblical themes in favour of liberation justified? What value is to be attached to the expression 'in the light of revelation' which plays some part in many official church statements?

I am not much concerned in this book with official church statements. But the crucial nature of our question can be seen from a brief look at some recent statements. The teaching of *Populorum Progressio* (1967) that the goods of the earth are for the benefit of all seems to rest on Genesis.[3] *Laborem Exercens* (1981) regards the 'revealed word of God' as the main source of its teaching on work.[4] The teaching of *Humanae Vitae* (1968) is 'founded on the natural law as illuminated and enriched by divine Revelation'.[5] The *Declaration on Procured Abortion* (1974) 'teaches moral principles in the light of faith' by citing a great variety of biblical texts.[6] The *Declaration on Certain Questions Concerning Sexual Ethics* (1975) refers to a revealed positive law and depends heavily on Scripture.[7] So also does *Familiaris Consortio* (1981).[8] The statement of the Irish bishops *Conscience and Authority* (1980) refers to the 'specific commandments of God'; the 'specific demands' of Christ and the specific actions which Jesus 'listed' as sinful.[9] The debate among the theologians in the period under review — a debate which still rages — is in effect about the legitimacy of the method adopted in such documents.

Many Roman Catholic philosophers have in recent years declared themselves puzzled and disappointed by the lack of intellectual rigour in moral theology — 'rich mines of fallacious argument and unexamined assumptions'.[10] The same criticism is heard outside of Roman Catholicism about Christian ethics in general — 'a relative absence of careful definition, clear statement, or cogent and rigorous argument'.[11] There are those who think that the period under review, in which a major renewal of moral theology was proclaimed by the theologians and by Vatican II, has only resulted in greater intellectual confusion.

Certainly there has been more movement in the last few decades in moral theology than for centuries before that. This was due especially to the impetus given to theological writing by what was called the renewal movement of the fifties and sixties. (The term is debatable, of course: the question is what is to count as renewal). But I begin a little further back — with neo-

Scholasticism. There are two reasons for this. First, it was the background to the renewal movement and one must understand it in order to see why a renewal was thought necessary. Second, its influence is still felt: there are authors today who still do morality in the neo-Scholastic mode. Neo-Scholasticism was a very settled system in which there were clear and unquestioned ideas about the meaning and norm of morality, the source of moral obligation and the relations between morality and God. It was predominantly a natural law morality and not the most distinguished account of natural law. In the forties and fifties many theologians began to question this conception of morality. I take 1940 as my date of departure. There is nothing very special about the date. But it is a useful starting-point. It is still within a strong neo-Scholastic tradition but a date at which the beginnings of renewal were being felt.[12]

The desire for renewal grew out of a dissatisfaction with what passed in neo-Scholasticism for Christian morality. The conviction of its authors was that there is more to Christian morality than was being offered by neo-Scholastic natural law. They set out to 'Christianise' morality, to insist on its specifically Christian character. That movement set off reverberations from which Roman Catholicism has not yet recovered — if by recovery is meant a return to a clear and settled system. The movement for renewal proved to be a more difficult undertaking than had been anticipated. Many authors adopted the new approach with enthusiasm but soon found that there were grave methodological problems. The result was a reaction in the late sixties and early seventies in which several authors — among them many of the best-known theologians and some who had been advocates of the renewal — began to drift from the movement. Their difficulties with the renewal's rather naïve appeal to the Bible, coupled with a desire to meet the new wave of secularisation and to dialogue with their non-Christian fellow-countrymen, led them to propose what they call an autonomous ethic within Christianity. The notion of the autonomy of morality vis-a-vis religion is a difficult one and its supporters have not found it easy to state their thesis. As we shall see, there are two strands to the thesis which correspond to two different but related concerns. One stresses that we should not expect to receive our moral norms from 'outside of ourselves' — from revelation — but should realise that we are meant by God to

3

discover them ourselves. The other maintains that when the Christian judges or discerns he or she does not arrive at any different content of morality from what is discovered by the humanist.

This movement for autonomy has, in turn, been bitterly countered in recent years by theologians who believe that the truth about Christian morality is found in the renewal proposals. Their crusade is to preserve the specific character of Christian ethics, to maintain that Christian faith has a moral content that is special to it. Their school is referred to by continentals as the *Glaubensethik* or faith-ethic. The seventies saw a sharp debate between these two parties. The debate has crystallised around the question of the specificity of Christian ethics. This in itself may not appear to be a matter of vital importance for Christianity. What is important is that a theologian's position on this debate involves and reveals his stance on method and sources in Christian ethics. It is not just a question for the theologian. It must make any Christian wonder about our everyday references to Christian values, Christian attitudes, a Christian society and about such common expressions as 'A Christian should/should not ...'

I am not attempting here a constructive statement about the nature of Christian ethics, although I believe that any such statement must take account of the ground covered here, and theologians would do well to learn from the experience of the authors discussed here. I am attempting to plot and evaluate a piece of theological history, to uncover sources of confusion, to identify questions, to clarify definitions. What interests me about the debate is that it has set in sharp relief some questions and problems on which any constructive approach to Christian ethics must take a position. How are theologians to approach any moral question? Are they, as Christians, to approach it differently from the philosopher? Are they to appeal to the Bible as an authoritative source of moral knowledge? Are they to derive moral truths from truths of faith: if so, can they demonstrate the logic of the argument? Can they, in effect, ignore the Bible and Christian faith in moral matters: can morality stand on its own legs? Can they expect from Christianity only an interpretation of the human reality of morality: is there any reason for thinking that there is a Christian morality any more than a Christian logic?

4

I have confined myself to the recent history of Roman Catholic morality. But the main issues discussed here are a problem for all the churches. There have been considerable convergences between Roman Catholic and Protestant theology in recent times, so there will be borrwing from and comparison with that tradition in an attempt to resolve the issues. Since it is important to see the question of Christian faith and ethics as an instance of the wider philosophical question of the relationship between religion and morality, an attempt will also be made to set it in that wider framework and to consider how the philosophical community has discussed the problems inherent in the notion of a religious ethic. The Christian must keep his eye on the philosophical ethic because the question of a Christian ethic contains an implied term of comparison. As the question has arisen and been debated by Roman Catholics in Europe and on the Anglo-American scene, that term of comparison has, naturally, not been the ethics of other world-religions but the ethics of the humanist, the citizen who does not subscribe to any religion. In fact, the possibility of communication or dialogue with such fellow-citizens has been the background to the debate in continental Europe.

PART I

The History:
Renewal and Reaction

1

From Neo-Scholasticism to Renewal

Section 1
THE NEO-SCHOLASTIC BACKGROUND

Neo-Scholasticism is the name given to the late nineteenth- and early twentieth-century movement in theology which took its inspiration from medieval scholasticism. It was a movement which resulted in a new interest in theology generally and which produced a whole crop of manuals of moral theology. These manuals purported to give a systematic account of Christian morality. They were of almost standard form and thought. They borrowed heavily from one another and showed only minor differences of opinion. They were enormously influential and provided Roman Catholicism with a strong body of moral teaching which few dared to question. They were used world-wide in the training of priests and were referred to by the central government of the church in its statements. They were incorporated into simple catechisms for the faithful.[1]

The movement of neo-Scholasticism was meant to be a new beginning. It had been encouraged by Pope Leo XIII to look especially to Aquinas and to take him as its model.[2] It did indeed look to him and references to him are liberally scattered through the manuals. But the moral manuals which it produced are basically in continuity with the morality of the earlier centuries and it could be argued that they missed the best of what Aquinas had to offer. They do treat morality, however, with a great air of security and certainty. They reflect a confident understanding of the identity of Christian morality. Since it was just this understanding which was found wanting by the movement of renewal and which sparked off efforts to find a new identity for Christian

9

morality, it is important for us to sketch in its main features.

What strikes one immediately about almost all the manuals is that the whole treatment of morality is dominated by a short introductory section on the last end of the human person. God, the neo-Scholastic said, created us for a purpose — the purpose of union with him in heaven. Our business on earth is to achieve that purpose. Morality falls into place as the way or the means to that end. So Noldin tells us that moral theology is the science which enquires what must be done by us so that we are directed to our last end.[3] Hürth-Abellan defines moral theology as the science about deliberate human acts in so far as they relate to the last supernatural end which is to be obtained by these acts.[4] Prümmer says that its principal purpose is to direct human acts to the last end, that is to the meriting of eternal life.[5]

That already tells us much. Morality is closely related to God. The whole enterprise derives from his purpose to offer us union with himself. It is not understood apart from that purpose. It is a means to an end. So the first rule or criterion of the moral goodness of an act for the neo-Scholastic will be that it leads to the last end.[6] Further, he clearly states that moral theology has to do only with what is necessary for the acquiring of the last end.[7] There were counsels of perfection, it was agreed. They were means by which one more securely acquired eternal life. They were admirable. But they were not regarded as strictly part of moral theology.[8] They belonged to an area which the authors called ascetical theology, regarded as dealing with the science of Christian perfection whereas morality was defined in terms of what was essential to remaining in the state of grace and reaching eternal life.

It is not surprising that the preferred way of referring to morality was in terms of the law of God. All of the authors have a central treatise on law. They begin by detailing the general features of law. They apply to morality all the legal language of the establishment of law, its promulgation, its abrogation, dispensation from it, etc. All of them cite Aquinas's celebrated definition that law is a dictate of practical reason which is made by one who has charge of a community for the common good and promulgated.[9] This becomes the key concept for the understanding of morality. Morality is the law of God, his eternal law.[10] Eternal law is truly a law *(lex proprie dicta)*, i.e. it fulfils all the conditions of the definition of law — it is a directive of the reason of God, who has charge of the world community, made by him for the common good and promulgated.[11]

It would be hard to overestimate the effect which this emphasis on law had on the understanding of Christian morality. The God who was presented by it was apart from human beings. His will was supreme. Morality resulted from his purposes and decrees. Prümmer puts it:

> By virtue of his supreme authority God prescribed for us the way by which we can reach him and our own beatitude. That way is made known to us by the laws made by Him.... Whence it follows that we cannot reach our beatitude except by obeying just laws, both divine and human.[12]

Two other ideas complete this understanding of morality. One is that of merit-reward. God the supreme legislator has it in his power to grant eternal life to us: we can merit this by our moral life; it is given as a reward for good living.[13] The other is that of sanction. According to the neo-Scholastic, God — conceived exactly in the image of a human legislator — can and should attach a sanction to immorality, i.e. to the failure of his subjects to obey his laws. So the manual recommends a sanction for immorality, regards it as necessary, discusses just how much of a sanction God owes it to his dignity to apply, and points out the appropriateness of the sanction of eternal damnation for one who has dared to disobey the law of God.[14]

We still have to come to grips with some of the key elements of neo-Scholastic morality. If morality is characterised as a means given by God to us in order that we might acquire eternal life, we still have to ask such questions as: what is the norm of morality; what are the sources of moral knowledge; is the morality of the Christian thought to be different from that of the non-Christian; what is the source of moral obligation? The neo-Scholastic answer to the question about the norm of morality is that there is a threefold norm. The morally good can be considered as what leads us to our last end or what is in accordance with the eternal law or what is in accordance with right reason: these are regarded as three different ways of looking at the same thing.[15] The eternal law has two parts. There is the positive divine law of the Old and New Testaments — the commands and prohibitions promulgated by Moses and by Jesus — which is found in the Bible. And there is the natural law. Together they

11

constitute the whole of morality.[16] God has freely given the decrees of the divine positive law for two reasons. First, because they repeat the natural law and so resolve the difficulty which we sometimes have in determining the natural law. Second, because we have been given a new supernatural end and it was fitting that God should give new commands in addition to those of the natural law.[17]

The human person is seen, therefore, as existing in two orders, that of creation and that of salvation. There are two distinguishable strata in his or her life, the natural and the supernatural. The neo-Scholastic distinguishes them sharply. By the natural order (nature, natural powers) he means what pertains to us as rational animal.[18] This is the area of natural law. Natural law contains what can be discovered about the conduct appropriate to the rational animal by our unaided reason.[19] This, we are told, would have been sufficient for our guidance if we had not been given a supernatural end.[20] Since we have been given such, it was fitting that God should issue the divine positive law. But the two orders remain distinguishable: the new law does not in any way destroy or interpenetrate the natural order of morality: it adds to it.[21] There are consequently two sources of morality — reason and revelation, natural law and scripture. We have, then, agreement about the important concepts of 'reason', 'rational', 'human nature', 'supernatural'.

If there were a specifically Christian or supernatural element of morality, then the divine positive law of the Bible would obviously be the source of it. But the authors do not claim any new moral content that goes beyond the natural law. Noldin says that the new law is supernatural because it comes from God who is the author of the supernatural order, is given to us who have been called to a supernatural order, is observed by supernatural powers and leads to a supernatural last end.[22] The only new content refers to obligations to receive the sacraments and to believe the truths of faith: he identifies the moral content with natural law. Most of the authors agree.[23] They allow that the new law contains counsels and proposes a greater perfection. But these are a matter of personal choice, do not oblige one by virtue of divine will and, as we saw, do not properly belong to moral theology.[24] One has a clear impression that the authors are not greatly convinced about the moral content of the divine positive law. When they do refer to the bible it is almost invariably to cite individual texts as corroborative proof of a position arrived at through natural law or taught by the magisterium of the church.

It was axiomatic for the neo-Scholastics that God is necessary to morality: many of them include a short section on the point in their works. They were particularly anxious to refute any suggestion that there could be such a thing as an autonomous morality and had an obsession with Kant and with what they called lay morality.[25] But in what sense did they regard God as necessary to morality? It was primarily as source of moral obligation. In the medieval scholastic tradition there had been a long debate reaching its climax in the debate between Vasquez and Suarez on whether law is an act of reason or an act of will. And there was no little controversy in the tradition on whether the intervention of God was required for moral obligation or whether reason alone was sufficient.[26] For almost all of the neo-Scholastics the answer to these questions is quite clear. Will was regarded as the primary element in law and without the intervention of God there would be no moral obligation. Noldin says:

> One must distinguish the principle of obligation from the norm of morality. It is one thing to ask why a human act is morally good or bad and another to enquire why a human act is morally necessary or why there is an obligation to perform it or omit it.[27]

But did they regard the distinction of good and evil as dependent on God? Does God command what is good or is the good what God commands? When they formally consider the matter they are clear that God commands what is independently good.[28] Yet one senses hesitation and confusion. This appears when they discuss the possibility of dispensation from the divine positive and natural laws. Most agree that God can dispense from the divine positive law and that Jesus can dispense from the new law.[29] The argument — that the legislator can dispense from his own law — emphasises the conception of morality as law of God. However, while they state the principle, they are not very forthcoming about giving examples. About dispensation from the natural law they are not so sure. The general opinion is that God cannot give a dispensation properly speaking. But, in effect, they allow that he can. They borrow an argument from Aquinas that since God is the lord of all life, all property and all bonds, he can

13

so change the order of things that in a particular instance the killing of the innocent, theft, the breaking of marriage bonds and extra-marital intercourse are not unlawful.[30] Some justify this on the grounds that there is sometimes a greater good involved.[31] If there is, it is hard to see why one would require a dispensation. If there is not, if God can so overturn the order of reality, it is hard to see how one can seriously maintain an order of morality independent of God.[32]

This, then, is the background to the renewal which we are to consider. This is the understanding of Christian morality which was in possession. The key points are the following. Morality arises from the precept laid on us by God to reach our last end. Morality strictly has to do with what is necessary to reach the end. The last end is given by God to us as a reward for good living. The content of morality is discovered by reason, unaided by revelation, reflecting on the nature of the rational animal. But it is confirmed by the divine positive law. Moral obligation arises not from the inherent rightness of an action but from the command of God. It was its position on these key issues which gave a particular shape or identity to neo-Scholastic morality. Our examination of the understanding of the identity of Christian morality in Roman Catholicism since the neo-Scholastic period will centre around the changing interpretation of these key issues.

Section 2

RENEWAL

The manual tradition continued through the forties and fifties. New editions of long-accepted textbooks appeared. But side by side with them, there emerged in Roman Catholicism a strong current of dissatisfaction with the morality of the manual and an urgent call for a renewal of moral theology. This was to throw moral theology into a state of excitement and confusion which would very soon leave piles of manuals to gather dust on the shelves of seminary libraries. It produced in the next thirty years a spate of articles and books which sharply criticised the understanding of morality proposed by the manual and enshrined in the popular catechisms of Roman Catholicism.

14

The central criticism was that what had been proposed as moral theology or Christian ethics was merely philosophical ethics or moral philosophy. It failed, so the criticism went, to present the distinctive character of the Christian vocation. It did not portray the supernatural character of that vocation. It did not stress that our destiny is to share the gift of life with God. It had none of the spirit of early Christianity. It lacked the dynamism and inspiration that one should expect from Christianity. It was not centred on Christ. The distinctive New Testament command of *agape* was not central to it. It was negative and minimalist.[33] It was concerned with, as some called it, the science of sin rather than with the riches of Christian life.[34] The basic reason for all of these errors, it was said, was that it sought its inspiration and method in the wrong sources — in philosophy and natural law ethics.[35]

The assumption in all of this was that religion should make a difference to morality, that it should give it a different content from ethics. So it was a primary tenet of the renewal movement that morality, if it is to be Christian, must be dependent on or derived from revelation. We are told by many of the authors that moral theology must be a purely theological science and not a mixture of philosophy, psychology and jurisprudence;[36] that it is unthinkable without dogma to which it is absolutely bound; that its point of departure and its source of knowledge must be the Bible.[37] This would reveal its true nature, its distinctiveness over against natural morality, its inner dynamism.[38] Christian morality, it was said, is in the order of redemption, the gifts of which cannot be measured on the basis of human nature.[39]

Above all else, it was said, morality must become biblical through and through. It must concentrate on the key themes of the Bible and not just be satisfied with random quotations to bolster positions arrived at philosophically. It must recognise that the reality of the kingdom creates new values; that the kerygma contains moral doctrine — a paschal morality — which is necessarily bound to the mystery of Christ; that the Bible shows us what our life is like when it is based on the mystery of Christ and the salvation brought in Christ;[40] that it gives us not only general moral bearings but guiding principles and even definite and concrete norms.[41] Moralists were even warned that their theological systematisation must be done with circumspection, because the mystery of God and of his dealings

15

with us defies any scientific and synthetical methods.[42] Within two or three decades many Roman Catholic theologians would be saying the exact opposite to all of this, among them many who at this time were enthusiastic advocates of a biblical morality. But that must wait: it is the story of the period of theology covered by this work.

The dependence of morality on revelation and the need to have recourse to the Bible was, of course, something that had always been a feature of the Protestant churches. It was something that was not unknown in Roman Catholicism. I mentioned the movement for a biblical and kerygmatic theology in early nineteenth-century Germany. It is interesting to note that many of the themes that were to be a feature of this twentieth-century renewal had already been canvassed — a morality of Christian perfection, a morality founded on the sacraments, a morality of charity, a morality of the kingdom.[43] But we saw that its influence was confined and, anyway, it suffered its own decline in the latter half of the century. We saw, too, that the manual had recourse to the Bible but that it was not as a source of its morality, rather as a corroborative proof for positions already arrived at philosophically. What was now being proposed — and what in fact took place — was so antithetical to the manual tradition that it could be said with truth that within a few years the manuals were rendered entirely irrelevant.[44]

The renewal in favour of a biblically-orientated moral theology did not happen out of the blue. For some years there had been taking place in the Roman Catholic church a general renewal of interest in biblical studies. The remote inspiration of this was probably the encyclical *Providentissimus Deus* of Leo XIII (1893) which said that scripture should be 'the soul of theology'. It received a very powerful boost from the encyclical *Divino Afflante Spiritu* of Pius XII (1943). But its vigour was especially due to the work of outstanding scripture scholars like M.J. Lagrange and to the foundation of the biblical school at Jerusalem. The influence on moral theology was enormous. Many works of high quality appeared on the general subject of biblical morality as well as many monographs on individual topics. They were mostly the work of biblical scholars but were quickly taken over by the moralists. One thinks especially of the work of Spicq, Schnackenburg and Lyonnet.[45] This movement reached its climax in the recommendation of the Second

Vatican Council about the study of theology in general and of moral theology in particular:

> Sacred theology rests on the written word of God, together with sacred tradition as its primary and perpetual foundation ... the study of the sacred page is, as it were, the soul of sacred theology.[46]

> Dogmatic theology should be so arranged that biblical themes are presented first. ... Special attention needs to be given to the development of moral theology. Its scientific exposition should be more thoroughly nourished by scriptural teaching. It should show the nobility of the Christian vocation of the faithful and their obligation to bring forth fruit in charity for the life of the world.[27]

Already it can be seen that what was happening in this period was a revolution in the structure and method of moral theology as the neo-Scholastic conceived it. In this chapter I want to consider the first wave of this renewal movement, roughly up to the time of Vatican II and its immediate aftermath. My interest is not in giving a survey of the literature, still less in covering all the authors of the period. I am interested in the change of approach and method, in the new understanding of the identity of Christian ethics which emerged. So I choose key themes and representative or influential authors. In particular, I want to examine how the proposal to base morality on faith or revelation fared and whether it realised its promises and expectations. I shall have in mind especially how the authors are seen to understand such key issues as the source of moral knowledge, the norm of goodness, the justification of moral positions and the foundation of moral obligation. It is important to point out that what was produced in this period does not represent the mature or developed thought of some of our authors. It will be part of the point of this work to show that some of them found that the proposal to base morality on revelation, which they so enthusiastically endorsed in the beginning, was unwise or unworkable. The history which we will survey is, in part, the personal odyssey of some of these authors. Indeed, even what is given later in this book as their developed thought may not be their final position. Happily, many are still pursuing the quest of Christian morality. It is not out of place, I think, to acknowledge here how much present-day Roman Catholic moral theology owes to some of these men — one thinks particularly of Fuchs and Häring — especially as, with the benefit of hindsight, I take issue with some of their views.

In the forties and fifties much of the discussion was about the possibility of finding one basic principle on which the whole structure of morality could be built.[48] This would be something which would replace the natural law as the dominant thought-pattern and which would be entirely theological in character. I shall consider three such proposals for a central principle of morality. They are (i) that Christian morality should be understood as the morality which corresponds to the new life of grace in Christ, (ii) that Christian morality should be organised around charity as its primary principle, (iii) that Christian morality should be understood as imitation of Christ. All of them are biblical themes. But it is instructive to look also at the more direct appeal to the biblical text as justification of moral positions: that shall be a fourth consideration for us. In fact, one often finds in this period that while an author has one central strategy, e.g. the new life of grace, he also uses other considerations, e.g. the imitation of Christ. One sometimes wonders whether his central strategy is meant to have the rigour of a principle, i.e. something from which all moral conclusions are to be derived or on which they all depend or against which they are all to be measured, or whether it is better characterised as a central idea or theme which, in a general way, informs his whole approach to morality. I have chosen three approaches. There were others, e.g. the idea of a morality based on the notion of the Mystical Body, a morality based on the kingdom, a morality starting from sacramental life, the adoption of Aquinas's teaching on the new law.[49] They seem to me to have been less important than the three mentioned above and to have been, in the end, largely dependent on them.

(i) *The Morality of the New Life of Grace in Christ*
Christian morality, it was proposed, should be based on the new life of grace. This view depended on the accepted interpretation of grace as an entitative elevation of the soul and its faculties. This was seen as giving the human being a new *esse,* a new ontology which was the basis of and which demanded a new kind of moral life. If Christian morality was to be genuine, it was

18

said, moral theology must take over from systematic theology an understanding of this new *esse,* this supernatural essence — just as ethics must take over a knowledge of human nature from metaphysics — and on the basis of it elaborate a new morality for Christians.[50]

This approach to morality, it should be remembered, was proposed out of a background which made a sharp distinction between God's creation and his redemption, between the orders of nature and of grace and between the baptised and the unbaptised. At baptism, it was said, a Christian receives sanctifying grace and this gives him or her a whole new way of being. A classic source of Roman Catholic theology put it like this: Sanctifying grace is a reality distinct from God, created, infused and inhering in the soul. It is a share in the divine nature. It is a quality which modifies the soul intrinsically. It is like a new nature, elevating the soul intrinsically to a new order which is absolutely above that of the creature, rendering the soul apt for supernatural activity. It is completed by the infused virtues which are the immediate principle of supernatural acts.[51]

For the moralists the anchor principle of their theory was the axiom, *Agere sequitur esse:* natural life, they said, demands natural morality, supernatural life must demand supernatural morality, which must be radically different from the natural. So Thils tells us that we should bring about in our actions the moral demands of the ontological being which constitutes our state as Christians, that Christian morality must be founded on the christification realised in us by justification, that there is a *vie morale christique* which corresponds to the supernatural status which has Christ as its centre, that we must act like Christ, because we are ontologically identified with him.[52] Lottin says that the rule of Christian morality is our supernatural nature, just as in natural morality it is human nature.[53] Mausbach's position is that since the axiom *Agere sequitur esse* operates, a precise conception of Christian action can be had only when the new supernatural essence of the Christian is analysed.[54] The Christian's new ontic status, he says, is participation in the life of Christ, so his action ought to be a development of life in Christ: the only principle which can be accepted as fundamental to Christian morality is that which proposes the laws deriving from the new being in Christ.[55] So we are given a definition of moral theology as follows: it is the theological science of the laws

19

deriving from the new being in Christ.[56] As such, he says, it must have close links with dogmatic theology and its chief source must be the Bible, which gives with absolute clarity the fundamental ideas of morality.[57]

The early Fuchs says that grace is the norm of Christian man and that the new law is based on our supernatural *esse:* human behaviour derives from our natural being whereas Christian living derives from our (supernatural) 'being-in-Christ'.[58] The early Böckle also cites the axiom. Ethics and moral theology, he says, are different in essence. The principles of Christian moral conduct are grace and the infused virtues. The concern of ethics is that conduct correspond to reason: the goal of supernatural morality is the realisation of that which the Christian is by reason of his incorporation into Christ.[59] The early Häring, too, insists on the distinction of two orders and two moralities. He says that the morality appropriate to the supernatural order of grace totally transcends the knowledge of unaided reason and can be known only from the revealed law of God.[60] Since the human being is the image of God, says Delhaye, he must act like God: the image must be transferred from the ontological to the ethical plane; Christian moral imperatives are intrinsic to Christian life.[61] Gillon says that we are absolutely bound to distinguish 'revealed' morality — this refers to what he calls the theological order — and natural law.[62]

To say that Christian moral activity must be supernatural was not to say anything new. It had long been taught that a Christian's acts must be supernatural. This was related to the doctrine of merit. It was the accepted orthodoxy that one could merit the beatific vision. But this required some equivalence between one's actions and one's supernatural end — how otherwise could human action merit a supernatural end? The equivalence was provided by sanctifying grace, which elevated one's soul and its faculties and ensured that morally good actions which issued from these faculties were supernatural. Lottin gives a neat summary of this:

> There exists an equivalence between the human action and the divine recompense ... every act performed by a person in the state of grace which is not morally bad is meritorious *de condigno*.[63]

But this did not require a special supernatural content to moral action: what mattered was the supernaturalised faculty and the charity by which it directed action to God.

> This notion of charity, form of the virtues, leaves intact the particular character of the moral virtues: the philosopher can examine the nature of them and elaborate a moral doctrine.[64]

One could not experience the difference made to moral acts by being supernaturally 'elevated': what one experienced was one's natural powers and natural morality. But what mattered was that one knew that there was an entitative elevation of natural moral acts so that they became supernatural: one knew that they were essentially (but only essentially, not psychologically) changed.

Now a new element appeared.[65] What was new in the renewal movement was that it suggested that Christians should live a new, different, higher morality, based on their new life, pursuing moral duties, as Ermecks put it, which went far beyond any merely natural thought and which could not be understood by it.[66] New, different, by comparison with what? By comparison with the unbaptised person, who bore only the natural image of God, who had only reason to guide him, who could be expected to live only the natural law and not the 'inherently supernatural' elements of the Christian life.[67] So we are told that the ungraced person must try to bring about his natural personhood, his likeness to God, while the graced person must try to bring about his supernatural personhood, his likeness to Christ:[68] for the many millions who live outside the kingdom of God and its morality there is natural morality and natural perfection, while for the baptised there is the perfection of being a child of God.[69]

The axiom, *Agere sequitur esse* means, most obviously, that a being can act only according to the powers inherent in it. To erect it into a moral principle or to make it the basis of a moral theory is, as many decades of philosophy have argued, a very difficult and, some would say, an impossible logical move. The theologians do not even nod in the direction of such problems. But, even if it be granted that there is an acceptable sense in which the axiom can become a moral principle, it should be noted that, so far, it is a purely formal principle. It tells us only that the morality of the Christian must be related to his or her being but nothing about the content of such morality. The

21

crucial question is whether the authors can derive from it new or additional content for morality. By 'new' or 'additional' I mean something that could not be discovered by or would not be expected from one who had not received faith and baptism.

We find, in fact, that the theologians do not follow that line. They do not argue from the structure of the new life, as Ermecke had promised. What they do is appeal rather to the will of God or to the imitation of Christ as found in the Bible and tell us that these show us the kind of behaviour that is appropriate to the new life.[70] Even here they are not very happy. Mausbach tells us that revelation gives supernatural truths and norms: he mentions truths about our eternal destiny, about the consequences of original sin, about redemption and justification, about sacrifice and abnegation of self.[71] It is true that such truths are relevant to moral life. But they are only obliquely relevant to its content and much discussion is required before content can be squeezed from them. Fuchs tries to go further but says rather weakly that it can hardly be denied that the new law contains materially new precepts that are beyond the natural law.[72] But he gives no examples. Lottin tells us that Christianity reveals to us new duties of filial love and obedience to God our Father as against duties of submission to our Creator, new duties to respect ourselves as children of God as against duties to respect our dignity as persons, new duties to love others in supernatural brotherhood as against duties to love them in natural love.[73]

The authors tell us several times that Christianity gives a more complete knowledge of moral truth or that it gives to morality a new climate, stimulus and motivation.[74] But this is a long way from the radically different morality which they had proposed for Christianity. Already we can see emerging some of the questions that will occupy us in this book: does the specificity or newness of Christian morality refer to content or does it refer to climate, motivation or stimulus? We also see emerging the question of the definition of morality. Not only does this movement treat 'filial duties of love and obedience' as morality. It also includes without differentiation acts of justice, interior acts of charity towards God, prayer, the reception of the Eucharist, voluntary mortification as an identification with Christ in suffering, acts of faith, etc — indeed, everything which can be regarded as contributing to growth of life in Christ.[75] But can all of this be properly regarded as morality?

22

How does this theory deal with the question of the source of moral obligation? We saw that the neo-Scholastics had a problem about whether reason itself was a sufficient source of obligation or whether a further command of God was required. Several of the renewal authors make a rather vague appeal to the obligation to be assimilated to Christ: their position seems to be that if reason dictates that the 'natural' person should live according to the demands of his or her natural being, it dictates that the Christian person should live according to his or her Christian being.[76] But they also appeal to the will of God or of Christ and one is not sure what force is to be attached to that. Mausbach says that morality is to be understood as submission to the supreme binding will of God.[77] Fuchs refers to the new order of Christian morality as God's will for us: he says that there is some glimpse of God in all recognition of moral obligation and seems to regard this as essential to the nation of obligation.[78] Häring sees the morality of the new life as a summons from God, as obedience to the divine will as having its foundation in religion.[79] Gillon situates moral obligation in one's unconditional attachment to the person of Christ.[80] We are in the end left with some vagueness: one does not know just how significant the axiom *Agere sequitur esse* is or what force it has as a source of morality.

This movement, therefore, sets out from the conviction that the natural law morality of the neo-Scholastics is unworthy of Christianity and it seeks to provide a supernatural morality. It does introduce into morality a climate, spirit, stimulus and motivation that were lacking in the neo-Scholastics. But its formal structure does not seem to be able to yield new content. And even when it appeals to the will of God in Scripture or to the imitation of Christ it still does not offer substantial content. The surprising thing is that while this renewal theme sets out its thesis about the newness of Christian morality with a great flurry, it ends up by proposing very little new content. The very sparse description of the Christian moral life comes as an anti-climax after all the rhetoric about the new ontology and the morality which is said to correspond to it. What one finds is enthusiasm rather than cogency of argument. Thils's conclusion to his book conveys something of the attractiveness and vagueness of the movement. It is vital for believers, he says, to orientate their life, their tastes and their affections towards Jesus Christ; to be always more aware of the ontological reality which constitutes the Christian; to possess a mystique of action and of the Christian sense of profane activities; to introduce themselves into the divine sanctuary of charity; to discover the significance of a growing interiorisation of life; to perceive how the norms of morality are organically realised in the different areas of life.[81]

(ii) *The Primacy of Charity*

The next movement is that which attempted to build moral theology on agape or charity as its central principle. This is associated with the work of the Jesuits, Gerard Gilleman and René Carpentier.[82] Gilleman's work especially was widely translated and had a great influence: many of the authors of the period acknowledge their dependence on him.[83] His point of departure is the difference which he finds between the text-books of morality of the time and the Christian revelation of moral life as portrayed in the New Testament. His purpose is to formulate moral teaching on revelation. The meaning of morality, he says, is bound to the meaning of the human person and it is only in revelation that the mystery of the person is revealed. This mystery is that God is love and that we are called as children of God to communion of life with him. The very soul of the moral life found in revelation is the fundamental law of love. This must be the source of all further systematisation. But this is not what he finds in the text-books.[84]

Gilleman's approach is dependent on the notion of an entitative elevation of the soul and of its faculties as sketched in the last section. But for him morality is not to be understood as some general actualisation of that life but, rather, as altogether an expression of its central principle, i.e. charity.

> Sanctifying grace is nothing but the communication of the 'Agape' that is God's being. In the soul which it divinises it gives birth to a new reality which we might call charity-love in the first act . . . Christian action will necessarily consist in transferring this particular way of being — which is loving — into second act. Adopting this perspective, we see at once all the commandments and, in fact, the whole of gospel morals converging towards charity.[85]

What was exciting about Gilleman's work was that it combined

24

the gospel spirit, which the renewal sought, with a philosophical grounding which was dependent especially on Aquinas.

Following Aquinas, Gilleman set out the structure of moral life as follows:[86] Morality or virtue has to do with the good of the person and goodness is to be defined in terms of one's end or perfection. We have a final or ultimate end and immediate or proximate ends. Our final end is the possession of God: this is our complete good. Our profound spiritual tendency is our tendency to love of God for whom we are made. This is our very nature. This is the fabric of our existence. Being moral means aligning one's life with this tendency by the virtue of love. This is complete or perfect morality. But we have intermediate perfections or ends. We order ourselves to them by the particular virtues — justice, temperance, etc. Such virtues share or participate in the profound tendency of love for the ultimate end: in fact, any goodness or virtue is goodness or virtue only because it participates in the direction to what is our ultimate end.[87]

There is, therefore, he claims, the imperfect morality of the virtues: he calls it also *bonitas obiectiva* and *bonitas prima*.[88] And there is the perfect morality of love. Perfect moral life involves the positive direction of all moral virtue to God by active love of God.[89] Gilleman does not wish to blanket out individual virtues. Each is specified by its own end — justice, temperance, fortitude, etc. But what is fundamentally important about them is that they can be, in their various ways, expressions of or — to use Gilleman's favourite phrase — mediations of love.[90]

To all of this there are two levels — the natural and the supernatural. Even in the moral life of the pagan, Gilleman says, there is this tendency to God and it is this which gives his moral life its value.[91] But the Christian has been divinised. This makes him capable of supernatural acts of love for which Gilleman reserves the name 'charity'. By charity we direct the whole of Christian life to the God who has called us into communion of life with himself, and thus merit the beatific vision.[92] This does not require that we always perform explicit acts of charity towards God but that we have virtual charity or a general disposition of charity.[93] So charity is to be, as Aquinas says, the mother, root, foundation and form of all the other virtues. It alone can give perfect form and shape to Christian moral life, directing all of it to its ultimate end.[94] Of such a life of charity,

Christ is the perfect example: Christian life is following Christ; here Gilleman refers with approval to the title of Tillman's book, which we will consider a few pages further on.[95]

What Gilleman gives is an interpretation of morality and of moral goodness. His major contribution is to identify what he calls the core of the good news — that God is love and has called us into communion of love — with his philosophical understanding of the profound tendency of the spiritual creature. But what difference is that supposed to make to the conscious life of the Christian and to the methodology of moral theology? He says that the Christian should become ever more fascinated with the presence of God and should harmonise his psychology with the profound ontology of his moral acts. This seems to mean that the Christian should realise that he is not performing impersonal moral acts, that he should learn to go beyond the immediate specifications of acts of justice, fortitude, temperance, etc., that he should pick up the direction to God which is implicit in such acts and make of them conscious acts of love of God, so that his whole life would be an expression of and would be unified in charity.[96] Gilleman sums up his approach:

> Our whole effort has been to restore not only the preponderance but even the universal and total presence of charity in moral life. . . . The task of Christian morality and of asceticism, which is intimately linked with it, is to render the intention and exercise of charity in us always more and more explicit.[97]

The task of moral theology, then, is to 'find in each moral act the innermost and universal presence of charity'.[98]

Does this mean that the Christian has a different content of morality from the non-Christian? Neither Gilleman nor Carpentier has any hesitation in saying that Christian and natural morality are radically different. They are different (a) because the being of the Christian is entirely new and (b) because the supernatural value of moral life arises from its impregnation by charity.[99] This same movement of charity 'all those who are related to God must attain', so that Christian society is nothing less than a society pervaded by Trinitarian love.[100] But granted that charity carries or directs all moral activity, how does one come to know the demand of charity, the

26

content of morality: does charity serve as some kind of knowledge-principle? How does one know what acts are good so that they can be made an expression or mediation of charity? Is the moral life of the Christian different from that of the non-Christian only in being consciously directed towards God in charity, or is the content of what is directed by charity different also? Gilleman says that what is directed or transformed by charity has a *bonitas prima* or *bonitas obiectiva*. Where does he get the norm for this?

The nearest Gilleman comes to explaining *bonitas prima* or offering a norm of goodness is in saying that our being and action are really structured and that there may be intrinsically evil acts which contradict a fundamental law of our being. Two examples which he gives are suicide and onanism.[101] These are contrary to what he calls natural morality: here he seems to be using some kind of natural law criterion. But he says that, besides this, there is a higher content to morality: Christian morality should be an imitation of Christ and the content of imitation will be derived from the gospels and from tradition.[102] So it seems that the source of moral knowledge is not to be found in the principle of charity but in natural law and the Bible. Moreover, among Christians, Gilleman says, the natural disposition of love is elevated and divinised and 'others are no longer seen as merely "fellow men" but as members of the same Body of Christ'.[103] So according to Gilleman, not only are one's soul and one's faculties elevated — as the earlier theologians had maintained — but one's perception of the other is also changed and this has consequences for action. This claim about the specificity of Christian love has become axiomatic for many Roman Catholic authors: it is the consideration most frequently adduced as evidence for the specificity of Christian ethics.

Christian morality, Gilleman tells us, cannot be reduced to natural law. The demands of natural law are not only reinforced for the Christian. They are changed because each new degree of being postulates a new law: so the ends or objects of the supernatural virtues of the Christian are different from the ends of the natural virtues of the non-Christian.[104] But it is not easy to see that Gilleman — or Carpentier — establishes a different morality for Christians. There is much imprecision in the writing here. Gilleman moves from 'requirements' of morality to the 'spirit' or 'sense' of morality, to 'motivation', to the 'influence' which the Christian context has on morality.[105] But the conclusion has to be that he finds great difficulty in showing a different content to Christian morality.[106]

What kind of identity, then, did Gilleman give to Christian morality? His interpretation of all morality in terms of love of God and his organisation of the whole of Christian life around this one principle was the kind of radical move which the renewal movement sought. But not all, not even all Roman Catholics, will agree with his understanding of morality, of grace or of agape. Some of these issues will be considered later.[107] It is fair to say that he did succeed in giving morality a new spirit and inspiration — in that sense he gave it an identity that was foreign to the neo-Scholastics. But we are left unclear about many things — about his norm of morality, about the source of moral knowledge, about whether charity is meant to be a knowledge-principle, about the relation between the onto-logical and the psychological orders. It must be said that at most he was only partially successful in his efforts to replace the morality of the manual with a radically new morality — a thoroughly Christian morality moulded on revelation — which was the task he set himself.[108]

(iii) *The Following of Christ*

A third strand of the renewal movement was that which took the following of Christ as its central principle or idea. There can hardly be any doubt that it is to the work of Fritz Tillman that the influence of this theme in modern Roman Catholic theology is to be traced.[109] Tillmann said that he was seeking a religious morality which would be quite foreign to natural law.[110] To this religious morality natural law could be at most some kind of ante-chamber *(Vorhalle)*.[111] Grace, he said, made one a bearer of a supernatural morality: morality is the science of faith *(Glaubenswissenschaft)*;[112] between systematic and moral theology there is an essential connection *('wesensmässiger Zusammenhang')*, an inner belonging-together *('inners Zusammengehörigkeit')*.[113] It is not just that morality is derived from dogma. They must both be re-inserted into biblical theology and re-united. In that biblical morality one finds that the key idea is that of the following of Christ. This is to serve as a unique principle on which all of Christian life is to be built. It is to inform all morality, he says, as the soul informs the body.[114] Thus moral theology can be defined as the scientific presentation of the following of Christ in individual and social life.[115]

'Following' admits of different interpretations. It can be understood as mere imitation of a copy. Or it can have the added sense of devotion and surrender of oneself to a person, as a disciple follows a master. Tillmann certainly included this aspect in his account. In this he was much impressed by Scheler's stress on the living presence of the model to the follower and by the vitality and plasticity afforded by personal, as against impersonal, norms. He says that Christ is not just a moral model to be imitated. One must share the religious experience of the disciples who followed him. The disciple should be a slave of Christ. He shares his life and being. He is mystically united to Christ.[116]

Tillmann gives two sorts of reason why one should follow Christ. In Christ the fullness of the Godhead has appeared on earth. He is due the highest possible evaluation by us. He answers to our native tendency to seek goodness.[117] But in addition to this, as Christians we have received a new being of grace which obliges to a new way of life. Of this new Christian personality Christ is the model. What contributes to the growth of this personality, measured against Christ as model, is morally good: what limits or destroys it is bad. That is the norm of morality.[118] There is some obscurity here. It is not quite clear what role Christ is playing. But when Tillmann asks how the Christian is to know just what is involved in the development of this Christian personality, he is clear about the answer. The Christian finds this, he says, in the Bible, in the person and teaching of Christ.[119] To be a follower of Christ is to exhibit in one's life all the characteristics and virtues which the Lord had. He is not demanding an exact copy of the life of Christ, however. Every following, he says, must be a new creation: what one is looking for is the 'how' of Christ's life.[120] This seems to mean that one is looking for the general spirit or the general virtues which informed the life of Christ.

Tillmann has no doubt that there is a specific morality based on the new life of the Christian, an originally Christian content, which is essentially different from and foreign to every other kind of morality.[121] He lists the key concepts of this revelational morality as our capacity for moral life, our responsibility, the notion of sin, the notion of the will of God as the highest norm of morality and source of moral obligation, our supernatural end, the grace that is available to us. Such are certainly relevant to morality but they may not have much to do with content and one would want to ask further how they yield such a distinctively different morality. In fact, like so many others, Tillmann has difficulty in detailing the content of a specific Christian morality.[122]

Although Tillmann sets out to make the following of Christ the one central principle of Christian life, he finds it hard to sustain this position. He had recourse to other sources. The will of God as revealed in the moral teaching of the New Testament is, he says, the basic law of Christian life and the highest norm of Christian discernment.[123] And, particularly in the later passages of his books, he seems to regard charity as the fundamental principle.[124] If these are taken with what he has to say about one's being-in-Christ and the new moral personality which derives from that, one sees that 'following' is a rather complex idea which tries to gather under its wing several different strands of approach to morality. This impression is accentuated when one tries to discover where Tillmann situates the source of moral obligation. It is true that in Tillmann's scheme one should try to realise one's Christian personality, should regard Christ as the model of this life, should submit oneself entirely to the master. But the ultimate reason which he gives for doing such things is that they are the will of God. God's will is the source of moral obligation.[125]

There remain questions. What finally is Tillmann's norm of morality?[126] Is it the realisation of the new Christian personality or is it the will of God or is it Christ's life — or are all of them to be taken together? How much will any of them yield in terms of content: what is the source of moral knowledge? Can one move from being-in-Christ to behaviour? Can one extract moral teaching from the Bible, even from the teaching of Christ? Is the following of Christ to be understood as an attempt to determine what Christ would do in our times and situations? Can Christian morality keep natural law at a distance as Tillmann proposes?[127]

Rudolf Hofmann follows Tillmann in taking the following of Christ as the fundamental principle of moral theology.[128] He sees it as a basic source (*Quellgrund*) which will work towards an understanding of the specifically Christian thing to do in all situations, even situations which have no precedent in the gospels.[129] It takes over for him the ground of any discernment of the kind associated with natural law.[130] Christian morality, he said must be the realisation of the new being. It cannot be natural law.[131] It cannot be known to reason, to conscience, to ethics. It cannot even be something developed by reason and deepened by revelation. It must be built out of faith and theology.[132] Its source is the Bible: the life, the word and the work of Christ constitute the final rule of morality.[133] Its expression is a supernatural love of God and neighbour that is radically different from natural love.[134]

One detects in Hofmann a stronger than usual rejection of any natural morality. He rejects all notions of the autonomy of morality or of starting from ethics. One must avoid, he says, any ethicising or secularising of moral theology — as would happen if the Christian understood his morality as a natural ethic which was specifically christian only in being heightened and informed by religion. There is only one good for the Christian, he says, and that is faith-knowledge of the will of God. The Christian should go to the primary source, revelation, with as few presuppositions as possible.[135] And yet when Hofmann gives what he refers to as the substance of revelation-ethics — the divine life, the power of God's kingdom, the inbreak of the last aeon — we are not much wiser about the implications for Christian conduct.[136]

Not alone is the Christian the only one who understands the content of morality. Hofmann says that the Christian alone understands moral obligation fully because the essence of moral obligation is the submission of one's will and conduct to the will of God. Morality is the claim and demand of the personal will of God personally given to us.[137] A morality not supported by faith is, in his view, only conditional and hypothetical.[138]

Two others who depended heavily on the idea of 'following' at this time were McDonagh and Fuchs. Christ, McDonagh said, is the way, the standard, the law, the norm.[139] Morality, said Fuchs, is centred on the person of Christ. Christ is the example of Christian life. We are to imitate Christ, pattern ourselves on him.[140] A different nuance here is the accent on the *logos* doctrine of St John and on the reference to Christ in Colossians and Ephesians as 'first born of all creation', 'first born from the dead', and one in whom all fullness dwells. These elements of Christological doctrine enable them to say that Christ is the

31

archetype for all human and Christian existence, that he is the centre not only of redemption but also of creation and so the standard for all people at all times.[141] The point they both make is that, as Fuchs put it, 'Seen ontologically, Christ is the archetype of each human being.'[142]

To consider Christ in this way is not, in the first instance, to say anything about the possibility of knowing his life or of imitating it. It is saying that, whatever the content of the good moral life, it is realised perfectly in Christ. What we are given is an interpretation of morality, the Christian interpretation in terms of the meaning of Christ, rather than any exposition of its content. How that content is to be known is another matter. Both writers insist, following Aquinas, that the new law is an unwritten law. It is the life which corresponds to the new being-in-Christ, according to the axiom, *Agere sequitur esse*.[143] It is 'the shape of our divine sonship as it seeks expression in our daily lives',[144] 'the natural law challenge to the individual human being together with the supernatural demands arising from the order of grace'.[145] It is found primarily in the Christian's understanding of his being-in-Christ, only secondarily is it found in the Bible.[146] So while Christ is seen as the model for all people in all ages, there is a specific morality proper to the life of grace and known to Christians.[147]

The following or imitation of Christ will remain for Christians an important theme. But it will be necessary to determine what role it is meant to play in moral methodology. To say that Christ is the norm or that morality means the following of Christ may have different meanings. It may be a Christological truth which declares that Christ is the perfect one. It may be a dogmatic truth which says that Christians share Christ-life and that this has implications for moral living. It may mean that the Christian is mystically united to Christ or that Christ is present to us as help and inspiration in our moral lives.[148] It may mean that the disciple is to commit himself or herself to Christ or that moral living can be referred to as discipleship or as following of Christ.[149] All of these ideas appear somehow in the literature of 'following'. None of them clearly indicates just how the Christian is to live, i.e. it does not give us the content of moral living. 'Following' or imitation may also mean that one is to take the content of one's moral life from what is known of the life of Christ, i.e. from the Bible.[150] Is one, then, to copy Christ exactly or is one to try to transfer the 'how' of Christ's life to to-day's world?[151] Is one to take one's general values from what is known of Christ's values? Or is one to allow the dogmatic truths which Christ has revealed about God, human life and the world to influence one's moral discernment?

All of these themes were biblical themes. But apart from such attempts to find a central organising principle, there was a more general and undifferentiated appeal to Scripture. It became standard practice in this period to introduce all moral topics with a treatment of the topic in the Bible. It became accepted in conferences of moral theologians that the correct procedure was to invite biblical scholars to introduce moral questions by outlining what the Bible had to say on the matter. Take Häring's *The Law of Christ*, for example. Few works of the renewal were as popular and it is doubtful if anyone contributed more to the general spirit of renewal than Häring. He tries to take seriously the tenet of the renewal that Scripture must not be just a corroborative proof of already established positions but the source of such positions. 'Moral theology in all its considerations', he says, 'must flow from the word of God.'[152] So almost every section of this work begins with a biblical prelude. But although the work is strewn with quotations from Scripture, it is not clear what role they play.

Sometimes Scripture plays a general contextual role. He introduces his treatment of property with the quotation, 'For creation was made subject to vanity ...' (Rom.8.19ff) and continues:

> With this revealed doctrine before us we now take up the following topics: the Christian evaluation of earthly goods. . .the just use of these goods ... and the basic outlines of a sound economic order in the light of creation-redemption. . .[153]

But it is not clear that the 'revealed doctrine' plays any role in the subsequent discussion. Sometimes the development of thought from Scripture is even more tenuous. He begins his section on truth as follows:

> Revelation places every truth and every relation to truth in the reflective splendour of the holiness of God. In this light we treat the following. . .[154]

He goes on to deal with truth under the following headings: The

33

Primordial Mystery of Truth in God; The Divine Witness to the Truth; Life Flowing from the 'Spirit of Truth'; The Bond of Fellowship; Sanctification in the Truth. Each element is heavily laced with a variety of references to Scripture, especially to the gospel according to St John. All of it leads to this conclusion:

> The obligation to truthfulness is not derived from the individual right of a specific individual to my utterance, but from the divine primordial source of truth.... But the Christian — perhaps only the Christian — can find this sacrifice (truthfulness) meaningful and obligatory, because he sees truth in the splendour of the holiness and love of God.[155]

At other times Häring takes Scripture quite literally and argues from the words of Scripture directly to moral values and rules. The argument for fruitfulness in marriage is tied directly to the text, 'Increase and multiply...' (Gen. 1:28): 'married life in its total context', he says, 'must be an uninterrupted consent to God's design'.[156] The argument for monogamy is taken from the words of the Old Testament scriptures and from the 'revealed concept in the image of Eve taken from the body ("the rib") of Adam and the two become one flesh'.[157] The argument for indissolubility is likewise linked to its institution 'in paradise as an indissoluble union'.[158]

Häring had declared in the first pages of his book that his aim was to 'expound the most central truths in the light of the inspired word of the Bible'.[159] But it can be seen from the above that it was not clear what role the text of Scripture played or in what sense it served as source or proof of a moral position. Furthermore, his selection of texts was often very uncritical: at times he simply gathered together all the scriptural references to the topic which he was discussing and, often enough, texts that had only the most oblique relation to his topic.

But what some found most disconcerting about Häring is that there often appeared to be no relation at all between his Scripture section and the rest of his treatment of a moral topic. The Scripture section was often followed by a treatment of a virtue that was very much what appeared in the older manual of theology or philosophy. For example, he introduced his treatment of the virtue of prudence with a section called 'The Inspired Concepts of Prudence'.[160] This was followed by what he called a philosophical-theological analysis and this was, for

34

all practical purposes, the standard manual treatment of the virtue. It is hard to see that the scriptural introduction had any relation to it. The same could be said of the treatment of justice and of the morality of such areas as life, property, the state, the economic order. Despite the biblical prelude, they were no more 'Christian' than what appeared in the standard manual.

Häring caught the mood of the time and at the popular level was very influential. But at this stage of his theology he had not produced a cogent and convincing moral methodology: this is compounded by a considerable looseness of style. One cannot find that in *The Law of Christ* he even once adverts to the exegetical or hermeneutical problems of the use of Scripture. One does not know how crucial Scripture is to his system or whether, in the end, he needs it at all. One does not know whether it is meant to give a general religious vision of life; or whether he sees himself as founding a moral argument on it; or whether it provides a context which influences judgment in an indirect way; or whether it is meant to give inspiration and motivation. This rather uncritical appeal to biblical morality was typical of the first enthusiasm of the renewal and did much to provoke a reaction. Twenty-five years later, a great deal will have been learned and we shall find Häring adverting to all of these problems and advocating a more nuanced use of Scripture.

What we have seen in these first two decades of renewal can be fairly described as a revolution in Roman Catholic theology. It produced an approach to morality that would have been unthinkable for and unrecognisable to the neo-Scholastic. But the result was, not unnaturally, some confusion about method, especially about the justification of moral positions and of moral obligation. The effect of the movement for a new identity for Christian morality was that a reasonably clear and well-tried natural law morality had been replaced by something much more woolly: one was not clear any more just how a moralist was proceeding or what weight was to be given to the different elements of his moral discourse. Many found themselves in agreement with the remark of Mackey that whatever the short-comings of the old moral theology it had a considerable advantage over the new moral theology in the clarity of its concepts and in the precision and consistency of its argument.[161] It began to appear that a new identity for Christian ethics could

35

only be achieved through much careful and painful analysis and clarification.

Yet anyone who looks at the neo-Scholastic manual or at the popular catechisms of Roman Catholicism in the early part of this century will regard the renewal movement as a blessing and will feel grateful to its pioneering authors. The first wave of this renewal movement lasted until the late sixties. The history of fundamental moral theology in Roman Catholicism since then has been one of reaction to the renewal, of debate about identity, of objection and counter-objection. It has been a period of growing pains but one in which much useful clarification was done.[162]

2

Reaction versus Continuity

Section 1

REACTION: AN AUTONOMOUS ETHIC

Within a few years the reaction had set in. In the early seventies we already find theologians writing as follows:

> ... there arises for Christians and non-Christians the same epistemological problem, that is, to recognise what really is in fact human and what is not.... The question is the same for non-Christians and Christians, the criteria for distinguishing between good and bad, honourable and dishonourable, are the same for them as for us.[1]

> The moral demands by which the Christian is obliged are basically intelligible to reason as far as their content is concerned. They are no different from the demands of natural law.[2]

> ... the Christian message gives no new material norms to an autonomous ethic.... The religious dimension of morality must be expressed in the autonomous structures of the world.[3]

> ... We should not use Scripture or Tradition as the ultimate authority for deciding any moral issue. These sources may provide confirmation of beliefs which we form on other grounds.... We should behave as though we really did believe that we stand on essentially the same footing as secular moralists...[4]

Such writing clearly understands Christian morality in a way that is radically different from what the renewal movement had proposed.

Some theologians of the renewal movement had held for a morality that would be completely different from natural law or secular morality.[5] Others allowed that natural law would be part of Christian morality but that the more important element would be a specifically revelational, supernatural element.[6] The great source of this was seen as the Bible: the Christian found what he was to do in the Bible; it was given to him by God. Recourse to the Bible was the touchstone of renewal, of morality as the science of faith (*Glaubenswissenschaft*). We now move into a situation in which all of this is reversed. There appears in Roman Catholicism a movement of thought in which emphasis is not on God as revealer of morality but on the human being as discoverer of it, not on the specific morality of Christians but on the common morality of all people. This is referred to in the literature as the movement for the autonomy of morality or for an autonomous ethic.[7] It is, as we shall see, a movement which has won over many of the more important names in Roman Catholic theology. But it has not completely ousted the renewal movement for the 'Christianising' of morality. A second phase of this renewal challenges the movement for autonomy — this has come to be known as the faith-ethic (*Glaubensethik*). The late sixties and the seventies have been marked in Roman Catholic theology by a debate between these two schools on the identity of Christian ethics. Most of the rest of this work will be taken up with an examination of that debate and of the strengths and weaknesses of the two sides.

Why did this reaction take place? One reason was that the enthusiasm of renewal came up against the hard facts of moral analysis. The theology of the renewal movement was loose in expression, kerygmatic in style, characterised more by enthusiasm than by careful analysis. Questions began to be asked about method, about whether moral theology still regarded itself as a science, about the justification of moral positions. An equally important factor was the feeling that the attempt to develop a morality 'out of the middle of the revelation', as Böckle put it,[8] could easily give the impression that Christians were a ghetto and Christian morality something esoteric. The ghetto-mentality went counter to the mood of the time especially in continental Europe where the talk was of dialogue and solidarity. We find this concern running through the writing of the autonomy school. They make the point that the Christian no longer lives in a

Christian society but that he should be able to dialogue in moral matters with all people of goodwill and be largely able to agree with them in matters of public policy.[9] They are also anxious to make the point to non-Christians that Christian morality is not a childish obedience to the commands of God. It is not irrational or infantile. It does not destroy responsibility. Christians do not obey arbitrary commands which they receive from 'out there', from 'beyond', from revelation. So the movement stresses that it is the Christian himself who is to discover the moral demand for himself and that every demand of Christian morality must be accessible to reason.[10]

Movements in general theology and in church thinking also gave support to the groping towards autonomy. The document, The Church in the Modern World, of Vatican II made this important statement:

> If by the autonomy of earthly affairs we mean that created things and societies themselves enjoy their own laws and values which must be gradually deciphered, put to use and regulated by men, then it is entirely right to demand that autonomy. Such is not merely required by modern man but harmonises also with the will of the Creator. For by the very circumstances of their having been created, all things are endowed with their own stability, truth, goodness, proper laws and order. Man must respect these as he isolates them by the appropriate methods of the individual sciences and arts.[11]

This was in line with general trends of theology. One finds that theologians were increasingly encouraging Christians to respect the structures immanent in the world;[12] to have a reverence for the true inwardness of things;[13] to suspect any theology which deprived the world of its intrinsic laws.[14] They were saying that the church should take account of the signs of the times and that it hears the voice of God if it listens to the world.[15] They were saying that a certain kind and degree of secularisation is demanded by Christianity.[16] All of this created an ethos which was favourable to the development of the autonomous ethic, and foreign to the idea of a specific or esoteric Christian ethic. The human person is seen as a creator, as having responsibility for himself and for the world. If it is God's will that he plan and explore and discover the laws of his life in other fields, is it not also God's will that he discover the laws of ethical life rather than receive them from revelation?

Two other developments in general theology appear to have contributed to the emergence of the autonomous ethic — one was the understanding of grace, the other the relation between the Christian (graced) and the non-Christian (ungraced) — but they can be more conveniently considered later. Let us now examine the understanding of Christian ethics which was advanced by some of the principal advocates of this theory. Josef Fuchs had made an important contribution to the movement of renewal. We find that by 1970 he had changed his mind. His 1970 article in *Stimmen der Zeit* was to prove to be a seminal article in the debate about autonomy. He says there:

> Christian morality, in so far as its categorial determination and materiality is concerned, is basically and substantially a human morality, that is a morality of true manhood. That means that truth, honesty and fidelity, in their materiality, are not specifically Christian but universally human values . . .[17]

Fuchs would go on to make many similar statements in the following years: we have already quoted one at the beginning of this chapter.

> The principles and commands of moral conduct are the same for a truly human morality as for Christian morality.[18]

> The content of this morality is 'human', not distinctively Christian . . . the moral consciousness of the communion derives knowledgewise from 'human' understanding . . .[19]

> Human and Christian morality are not to be distinguished in their material aspect.[20]

> . . . the Christ-event . . . leaves unimpaired the essential structure of the person's this-worldly situation and therefore the material content of the ethical order between persons.[21]

By human morality Fuchs says that he means a morality that could be recognised and acknowledged by anyone: that excludes everything we know about the human person from God's revelation.[22]

Fuchs bolsters his position by making three further points: (i) The classic Roman Catholic position from Aquinas did not acknowledge any 'new' moral precepts, i.e. any moral precepts which could not be known by reason. The position of autonomy, therefore, is not original but traditional.[23] (ii) Many biblical scholars accept that there are no new moral precepts in the bible, i.e. no precepts which have not been found in extra-biblical material.[24] (iii) One might have tried to argue that some moral ideals were specifically Christian. But many non-Christians follow a morality not only of basic duty but of high ideals — they love enemies, practice non-violence, sacrifice themselves, etc.[25]

His substantive position, therefore, is that the content of Christian and non-Christian morality is the same. That means for him that the fact of being a Christian makes no moral demands which do not also arise for the non-Christian. One takes this to mean that if the Christian and the non-Christian attend equally seriously to the business of morality they should arrive at the same content of moral demand and that there is nothing in the Christian consciousness or tradition which would demand a different or additional morality. What Christians call morality, he is saying, is available to the reason of the non-believer. This is what Fuchs means by the autonomy of morality and this is his interest in it. He acknowledges that the Christian will have what he calls a natural obligation to realise some moral demands of which only he is aware, for example obligations to receive sacraments, to be grateful to Christ, etc.[26] But that does not touch the heart of the matter. The question for him is whether in the different inner-worldly situations of life the Christian understands the content of moral life differently from the non-Christian.[27] His answer, we have seen is that the epistemological problem is the same for both, the criteria of judgment are the same, the principles and commands of conduct are the same.

Does Fuchs see any point, then, in referring to *Christian* morality or moral *theology* or *Christian* ethics? Does faith have any bearing on ethics? Yes, he says. He presents a group of considerations which justify calling morality Christian. They do not have to do immediately with the content of the moral demand. (Whether he can sustain the position that they have *nothing* to do with content we will have to consider.) He says that there is much more to Christian morality than content. There are the Christian significance (or context), motivation and inspiration of morality. It is such elements, he says, which identify Christian morality and give it its specific character. Later we find Fuchs insisting on the distinction between religion and morality. In the religious field, he says, there are specifically Christian realities but not in the

41

moral field. The Christ-event is not ethically normative: its significance is in the theological and religious areas. So one should not expect to derive new moral content from the Christ-event. Rather one should see that the religious realities — the Christian truths — give a new significance and meaning to morality without changing its content.[28]

This means, above all, that the Christian sees morality in a different light or framework from the non-Christian. Fuchs sometimes expresses this by saying that the morality of the Christian has a specific intentionality.[29] It has a goal. It is going somewhere. He means that the basic reality for the Christian is his relationship to God and that morality is important to that relationship. The relationship cannot be maintained or grow unless one is morally faithful in everyday life. One cannot love God or follow Christ or walk in the Spirit if one is not morally upright. This is the further significance or meaning or depth of moral life. So for the Christian true morality contains within itself a 'theologal life' and is that life's practical expression. It is that life which gives morality its real depth.[30]

For Fuchs the difference between Christian and non-Christian morality is not in their content but in the fact that the Christian can be aware of and should try to live out the religious significance of his moral action. Morality, while remaining itself, is pervaded by religiousness. There is, he says, an *extra* in Christian morality. But it is not primarily an ethical *extra*, rather a religious *extra*.[31]

Not only does Christianity give this basic significance. It gives an added dimension or enrichment to particular moral stances. An example is the new depth it gives to one's response to one's fellow human being who is seen by the Christian as child of God and brother or sister in Christ.[32] It also gives motivations to Christianity which he says are specifically Christian, for example, motivations for truthfulness and for chastity.[33]

> Think for example of St Paul: in order to keep Christians free from the sin of fornication or of lying, he does not refer to human or to philosophical considerations (1Cor.6.12-20; Eph.4.25). Rather he invokes the special dignity of the body of the Christian and the mutual relationship of Christians in a Christian community.[34]

'Motive' or 'motivation' is important to Fuchs's scheme but the word is used very loosely by him. Sometimes he applies it to the basic significance which the Christian is to give to his morality. At other times he applies it to the giving of extra reasons for truth-fulness, chastity, etc. — the added reason that one is a member of Christ's Body. At other times the motive seems to enter more fully into the content of the moral action.[35] There is need for clarification here.

Fuchs's general position is clear, however. His strategy is to distinguish the content or materiality of morality from its context or significance, and from its motivation. He agrees that faith pervades moral life but in such a way as to leave the content untouched and detachable from faith. The result is that Christian morality can be presented to non-Christians as entirely reason-able and one can dialogue with all people of goodwill about the problems facing the world.

His autonomy thesis, however, is ragged at the edges. There are times when he appears rather uncertain and less than consistent. (a) He says very frequently that the demands of Christian moral behaviour are 'substantially', 'basically', 'largely' the same as those of proper human behaviour or that they are 'very similar' and that moral theology must proceed 'largely' by means of the ordinary disciplines of human thought.[36] (b) He seems to be in some doubt about whether the non-Christian can know the content of the moral life fully. He says that the revelation is not only a great help to the discovery of morality but that it is necessary to discover the totality without error. There are truths which are accessible to non-Christians, he says, but which are not known to them. They are 'per se accessible' or 'not inaccessible'. In his recent writing Fuchs recognises that the gospel gives not only 'maieutic and paraentic' emphases, not only a radicalisation of ethical demands but also 'important basic insights for ethical understanding, truths which 'condition a Christian ethic' and 'specifically Christian ideals'.[37] (c) He has difficulty about the notion of a Christian anthropology. In 1969, while advocating autonomy, he was still saying that the 'is' of Christian anthro-pology should have an effect on the content of the 'ought' of Christian living.[38] Later one finds him saying that the newness of the Christian is in his freedom from sin and that the 'ought' which should realise the 'is' of his life is the call to realise that freedom in action.[39] (d) He makes much of the fact that one finds among non-Christians people who are ready to love enemies, make sacrifices, etc.[40] This is true, of course. It is also true that many moralities distinguish sharply between duties and ideals. One would need clarification about the status to be given to moral ideals in Fuchs's own vision and about the relation between norms and ideals. All of these questions will occupy us.

Alfons Auer states his position thus: God did not first create the human person and then give him a code of ethical rules; he created him with reason so that he might give himself moral norms.[41] The discovery of moral norms, therefore, is a matter of human reason. The *proprium* or special character of Christian ethics lies not in its content or in additional norms developed from faith.[42] The Christian message, he says, gives no concrete ethical normativity: its ethical relevance lies in something other than material norms.[43] Its content is 'human' not 'Christian'.[44] Auer sees the great value of the formula of autonomy in its insistence that the ethical experience can be shared with those who do not subscribe to any metaphysical or religious viewpoint.[45] Neither the individual Christian nor the church, he says, has any revelation about what is or is not the concrete expression of the moral demand. Indeed, he sees no reason why the elaboration of ethical directives should be automatically regarded as part of the church's function. There may have been historical reasons why she assumed this role, just as there are historical reasons why she assumed a role in education or in social work. But he can see no reason why she should any longer regard herself as having any special competence, since it is clear that the elaboration of moral norms is a matter of reason. The role of the church, Auer says, is to accept moral positions which have been well-formulated by the human community, realising that the humanly and morally good is the same for all people.[46] This, he maintains, is just how one finds morality in the Bible. What is specific about Old Testament morality is not content but the anchoring of morality in the authority of God. What one finds in the teaching of Jesus is not new or unique moral norms but the call to moral conversion, the awakening of a hunger and thirst for a better life and the situating of morality in the context of salvation and eschatology. What Paul offers is not material norms but morality seen in the perspective of the kerygma.[47] This, too, he says, has been the Roman Catholic tradition.[48]

Can Auer give any sense, then, to the notion of a Christian morality? He says that the specific character — the *proprium* — is found in the new context or horizon of meaning (*Sinnhorizont*) which Christianity gives, and in the new motivation and stimulation.[49] By new context he means that the Christian sees the autonomous moral demand as a divine claim, interprets the moral enterprise as part of the creative purposes of God and of the redemptive mission of Christ, hopes that moral goodness is a possibility in Christ, and accepts success and failure in his moral undertakings in the light of the *parousia*.[50] So Auer says that his view of morality is not one of absolute autonomy but of what he calls 'relational autonomy'.[51] But he insists that this leaves the content of moral life exactly (*genau*) the same for Christian and non-Christian.[52] By saying that the Christian has new motivations, Auer means that he is to see his moral activity as a partnership with the God of creation in the bringing about of the world's possibilities, as a partnership with Christ in the ordering of all things to salvation, as a partnership with the Lord of history who brings about the fulfilment of all things, as a response of gratitude to the God who has loved and forgiven him.[53] It is in the intergration of autonomous natural morality into this relationship with God that Aner finds the distinctive character of Christian ethics.[54]

Christianity also has a stimulating effect on morality. Two rather different examples give us an idea of Auer's thinking. (a) He says that the realisation that we have been forgiven in Christ should effect in us a new spirit of moral goodness: this should find expression in an attitude of love for others for which God's own love can be the only measure.[55] (b) He makes the point that Christian teaching about the equality of all people before God has contributed to the struggle for civil rights, to the abolition of slavery and to the securing of equal rights for women.[56] He sees this stimulating effect as a continuing process in Christianity.

So for Auer, as for Fuchs, the content of Christian morality is self-contained. It is a matter of natural morality: it is discovered by reason and is available to all. This core is untouched by faith but is set into a context of Christian meaning, motivation and stimulation. But there is some obscurity here. Meaning and motivation sometimes seem to be the same. Are stimulation and motivation the same — Auer refers to the 'power of motivation'?[57] In five different treatments of the subject he makes separate mention of Christian motivation and stimulation.[58] But the basis of the distinction remains obscure.

There is a more significant problem. Auer states his main

thesis quite firmly. But one wonders if he is entirely happy with it. In his 1971 book he said that revelation has a critical function with regard to the discovery of moral norms. By this he means that the autonomous model of morality must always be placed under the judgment of the Word of God — because the human person is always the victim of his or her own sinfulness and error.[59] In later writings he uses the language of hermeneutics for this process. The stress now is on the fact that our moral judgments come out of a background, a pre-understanding of the moral, which is a composite of the insights of humanity, of philosophical considerations about the meaning of life, and of the data of revelation. This affects our arriving at moral judgments and must be constantly purified. Auer sees revelation making a special contribution to this process. He says that it will criticise every deviation from the biblical and Christian view of the person (*Menschenbild*).[60] But at the same time he says that revelation does not criticise the autonomous ethic as such or rationality as such but only deviations from the human.[61] Of this he gives two examples: (a) Revelation should prevent ethical judgment from lapsing either into a naïve notion of a utopia here on earth or into unwarranted pessimism.[62] (b) When ethical norms fall to a minimum, revelation is always present to give an impulse to a high ethical level (*hochethische Impuls*): it draws us beyond mere commandments to the pure model of morality which is found in God who is love.[63] Is Auer saying here that the Christian consciousness has certain points of view on the person and on the world which will be significant in arriving at moral judgments — and, if so, is this compatible with the autonomy thesis? Or is it that revelation helps one to keep clear what is accessible to the non-believer but is in danger of being lost sight of by him or her — and, if so, is he not making too much of the biblical and Christian view of man? Is he holding, as Fuchs does, that all morality is *per se* accessible to the non-believer but more easily discovered by the believer? Does this apply equally to moral ideals (*hochethische Impuls*) or is the thesis of autonomy limited to moral duties? The question of the status of ideals arises again, as it did with Fuchs.

The autonomy position has been most extensively set out by Fuchs and Auer. They are, however, part of a movement. The position is supported by many of the best-known Roman Catholic theologians. Among German speakers one thinks especially of Schüller, Mieth, Furger and Korff.[64] Schüller has been very active. He sees the movement as a rehabilitation — after what he calls a temporary crisis — of natural law and of the traditional opinion that the Christian is subject to the same moral demands as anybody else.[65] This is certainly his own position. He defines natural law as the sum of the moral demands which can be known by reason and which are logically independent of revelation.[66] This, he says, is what is demanded of the Christian and only this: by recognising the natural law one is by that very fact recognising what God demands of us in virtue of the *lex gratiae*.[67] So the demands of Christian morality are in principle accessible or fundamentallly intelligible to reason: he includes here the biblical command of agape and even love of enemies.[68] To hold this, says Schüller, is simply to follow the practice of the early church and to adhere to traditional theology which maintained an identity between natural law and the precepts of Jesus.[69] This does not mean that the Christian should not become a disciple of Jesus and surrender himself to him as his moral authority. He should. But the Christian has no reason for thinking that the ethic proposed and lived by Jesus is beyond the understanding of reason. Schüller says that the role of Jesus in morals is what he calls maieutic or pedagogic — a point also made by Fuchs, Auer and Mieth. What Jesus does is help us to understand the demands of our own reason. Jesus clarifies the moral demand.[70] Does Schüller see any point then, in referring to *Christian* morality? Yes, he does, provided the 'Christianising' of morality is not regarded as referring to content. It refers to the horizon of meaning and final grounding which the Christian can give to his morality. For the Christian, morality is the will of God; it is the expression of his response to God.[71] It refers to the new motivation which the Christian has: he lives his morality in faith, hope and love as one who has been forgiven.[72] It refers to the fact that the Christian has not only been forgiven his sins but has been called to a life of union with God and that this is the source of new possibilities.[73] This last suggestion seems to mean — although Schüller is not very explicit here — that such inner power arising from one's awareness of God's action on us in Christ might open up for the Christian demands of love for the neighbour which go beyond the natural. If this is right does it not raise for Schüller at least some marginal questions about his autonomy thesis?

47

In 1969, just as the autonomy position was beginning to emerge, French moralists held their conference on 'Christian Ethics in Search of its Identity'.[74] There are questions asked there about the renewal movement and especially about the appeal to Scripture.[75] There are suggestions that the contribution of Christianity is to call one to moral conversion, to encourage one to go beyond the minimum, to give a new significance to one's moral life.[76] There is the insistence of Aubert that the material content of the morality of the Christian is not different from that of the non-Christian: the specificity of Christianity, he says, is in the new spirit, dynamism and significance which it gives.[77] There is support from Simon for the thesis that the newness consists less in content than in new significance.[78] It is a position which Simon goes on to develop in a number of other places. The person is to discover his own moral norms, he says, not receive them from revelation: in this respect the church is on the same level as the rest of humanity.[79]

It was among the Dutch that the first murmurings about the renewal movement were heard and the first suggestions about autonomy. Blank, Van der Marck, Beemer, van Ouwerkerk and Schillebeeckx were all early supporters of the autonomy position. In Christian ethics, says Schillebeeckx, the exact content of the natural law is not altered: there is no Christian anthropology and no supernatural ethic beyond a natural ethic; the church does not impose one demand beyond the content of natural law.[80] But revelation, he agrees,, does confirm our rational insights, it is a remedy for our sinfulness and for the confusion of our consciences, it is a new enlightenment.[81] More than most, the Dutch theologians, accepting the autonomy of morality, have concentrated on raising the question of the Christian interpretation of morality, of the relationship of morality and salvation, of the integration of the secular into the Christian scheme of things.[82] Several Italian theologians, too, have adopted the same position. It is squarely stated by Compagnoni: the material content of Christian ethical life is not different from that of human life.[83] It has also won support among Polish moralists.[84]

Among theologians writing in English, Charles Curran and Richard McCormick, while they introduce their own qualifications, support the same position. Curran says that non-Christians can and do arrive at the same ethical conclusions and embrace the loftiest of motives, virtues and goals which Christians have wrongly claimed for themselves.[85] McCormick agrees that there is material identity between Christian moral demands and those perceivable by reason. Christ, he says, did not add any new moral claims and Christian ethics cannot add any to what is available to human ethical self-understanding.[86]

In his writings through the seventies Enda McDonagh does not formally consider the question of identity or specificity: he is interested in the approach to Christian morality — the starting point. But this in itself is an indication of one's conception of morality. He had been an advocate of the renewed biblical morality but acknowledges a change of approach in 1970. He says that one must begin the study of moral theology by examining human experience and subsequently seek to understand that experience theologically. So he regards the order of words in his article, 'Morality and Christian Theology' as important. What he is interested in is the light thrown on — the interpretation given to — morality by theology. The thrust of his position is that this light refers not to content but to the meaning, significance, hope and possibility of morality in the Christian vision. It is a matter of the relationship between faith and the frontier questions raised by moral experience. (McDonagh has developed his position further in his most recent book.)[87] James P. Mackey, in a review of McDonagh's book, agrees:

> The relationship between Christianity and morality has to be discussed less in terms of distinctive additions and more in terms of harmony between questions innate [to morality or Christianity] and answers independently preferred [by Christianity or morality]...[88]

Most uncompromising of all is the position of Gerard Hughes. Hughes writes out of the Anglo-American philosophical tradition rather than out of the continental theological tradition. He has been critical of the method and mode of argumentation of the theologians. Part of the criticism refers to their appeal to faith in moral argument. Hughes says:

> We stand on essentially the same footing as secular moralists. . . . Our Christian faith cannot supplement the knowledge of ethics which is available to us apart from Christian revelation.[89]

> To the extent that we do succeed in discovering in the tradition of the church what God is saying to us, we shall do so by the patient methods of moral philosophy which enabled us to hear him in the first place.... There are no good theological reasons for supposing that reflection on our human nature cannot enable us to arrive at moral truth.[90]

> We should not use Scripture or Tradition as the ultimate authority for deciding *any* moral issue.[91]

My aim has not been to give a survey of the literature but to indicate, first, the thesis of the autonomy position and, second, the extent of its support among Roman Catholic authors — on any reckoning the authors mentioned must count among the most important and influential in moral theology in the seventies. The movement has been a reaction to a renewal movement which proposed that revelation/faith is the source of morality and that this gives Christian morality an identity which relates particularly to its content. The authors under review say (a) that morality is not to be regarded as the command of God imposed on us in revelation, (b) that morality is discovered by human reason, (c) that the content of Christian morality is not specific but is available to us without revelation, (d) that the special character or identity of Christian morality is in something other than its content. The movement is best presented in Fuchs and Auer. But it has not been content to set out its thesis. It has, as we shall see later, engaged the faith-ethic more closely, challenging it to demonstrate how faith yields ethical truth and pointing particularly to the difficulty of its appeal to Scripture.

The autonomy position looks straightforward enough. But there are obscurities lurking in it which require further exploration. This can be most conveniently done by considering the contribution of Franz Böckle. Böckle is generally regarded as one of the autonomy school and much of what he says is held in common with the other authors of the school: the person must give himself of his own norms; morality must be rational; the specific character of Christian morality is the new horizon of meaning, the integration of morality into theologal life, the new depth, the special motivation.[92] It is when Böckle asks the question about identity of content that confusion occurs. He regards it as a non-question (*Scheinfrage*).

If we take the inner unity of the order of creation and redemption as our point of departure, this question will inevitably prove to be illusory. The Christian message is nothing but the fulfilment of man's deepest expectations. It cannot estrange man, nor can it ultimately seem strange to him.[93]

Böckle's position is that the only true morality — the only morality worth talking about — is Christian morality. All morality is in some sense Christian.[94] This is a pointer to a difficulty which troubled the developing autonomy position in the seventies and which reflected the changing theological background. In fact a number of theologians, especially Fuchs, were attached to the remark that all morality is Christian. It is important that we sort this out. I said early in this chapter that the developing autonomy position was helped not only by the trend towards a theology of secular realities but by two other movements. Let us look at them briefly. One was the change in thinking about the doctrine of grace. One of the great cries of the renewal movement was for a morality that would be appropriate to the new life of grace: the ontological change in us demanded a supernatural content of morality, it was said, on the basis of the axiom *Agere sequitur esse*. Some have referred to this as the two-tier or superstructure model of nature-grace. In the sixties and seventies many theologians moved away from this model. We find them putting the stress more on the fact that grace is primarily God's love for us, and less on the aspect of created grace, i.e. the effect of such love in us. We find them saying that the doctrine of grace does not tie one to the concept of an entitative elevation of nature with its faculties and powers. There are other models for the change wrought by grace. One who enters into a new relationship is a changed person. One with new insight about the meaning of reality is a new creation. So is one who trusts that the creator of all things is his or her loving Father. Why not think of grace in such terms, they asked?[95]

The different models do not greatly concern us. What does concern us is that the strict analogy of nature-supernature, each with its own appropriate morality, on the basis of the axiom, *Agere sequitur esse,* was no longer widely acceptable. The autonomy school was encouraged to ask whether, in fact,

Christian morality was to be different in kind — specifically different — from that of the non-Christian. Could it be that what was required by Christianity was not a new morality but a new person? Could it be that what was given by the Christian experience was a new inspiration and a new readiness to live the autonomous morality that was common to all? This is just what authors like Fuchs and Auer began to say:

> I would be inclined to put it like this: what Christ preaches in the Sermon on the Mount as something new is not really a new — Christlike as distinct from simply human — morality, but a new mankind vanquishing the 'old mankind of the Fall'.[96]

But the issue had become more complicated than that. Not only did the model of grace change but the conception of the relationship between the graced and ungraced person changed also — this is our second theological development. During the days of the renewal movement there was still the traditional sharp distinction between baptised and unbaptised. The state of the question, therefore, concerned the distinction between the new Christian morality of the baptised and the natural morality of the unbaptised. In the forties there was some questioning of the theory that there are two orders existing side by side, the natural order of the unbaptised and the Christian order of the baptised. By the sixties, authors were saying explicitly that God created but one order, the supernatural order; that everybody exists in that order; that to everybody the one destiny of union with God is offered; and that a person refuses this gift only through his own fault. So that, to use Rahner's celebrated and controversial expression, many pagans are anonymous Christians.[97] This meant also that, since pagans live in the supernatural order and are likely to be in union with God, their knowledge cannot be described as natural knowledge: it has supernatural elements.[98]

Some moral theologians were quick to adopt this thinking. It had the effect of changing the state of the question about the identity of Christian morality. The problematic can be put this way: If there is, as Rahner and others put it, but one order, if all are in the order of Christianity, if all have the possibility of being anonymous Christians, what are we talking about when we compare Christian morality to human, natural, non-Christian morality? Can we any longer talk about two moralities? How are we to define natural law if all morality has supernatural elements? We find Fuchs saying in 1966:

It would be better to say that non-Christians largely share Christian morality and this is true despite the fact that Christian morality contains 'supernatural' as well as 'natural' elements, since its prototype is the God-man, Christ. And it cannot be objected that non-Christians have, so to speak, no right to Christian morality on such terms, for all mankind are rightful heirs to it. Moreover, there is good Catholic authority for saying that non-Christians share more than the 'natural' elements of the Christian vocation. And it cannot be presumed that non-Christians are incapable of perceiving the grace of Christ: its insistent prompting can affect their moral outlook. . . . Indeed there are many grounds for supposing that even those who in all sincerity declare themselves atheists may encounter God, on occasion, in their inmost consciousness. . .[99]

So Fuchs says that, instead of dividing morality along traditional lines into Christian and non-Christian ('natural law morality'), one should realise that the Christian morality described by Vatican II as 'our exalted vocation in Christ' 'appears to be the one and only morality appointed for all humanity'.[100] The quotation from Fuchs gives a fair idea of the development that was taking place and of the confusion of ideas and terminology. He would go on in later years to say often that the Christian understanding of the human person describes the genuinely human order as Christian and that every serious non-Christian morality is a participation in Christian morality and, in this sense, not simply non-Christian.[101]

Böckle went through the same process. He moved from the sharp distinction between baptised and unbaptised — '. . . man viewed from faith, in his becoming and being a member of Christ, is radically distinguished from man understood purely naturally'[102] — to an explicit acceptance of the position of Rahner. Since the whole of the human race is accepted into the supernatural order, he says, everyone is in a position to receive understanding that would not be available to mankind if God had left it in a purely natural state. That means that moral knowledge without revelation is not pure natural knowledge: it

53

is always supernatural and supernaturally modified. What appear to be purely natural acts, i.e. acts performed by someone without faith, belong to the supernatural order. What one would have once called natural morality is really Christian morality.[103] It was this thinking that led Böckle in his major work of 1977, the aim of which was 'to provide a comprehensive answer to the question of the distinctive aspect of Christian ethics: what are specifically Christian ethics',[104] to say that the question about content is an illusory question — given the unity of the orders of creation and redemption.

This appears to me to be a mistake and to throw the whole issue of the identity of Christian ethics into confusion. It is surprising that Böckle, who set out to promote dialogue in morals with humanists and other world-religions, takes this position.[105] It is rather his remark that all morality is Christian which must appear illusory to non-Christians. The question about distinctive content is an important question.[100] There is a genuine term of comparison for Christian ethics and that is the ethic of one who does not subscribe to the Christian religion — however such a one is to be described. That, in systematised form, is what we call philosophical ethics. Some theologians, such as Schüller, have never lost sight of that question. Fuchs has clarified his own thinking recently by referring to thematic revelation. Philosophical ethics he now defines as the ethic that is available to us without *thematic* revelation. His concern is to explore the possibility of dialogue with such human, natural, non-Christian morality: the validity of this concern, he says, is not affected by the fact that everyone is under the influence of grace and that the grace of Christ can operate in the moral knowledge of all.[107]

The comparison between such a philosophical ethic and the ethic of the Christian is now more clearly seen by the autonomy movement as the crucial question — although they recognise that it is not the whole of the question about the identity of Christian ethics. One has to agree that it is an important question for several reasons. (a) It is important to know how Christian theologians and Christian churches argue to their moral positions and what their sources are — we have seen that even philosophers sympathetic to Christianity are often puzzled about this. (b) It affects matters of public and legal policy: are there necessarily differences between Christians and others and,

54

if so, for what precise reasons? (c) The document 'The Church in the Modern World' of Vatican II is addressed not only to Roman Catholics but to all people of good will and it encourages 'common solutions' to moral problems:[108] This requires that different groups be clear about their methodology and about the possibility of such common solutions. None of this is helped by blurring the distinction between Christian and non-Christian morality.

So one can say that, while the background developments in general theology led to confusion about the state of the question, the end result has been a clarification of the issue against the background of the new theological thinking on grace and salvation. The major concerns of the autonomy movement remain: can the Christian theologian reach agreement with the humanist in moral matters or is he or she necessarily committed to a different content of morality; can the Christian convince the humanist that Christianity encourages the human person to discover his morality and is not an unquestioning acceptance of a revealed moral code? Its answer is a firm 'Yes': it is the design of God that the person is to be his own lawgiver; there is nothing required of the Christian that is not also perceivable by and required of the non-Christian; what is distinctive about Christian morality does not pertain to content but to context and motivation. This is its vision of the identity of Christian morality.

Section 2

CONTINUITY: A FAITH-ETHIC

The autonomy movement was a reversal of everything that the renewal hoped for. One can understand the bewilderment of Ermecke, one of the advocates of renewal, as he saw how theology was developing. He finds that whereas a few years previously theologians regarded it as natural to demand that the teaching of morality should be theological, i.e. 'conceived in terms of scripture and of salvation history' things have been entirely reversed 'so that Christian morality is understood in rational, philosophical terms, i.e. in terms of empirical human science'.[109] However, not all Roman Catholic moralists were to go along with the autonomy thesis. Schüller had said in 1970 that the doctrine of the identification of Christian morality with rational morality or natural law had overcome the temporary crisis of the renewal movement, and had been rehabilitated.[110] That was to prove a rather optimistic forecast. A stiff opposition to the autonomy movement began to appear. One could call it a counter-reaction. I prefer to regard it as a continuation — a further phase — of the renewal of the fifties and sixties. The justification for taking it separately is that it is a response to the developing autonomy position. It joins battle with it. One of the results is a greater sophistication in some of its proposals for renewal.

Already in 1966 Häring was casting scorn on theologians who had 'the incredible idea that the moral teaching of the New Testament does not provide any new content to natural law morality but only new motivation'.[111] In 1973 Philip Delhaye attacked the positions of Blank and Valsecchi but particularly that of Fuchs's article, 'Is there a Specific Christian Morality'?[112] The tone of the criticism became sharper. Gustav Ermecke spoke about a fundamental crisis in Christian morals for which the writings of Auer, Schüller, Böckle and Fuchs were responsible. They were separating Christ from the world, he said. They were too influenced by psychology and sociology. They were responding too much to the thinking of the time and engaging in what he referred to as *ad hoc* theology.[113] Bernard Stoeckle was also alarmed. It is no wonder, he says, that the question of the identity of Christian morality is receiving so much attention: as he sees it, the whole fate of Christian morality is involved.[114] He accuses those who espouse an autonomous ethic — he mentions especially Fuchs, Auer and Blank — of being affected by the general trend towards secularism, which, he says, denies all transcendence, makes reason absolute, makes the human person the measure of all things and encourages absolute self-determination. The movement, he says, also leads to over-emphasis on personal judgment, uncertainty in morals, the destruction of moral obligation and a utilitarian style of ethics.[115] Most strident of all is the criticism of Konrad Hilpert: his main targets are Fuchs and Auer. He traces the long history of movements for autonomy in ethics and their attendant evils. The term 'autonomy', he says, cannot have an innocent meaning: it is historically tied to attempts to free oneself from theology, from the church and from religion.[116] It also has an

56

affective content — it has suggestions of freedom from repression and from everything 'merely theological'. It is in the same category as 'alienation', 'emancipation', 'liberalism', 'secularisation' and 'enlightenment' — all of which he regards as inimical to Christianity. So the movement, he warns, involves one of the greatest dangers to Christianity and Catholic faith.[117] The fear of Joseph Ratzinger is that the movement for autonomy is tantamount to a denial of the teaching authority of the church.[118] It is hardly surprising that the autonomy movement found it necessary to hit back, accusing its critics of distorting its position and of making unsubstantiated charges. Nobody had ever advocated the absolute autonomy of the human person, it said, and nobody had denied the teaching office of the church.[119]

If the *Glaubensethik* does not agree with the autonomy movement's understanding of Christian morality, what does it propose instead? As we might expect, the main elements of its thesis are (a) that Christian morality is not to be discovered simply by unaided reason, (b) that its content cannot be identified with philosophical ethics, (c) that its specific character cannot be limited to considerations of context and motivation.[120] Its morality must be developed 'out of the middle of the faith.'[121] There are a number of different strands to this position which I shall now consider.

Ratzinger and the biblical scholar, Heinz Schürmann, answer the autonomous position by saying that the Bible is an indispensable source of moral teaching and that it is possible and necessary to have recourse to it. Reason will not do for morality, says Ratzinger. Reason is not clear. It capitulates to the spirit of the times. It is not easy to distinguish what is true rationality and only the appearance of rationality. Christianity, he says, was never satisfied with reason: he particularly objects to the suggestion that the Judaeo-Christian tradition simply accepted the morality of the time and culture in which it found itself. His position is that there has always been a close relationship between faith and ethics. The Decalogue, he says, was tied to faith in God: it showed the nature of God. In particular, there was a relationship between the holiness of God and morality. This gave a new level to morality and served as a criterion for discernment and choice.[122]

So he sees faith as a critical and discriminating factor. Paul did not simply accept pagan philosophical morals, he says. In fact, there was no such thing as a contemporary morality. There was only a confusion of conflicting opinions among which Paul had to choose in the light of the tradition of the Old Testament and the 'mind of Christ'. Paul knew that he had power to teach and that the mind of Christ was to be the measure of Christian moral life — Ratzinger cites 1 Thess. 4.1ff and Philippians 2.5 and 4.9. So, in his opinion, Paul sets out 'the inner necessity of grace.'[123] His directives are 'not a moralising appendage, the contents of which could be changed but the concrete designation of what faith is', [124] 'not a variable accessory to the gospel but something guaranteed by the Lord'.[125]The conclusion for him is clear: faith includes judgments of content; it is the task of Christianity to continue to elaborate moral norms from faith and to refuse to capitulate to reason. In doing so it is to remember that the clear content of biblical morality is a constant for Christianity and not a variable.[126] As we shall see, the autonomy school was to remain unconvinced.

Schürmann, too, set out to refute the claim that New Testament directives are time and culture-conditioned. There are, he says, unconditionally binding demands, which remain valid for us. (a) There are what he calls the transcendental values and directives, i.e. that we are to respond to the love of God, to the inbreak of the eschatological times in Jesus, to the nearness to the end. (b) There is the example and there are the words of Jesus. The following of Christ must remain the basis of the Christian moral life, although it is true that his words must be interpreted according to their literary character. (c) There are the general directives, such as exhortations to joy, thankfulness, unceasing prayer, indifference to the world. These remain valid although their concrete expression may change from age to age. (d) There is the command of *agape*. It is a specific demand of Christianity: it is from the love of Christ that the demand of love in human life gets its motivation, its specificity and its content. There are also the biblical expressions of this demand in social life — as in 1 Cor. 13, 1 Thess. 5:14 and Col. 3:12. To the extent that these are general expressions they remain valid: their precise and concrete bodying-forth may require an analogous expression from one age to another. (e) There are more specific directives for various areas of life. These, he says, may require to be subjected to a more exacting hermeneutic. He considers that the directives of the baptismal catechesis in Eph. 4:17 and 5:5ff. and the directives of 1 Thess. 4:3 must be regarded as having a greater binding force because here the baptised were given a basic moral teaching. But that binding force does not apply to other directives, such as the place of women or of slaves or the attitude of the Christian to the state: about them, he says, the Spirit has led the church into a deeper understanding.[127]

Schürmann's overall position is that one must not jump to the conclusion that all New Testament precepts or directives are time-conditioned, even those mentioned in (e).[128] But it could hardly be said that he advanced the argument much beyond that. He seems to set out the problem rather than solve it. The critical question is how one discerns — and how the church is led to differentiate — between what is permanently valid and what is time-conditioned. Schürmann slides out of the difficulty. It is a job, he says, for the expert in hermeneutics and not for a mere exegete like him.[129]

What Ratzinger and Schürmann insist on is that there are moral norms in Scripture that are permanently valid. What disturbs them is the suggestion of some of the autonomy school that all the norms of Scripture are merely models or paradigms, which have to be re-interpreted by the Christian of today. Their fight for the validity of revealed norms is supported by several other moralists and biblical scholars: one finds that most contributors to the Italian Biblical Association's 1972 meeting on biblical morality deplored the autonomy position and urged that Scripture contains valid norms which are tied to Christian faith and specific to it.[130]

A number of authors who insist on specificity appeal to the Bible for something less precise and concrete than revealed norms. They acknowledge the need for what Häring, an early enthusiast for biblical morality, now calls 'a thorough going hermeneutic' in the application of biblical texts to moral problems.[131] They say that the Bible gives us truths — about our relationship with God, about the incarnation, about the new creation, about eschatology — which imply a specific Christian content.[132] There is not a single Christian truth, says Johannes Gründel of Munich, which does not have consequences for behaviour, some of which are unavailable to the non-believer.[133] They say that the Bible gives us new vision or intentions or values — such as poverty, renunciation of power, hope in the

59

face of suffering, mercy — or that it speaks to us of the virtues of those who have known the Lord.[134] There seem to be thrown together here two kinds of dependence on the Bible which ought to be distinguished. (a) The Bible may be appealed to as an authoritative revelation of moral values, intentions or dispositions, which are of permanent validity: that means that the Christian regards himself as, in some way, directed by God to have such values, intentions and dispositions. (b) The Bible may be appealed to as a source of Christian beliefs — something acknowledged by all Christians — which may be thought to imply or entail for the Christian a specific behaviour because of the world-view which they give him. It is not clear to what extent the authors are holding that the Bible is the authoritative revelation of values, intentions, dispositions, etc. The remark of Hans Rotter of Innsbruck is a statement of the problem rather than a solution to it. He says that to the extent that the values of the Bible express the Christian's new faith in God, in the human person and in eschatology, to that extent they are a requirement of Christian living in all ages.[135]

Two authors have suggested an approach to Christian ethics that is a development of this line of thought. They are less interested in the precise issue of specificity than in the question of how one is to approach the doing of Christian ethics. But they are convinced that the autonomy approach is inadequate. Their suggestions may offer significant possibilities for the future of a faith-ethic. Klaus Demmer criticises fellow-theologians for an approach to Christian morality that is too static and historical. Their approach, he finds, has in the main been limited to looking for additional moral material in Scripture, i.e. moral precepts that could be referred to in all ages. Such an approach, he believes, is doomed to failure. One should look rather to what he calls the specific self-consciousness or auto-experience of the Christian. One should look to the way in which nature and grace, faith and reason compenetrate one another and form a unity of consciousness which penetrates the whole of Christian thought and action. This 'anthropological predetermination', this Christian anthropology, gives fundamental attitudes which characterise the believer in all ages and which serve as a criterion in all moral judgments. Christian morality is the spontaneous result of this specific moral consciousness. Since the moral consciousness is not shared by the non-believer, neither will there be coincidence between the moral judgment of believer and unbeliever.[136] A similar line is taken by Michael Simpson in a reply to Gerard Hughes. He is strong on the need to think of Christian ethics not in the sense of additonal moral content given by an authority external to us but in terms of our self-awareness, of which our religious awareness forms an important part. The Christian's religious awareness, he says, has an influence on his moral consciousness, on the source of his moral discernment, and so must issue in distinctive moral content. So 'the distinctive (but not totally exclusive) features of the christian ethic are justified by reference to the distinctive and religiously differentiated awareness of Christians.[137]

The counter-attack of the *Glaubensethik* has taken other forms also. Ermecke and others have revived the *Agere sequitur esse* argument of the fifties: the responsibilities of the *agere in Christo* which follow from the new being in Christ can only be discovered by faith, he says.[138] With this, one can couple the contribution of the influential Swiss theologian, von Balthasar. He writes:

> A Christian ethic ought to be formulated taking Christ as its foundation... he is the concrete and absolute norm of all moral activity... The concrete existence of Jesus, his life, suffering, death and resurrection, assumes into itself all moral systems.... Morality is only answerable to this norm...[139]

For him the new form of existence of the Christian appears to invalidate every other kind of morality and moral thinking. He says that pre-biblical and extra-biblical morality are at best fragmentary: moreover, whatever is of value in the morality of the good non-Christian must be admitted to come either from the revelation of creation or from a Christian light that is found in pre-biblical or extra-biblical sources. But von Balthasar does not tell us how one is to derive moral content from one's life in Christ. He does not raise any of the problems of taking 'the concrete existence of Jesus' as a source of morality. The only suggestion he makes about content is that the Cross will issue in content for Christian life and that only the Christian can reach the golden rule of agape.

This last claim — that the moral requirement of agape is something specific to Christian ethics — is the one most widely met in the *Glaubensethik*. Almost every author mentions it: some of them express amazement that the autonomy movement should be blind to it.[140] The claim for the specificity of agape has a slightly different nuance from one to another. But none of them gets beyond a brief assertion of the fact: there is no extended treatment of the claim. On this point there does not seem to have been any development from the early renewal days.

A few other strands of the *Glaubensethik* deserve mention. Norbert Rigali has aroused some interest by his proposal that the issue of the identity of Christian ethics cannot be approached without a distinction between essential and existential ethics: by 'essential' he appears to mean the moral demands which are common to and expected of all men. The case of the autonomy movement for coincidence of content between Christian and secular ethics can at most apply to essential ethics, he says.[141] At the existential level there are personal choices made by Christians — especially choices of vocation — which are specific to and dependent on faith. Related to that is his assertion — found in the early renewal and now found widely in the *Glaubensethik* — that a secular ethic is static, limited and calculating, while Christian ethics is dynamic and seeks perfection:[142] Häring makes the provocative remark that those who exclude or minimise a specifically Christian morality are dominated by a static code morality.[143] Finally, we find that these authors include in their general position the weaker claim that Christianity gives a new depth, grounding, strength and clarity to moral demands.[144]

There the issue stands. The history which we have surveyed is, in some respects, cyclic. Since the upheaval of the fifties — the first major change in Roman Catholic thinking about morality for hundreds of years — we have come from the natural law ethic of neo-Scholasticism through the attempts to 'Christianise' morality in the renewal movement and back to natural law in the autonomy movement. We have come from the renewal through the reaction of the autonomy movement and back to further attempts to continue the line of renewal. Roman Catholics find themselves deeply divided on what all agree is a crucial issue. The division is not about a few additional moral demands by which the Christian is thought to be bound. It is about the source of morality, about where Christians seek their morals (the biblical revelation or the general human community). It is about the norm or standard of moral living (Christ or the rational man of philosophy). It is about the source of moral obligation (the will of God who reveals or human reason). And, as some have pointed out, it involves the question of the teaching competence of the church. No wonder McDonagh could say that, after twenty years of intensive activity, the quest for a renewed moral theology remains unfinished and confused.[145]

The situation is usually characterised as a clear division between the autonomous ethic and the *Glaubensethik*. The autonomy movement, as we saw, has two concerns: (a) that moral norms should be seen to come from within us rather than from outside of us; (b) that it be recognised that there is no specific Christian content — so that dialogue is possible. The *Glaubensethik* authors have defended the case for a specific content. This is understood by some of them as a revealed morality: that means that the Bible is the source of moral directives, which are obligatory for Christians, just as surely as it is a source of Christian belief. But there are intermediate positions. Böckle is usually placed in the autonomy school. But we saw that his interest seems to be point (a) above: moral norms, he says, are to be discovered by us but by us as Christians, i.e. by people enlightened by faith. Demmer, too — and perhaps Rotter and Gründel — occupies middle ground. His approach favours a specific content but he rejects any idea that we are to receive from revelation a set of revealed moral directives. For him morality — now as in New Testament times — is the product of a distinctive Christian self-awareness.

I have referred to a wide range of authors but have tried to deal with themes and approaches rather than with individuals. The debate about identity hangs on certain key issues. We can best examine the claims, the strengths and the weaknesses of each side and best advance the discussion by isolating these issues. I believe that some light can be thrown on them and some sharpness given to the discussion. There has been much talking at cross purposes. Part, at least, of the problem has been looseness of terminology and disagreement about the terms of the debate. Even to deal with this may be to offer some pointers to the way forward.

The questions which I believe to be central to the debate and which will occupy us for the rest of this work are as follows:

(i) The *Glaubensethik* appeals directly to biblical norms in support of its claim for specificity of content: the autonomy movement regards this as illegitimate. What is at issue here? Is there confusion about the notion of revelation?

(ii) The autonomy movement says that there is no specific content to Christian morality, only specific motivation: the *Glaubensethik* claims specificity of content. Very much depends on how one defines 'morality' , 'content' and 'motivation' but none of the authors from either side has examined the terms.

(iii) The *Glaubensethik* asserts that, even if there are no revealed norms, there are specific Christian truths and values and a specific Christian self-awareness and that these lead to a specific concrete behaviour. Can it show this: can the oppositon disprove it?[146]

(iv) The *Glaubensethik* asserts that the moral requirement of agape is specific to Christianity. Will this claim stand up to examination?

(v) To what extent is the disagreement about specificity a disagreement about moral ideals rather than about basic moral content. Both sides need to clarify their position on the status of ideals.

(iv) The autonomy ethic says that Christianity gives a specific context to morality. How useful is this term? Does the autonomy scheme ignore some important elements of Christian morality: in particular, does it have a consistent position on moral obligation?

Before we proceed to an analysis of these issues, a few general remarks may be helpful.

(a) I have retained the language of 'renewal', 'Christianising', etc. This, of course, begs the question. The question is whether it is the faith-ethic or the autonomy movement that offers genuine renewal and the authentic Christian understanding of morality.

(b) The debate has remained largely at the level of theory, of fundamental moral theology. We do not know how much specificity the *Glaubensethik* claims. The early renewal wanted to distance itself from natural law or mere ethics. It is not clear how much coincidence the *Glaubensethik* would allow between the discernment of the believer and the unbeliever. Its concern has been to defend the claim that Christian morality has a different source and a different standard from secular ethics. But it has not pursued the significance of that very far into the different areas of morality.

(c) The autonomy position is also largely theoretical and does not seem to test itself against reality. It says that the content of Christian morality is '*per se* accessible' to the unbeliever: one finds equivalent terms — 'theoretically possible', 'fundamentally intelligible', 'substantially equivalent'. Are these escape clauses ? One needs to ask: accessible to whom? Is the thesis saying that without Christianity anyone would arrive at the fullness of Christian morality if he or she attended seriously to the business of morals? Is it saying that, in practice, many/most people do? Is it saying that all people have the mental equipment for this but, for some reason, do not arrive at it? Is it our fallen state that is the reason? (If so, what is meant, in effect, is that the only human beings we know in the only world we know cannot arrive at the fullness of morality without revelation.) Would it be sufficient for the thesis of autonomy that some rare genius could arrive at full understanding but that it is not available to the generality of people without revelation? Is this what is meant by saying that the fullness of morality can be arrived at only with difficulty?

The same vagueness surrounds the terms 'human', 'secular', 'non-Christian morality': with what is Christian morality being compared? The term of comparison is elusive: as it is presented by the autonomy school it fades into ideas of what human beings could do, have the possibility of doing etc. It might be better to try to make a comparison with the judgments which people actually make about morals without Christian faith or thematic revelation. If the thesis of autonomy is to be true in any interesting sense it must mean that the content of what is proposed by Christian morality is available to people generally or, at least, to those who engage in morality seriously and scientifically. There are some areas of ethical thought where it should be possible to compare Christian morality more closely with the very considerable philosophical tradition, rather than make a hypothetical morality the term of comparison. Some attempt will be made to do that in Chapter 6. If philosophical ethics — or some of its more important and more representative systems — does not show an overlap with theological ethics there does not seem to be much point in continuing to say that human morality can reach or has the theoretical possibility of reaching the same content as Christian ethics. (Fuchs, repeating Vatican I, says that there are moral truths which are *per se* accessible to non-Christians, although they are not in fact known by them — does this mean never known by any non-Christian? How does one test this thesis and how useful is it for dialogue?).[147]

But it must be acknowledged that it is hard to pin down the terms of comparison. While, at first glance, the question of specificity looks straightforward and has been treated as such it becomes more elusive as it is examined. Even the meaning of the term 'Christian ethics/morality' is not entirely clear: are we talking about the actual morality of individuals or of churches? I take it to refer to the moral judgments that arise for individuals and communities from a faith that is alive, that is conscious of its tradition and that shapes world-view. The assumption of the question of specificity is that one can compare this Christian morality with the moral outlook of the citizen who does not subscribe to Christian belief.[148] The question is a valid and important one and I shall continue to pursue it in those general terms. But it is a more complex question than it looks. One can certainly try to isolate the factors that enter into Christian morality — if there is a specific morality. But it must be remembered that those who do not subscribe to Christianity do not share a common world-view: there are differences among them of moral outlook and of moral systems. It must be asked if judgment about the question of specificity — and about the possibilities of dialogue — will not depend on the precise term of comparison.

PART II

Analysis: The Issues

3

A Revealed Morality?

Roman Catholic moral theology does not have a long or rich tradition of appeal to the Bible. The renewal movement opened up for it new and exciting horizions. But it quickly began to emerge that appeal to biblical morality is more complex than had been anticipated: the new enthusiasm was soon dismissed as 'naive biblicism'.[1] The autonomy movement, in effect, says now that direct appeal to the Bible is neither necessary nor possible. The *Glaubensethik* position is that one must recognise that there is a revealed morality and that one is not doing Christian ethics if one does not do so.

The terms 'faith-ethic/morality', 'revealed ethic', 'specific ethic' are not synonyms. A specific ethic is not necessarily a revealed ethic and a revealed ethic is not necessarily specific. There could be a faith ethic that is not a revealed ethic in the traditional sense — as we shall see. It is the traditional Roman Catholic position that some natural truths of morality are revealed. But it is the position of the *Glaubensethik* that part of Christian morality is not only revealed but specific and therefore closed to unbelievers. Since this is found primarily in the Bible, approach to morality, they say, must be through the Bible.

The current orthodoxy of Roman Catholicism with regard to the authority of the Bible is summed up in the constitution *Dei Verbum* of Vatican II:

By this revelation then, the deepest truth about God and the salvation of man is made clear to us in Christ. ... Sacred Scripture is the word of God in as much as it is consigned to writing under the inspiration of the divine Spirit. ... The books of Scripture must be acknowledged as teaching firmly, faithfully and without error that truth which God wanted put

69

into the sacred writings for the sake of our salvation. . . . For the sacred scriptures contain the word of God and, since they are inspired really are the word of God; and so the study of the sacred page is, as it were, the soul of all theology.[2]

There is difference of opinion about whether this extends to morality or whether there is an essential difference here between faith and morals. The *Glaubensethik* maintains that God has not only communicated through the Bible some understanding of himself and of his purposes for us — the faith of Christianity — but that he has also made known how we are to live — the morality of Christianity. This means that through the Law and the prophets, through Jesus and the apostolic church, God has given us moral directives which are to be accepted on his authority as revealer. The stronger form of the claim is that he has revealed moral rules which are clear and valid in all ages. The weaker form is that he has revealed moral values, dispositions, intentions and attitudes which must characterise our moral life if we are to live truly as children of God; or that what we have are revealed moral paradigms or models. Some of these moral directives, it is maintained, are specific to Christianity so that Christian morality has a strong identity. This position is supported, as we saw, by the statement that the sharp distinction between faith and morals is unacceptable and that the rules, values and dispositions of the Bible are to be seen as a necessary expression of faith.

What we are dealing with in this chapter is the debate about a revealed morality, i.e. with the direct appeal to the Bible as a source of such rules, values, etc.[3] This differs from the much wider claim that the Bible is the source of a faith — of beliefs, stories, symbols — which influences discernment and which leads the Christian in any age to moral judgments that are specific. That also forms part of the *Glaubensethik* position. It appears to me to be a more profitable and more important approach to Christian morality and will occupy us in the next chapters.[4] It would be a mistake to make too sharp a distinction between the two. The frontier between prescriptive and indicative forms of language is blurred. More important, it can be argued that the revealed biblical morality is related to or issues from faith. But it is necessary to maintain the distinction of the two approaches.

70

The issue which immediately concerns us is that of direct appeal to the Bible as an authoritative source of moral teaching — whether of rules, of general moral orientations or of moral paradigms. It matters greatly in what sense it is regarded as authoritative. I take it as read that there is a wide range of ethical teaching in the Bible. About that fact there is no argument — I need only note that such teaching comes in various forms, that it can be general or particular, that it can be traced to different sources, that it appears in a religious setting with a variety of religious motivations and that the mind, words and example of Jesus are of special importance to it. Our problem is not one of biblical theology, of laying bare the ethical teaching of the Bible, and so it is not to my purpose to try to give a comprehensive account of it. Our question is (a) about the necessity and possibility of appealing to the Bible as a source of morality and (b) about whether, as such a source, it yields a specific morality. Most of what I am considering refers to New Testament morality. That is for two reasons (i) It is to this that our authors mainly refer. (ii) We are concerned with problems of use: whatever problems arise for New Testament morality arise even more sharply for Old Testament morality; if direct appeal to the New Testament as an authoritative source is invalid, appeal to the Old Testament is at least equally invalid. Our problem is, of course, part of the wider problem of the authority of the Bible as it is discussed in my church and in all the churches.[5] I consider it only as it applies to the debate about the identity of Christian ethics.

The autonomy movement rejects the appeal to the Bible as the source of moral directives. Any such appeal, it says, runs into so many philosophical, exegetical and hermeneutical difficulties as to invalidate it. The most radical objection concerns the manner in which moral positions are justified. All appeal to a revealed morality, it says, is a form of the divine command theory of morality. So it refers to the *Glaubensethik* position as 'Christ-positivism', 'revelation-positivism', 'theological positivism', 'obedience-morality'.[6] It rightly points out that the *Glaubensethik* fails to distinguish between the explanation of moral positions (or the genesis of them or the psychological process by which one arrives at them) and the justification of them: to say that one gets one's moral position from the Bible may explain one's having it but does not necessarily justify one's holding it.[7] The objection is very familiar to religious moralists. It says that appeal to the Bible — an argument of the form, 'One finds in the Bible . . . therefore . . .' or 'God has revealed . . . therefore . . .' — cannot be the ultimate justification of a moral position because one is appealing to what God commanded, said or did and that, in itself, can never be an adequate justification. Why should one do what God/Christ commanded or did? We are faced, it is argued, with a dilemma. Either one says that the good is what God commands and, in that case, one is making goodness a purely arbitrary matter with no relation to the structure of the universe and making morality a matter of the prudence involved in obeying the will of the stronger. Or else, one introduces into the argument an ethical notion, saying that God is or must be perfectly good and that, therefore, it makes perfectly good sense to obey what he has commanded. One is now postulating that there is an order of goodness independent of God and that we know something of this order: otherwise how could we recognise our God as the true and moral God and recognise that he ought to be obeyed? But if one knows morality independently of God, what need is there to appeal to a special revelation: will one's moral experience not suffice?[8] An additional strand to the objection stresses that to receive a moral command from God without being able to see why it is morally required is to render genuine moral response impossible.[9]

The short answer for the *Glaubensethik* is to accept that we do have some moral understanding independently of revelation and to recognise that what God commands is what is independently good. That, as we saw, is the traditional Roman Catholic position, even among the neo-Scholastics: Eric D'Arcy's summary of it is accurate:

> God forbids certain kinds of action because they are wrong, not vice versa; God commends, commands, or forbids certain kinds of action and certain frames of mind because he is essentially holy, and they are intrinsically good, or evil.[10]

(While this is certainly the tradition, I should like, in parentheses, to enter a few reservations. The first concerns the way in which von Balthasar states his position. 'A Christian ethic', he says, 'ought to be formulated taking Christ as foundation. . . . Christian morality is answerable only to this norm.'[11] Is this to be interpreted as a rejection of the human experience of morality? The second reservation is about some other expressions found in the *Glaubensethik*: we are told that morality is response to the love of God, is perfect submission to God, is the following of Christ, is walking in the Spirit.[12] Some of this, certainly, refers to the motive and the context of morality. But it also raises questions about definition and about how one assesses the human experience. A third reservation is that, while the tradition is as given above, the neo-Scholastics did slip into occasional aberrations, as indicated earlier. Not all modern authors avoid them either.)[13]

If we have an independent moral experience, why do we need a revelation? The obvious answer is that we do not have a complete understanding of morality and need to receive some moral directives from God. Two considerations might be adduced here. (a) The science of morals, as generations of moralists have reminded us, is a difficult one and one in which an authority might well be welcome. (b) There is, it could be argued, a Christian anthropology or view of reality and a corresponding Christian value system. If this is so, it could well be that one needs to receive from revelation some enlightenment about the moral inplications of such an anthropology. So there is a middle position between holding that all moral knowledge must be available to us without revelation and holding that all moral knowledge for Christians comes from revelation, and that one otherwise has no access to moral understanding. This middle position is the one which corresponds most to the tradition of Roman Catholicism. Hughes spends some time exposing the dilemma of one who holds that without revelation we have no access or only very limited access to moral understanding.[14] There was, as we pointed out, some tendency to this in the early days of renewal, especially in Tillmann and Hofmann. But, von Balthasar apart, it does not seem to be widely held at the present time.

Does a revealed morality render genuine moral response impossible? Not necessarily. There seems to be no good reason why revelation would not teach moral truths which find some resonance in our moral experience but which, without revelation, we cannot completely reach. One may have a basic or general sense of moral goodness but may require guidance in working out the details: recourse to Aristotle's *phronimos* is not

73

viciously circular.[15] This is accentuated if morality is, in any way, related to beliefs and stories that can only be known from revelation. The sensitivity and imagination that are required for the appreciation of a revealed moral directive may be awakened in one by sayings and directives that are related to the great ethos-shaping Christian stories of God's dealings with us. A good teacher extends one's understanding. A moral revelation may throw light on one's groping or confirm one's leaning towards a particular position.[16] But it should be remembered that it is a groping that is being done within a community that reflects on the whole of the revelation. Some Christians hold that the indissolubility of marriage is revealed, for instance. Does this render a genuine moral response impossible? May it not be that one has a sufficient appreciation of the importance of human relationships and commitments to be at least open to the possibility of the indissolubility of marriage and to be able, with the further light which revelation throws on human relations, to appropriate a revealed teaching on the point?

Thus far I have only been concerned to ask whether the notion of a revealed morality is at all tenable and whether it can, in any sense, serve as a justification for a moral position. But is there a revealed morality? Some of the autonomy school maintain that there is not, that revelation does not extend to morality. If there is no moral revelation, then the Bible is not authoritative in this respect and there is no reason why one should feel obliged to appeal to it. Fuchs and Auer many times make the point that the Christ event is of religious and theological, but not of moral, significance. It is concerned with salvific liberation, they say, rather than with moral doctrine.[17] It is true and obvious that there is much moral material in the Bible. But the Vatican II Constitution on Revelation tells us that what we must seek is 'that truth which God wanted put into the sacred writings for the sake of our salvation': it says that we should carefully investigate 'what meaning the sacred writers really intended and what God wanted to manifest by means of their words'.[18] Hughes puts the objection forcibly:

> From the fact that the biblical writings are everywhere inspired, it does not follow that everything which they appear to us to say is what their writers intended to say; nor that everything which their writers intended to say is true; nor that everything which is truly said is a revealed truth...[19]

74

A number of subordinate ideas appear in the objection. We have seen that, in their effort to preserve the uniqueness of Christian morality, the *Glaubensethik* authors point to the close link between faith and ethics — something that is a commonplace among biblical moralists. The objection says that they make too much of this. It is undeniable that the link between faith and ethics is a constant of the biblical tradition. Not all Christians understand the link in the same way. But that there is such a link is hardly in question. It was an important contribution of the Mosaic tradition, based on ancient near-Eastern treaty formulae. It was insisted upon by the prophetic literature. It was stressed by the New Testament writers, so much so that one may justifiably claim that the fact of such a link is part of the revelation, a salvation-truth which God wanted to make known. But does the revelation go beyond this very general truth? Perhaps, all that is revealed to us is that there is a bond between faith and ethics, that God does require us to be morally good. The *Glaubensethik*, as we saw from Ratzinger and Schürmann, seeks to hold that the individual moral positions, which are related to faith, especially in the writings of Paul, are the 'inner necessity of grace', not 'a variable accessory to the gospel' but something guaranteed by the Lord and thus constituting part of revelation.[20] But is there any reason for thinking that these individual moral positions are anything more than the opinions of the writers offered in the course of reinforcing the general truth that our moral behaviour is intimately connected with the kingdom?

It is difficult to see how this fundamental question can be answered in a straightforward manner. But there are a number of related considerations which the authors of the autonomy school have not been slow to fasten on. Such cast further doubt on the acceptance of a moral revelation. The first is the fact that the New Testament writers, especially those in the Pauline tradition (it is not necessary for our purposes to discuss what letters can be attributed to Paul himself) are so dependent on the ethic of the time. The outstanding examples are the *Haustafeln* of Colossians 3:18-4:1, Ephesians 5:22-6:9, (cf. 1 Peter 2:13-3:7) and the lists of virtues and vices of 1 Corinthians 6:9-11 and Galatians 5:16-25. There can hardly be any doubt that these are Hellenistic Jewish (originally Stoic) in origin.[21] It is true that they are put in a Christian setting. They are given a Christian

75

motivation. There is even an attempt to proclaim a distinctively Christian way of life, which would mark Christian off from pagan. 'Wives, be subject to your husbands, as is fitting in the Lord' (Col.3:18); 'For the husband is head of the wife as Christ is the head of the church...' (Eph.5:23); 'You must no longer live as the Gentiles do' (Eph.4:17). But there is much reason for thinking that what is proposed here is not a new standard of conduct derived from Christian theology but a familiar standard of conduct that is given a new base or motivation. There is no indication that the lists of virtues and vices relate to or are derived from Christian faith or hope.[22]

If this is so, does it not weaken the likelihood that we have in the Bible a revealed morality valid for our time? So the case has been made by some authors expounding autonomy that what is revealed is rather the power and motivation of Christianity as an energy for moral goodness. What one learns from the Bible is that one must constantly engage with the values of the time, that the Christian must proceed in the world *modo humano*.[23] Perhaps we should go further and say with Blank that what we are to learn here from Paul is the relativising of all law. If Paul could see fit to jettison God's Old Law, Blank says, he teaches us that we are not to seek our morals by fastening on to the New Testament as a law, either. What we are to learn from him and from his use of the morality of his time is that every human, historically conditioned statement of moral norms is relative. In every age the Christian must discover the expression of the Christian spirit.[24]

Some of the *Glaubensethik* authors have tried to meet this objection by saying that Paul did not simply accept the morality of his time but made a critical choice of faith. Thus Ratzinger insists that there was no such thing as the morality of the time but, rather, conflicting moralities, among which the early church had to choose. This choice, he says, was determined by Old Testament standards and by the 'way of thinking of Jesus': it was a faith-choice.[25] However, the fact that Paul or the other writers chose between pagan virtues or mores is hardly, in itself, decisive. Presumably, the good pagan would also choose. What Ratzinger needs to do is to bring forward instances in which faith served as a hermeneutical key in the confrontation with paganism and to show that this gave Christians a specific morality. That he does not do.

A further consideration which tells against the possibility of a revealed morality is the fact that Paul and the apostolic writers were clearly limited by the horizons of the time in moral matters. The most obvious instances are well known. Paul accepts an inferior position for women and this does not seem to be affected by other assertions of his about the equality of all the sons of God. What must be even more disturbing is the fact that his position about the obedience of women, their silence and their being veiled are attached to or derived from what seem to be theological or faith-assertions. 'For man was not made from woman but woman from man. Neither was man created for woman but woman for man.' (1 Cor.11:3). 'I permit no woman to teach or to have authority over men; she is to keep silent. For Adam was formed first, then Eve; and Adam was not deceived, but the woman was deceived and became a transgressor' (1 Tim.2:9). 'Wives be subject to your husbands as to the Lord. For the husband is the head of the wife as Christ is the head of the church' (Eph.5:22). The same is true of the argument about slaves. Servants are to be subject to their masters, as to Christ, 'doing the will of God from the heart' (Eph.6:5). In 1 Peter 2:18, the slave is to submit to his master: 'For to this you have been called, because Christ also suffered for you, leaving you an example that you should follow in his steps.' One must take seriously what Weidinger says about this: 'The rule about slaves in this *Haustafel* has the deepest motivation that we encounter in early Christianity for the demand to persevere in slavery.'[26] About the rules for slaves and the motivation given for them Sanders says that we must recognise that a truly horrible thing has occurred here to the Pauline ethical norm of concern for one's fellow-man.[27] It could be argued, on the other hand, that Paul was giving the best and most practical advice in the circumstances of the time and that he was motivating his Christians to bear their difficult lot. Perhaps this was part of what he was doing. But he also seems to use faith-considerations to support or justify positions that we would now regard as morally unacceptable. Even our very difficulty here in determining what Paul was proposing sets in relief the problem of appealing to the Bible for one's ethic.

None of this decisively proves that there is no revelation of morality. But the cumulative doubts which can be raised against many of the precepts of the early church make one wary of accepting any biblical moral precept as of faith. One could go on to fault the *Glaubensethik* further for failing to distinguish, in the Bible, between normative ethics and paraenesis. By normative ethics one means the teaching of ethical values, norms, attitudes. By paraenesis one means the attempt to move or encourage the hearer to be moral, to follow what one already knows to be the Christian way. There is no doubt that much of the biblical material on ethics is in the latter style: it involves linking the moral encouragement or warning to some aspect of faith. There is, therefore, an indicative-imperative structure, as it is said, in Christian morals: given the richness of early Christian theology, the indicative admits of almost endless variation. Much of the energy of the biblical theologians went into detailing this link between faith and ethics and it was taken up enthusiastically by the moral theologians. Schnackenburg is a fair example of this style of writing:

> St Paul varied these basic ideas in his moral teaching by the use of constantly changing new images and points of view. We are transferred from slavery or military service under sin to the service of God (Rom.6:12-14,16-23). Through Christ we are reconciled to God, but we must also reconcile ourselves with God (2Cor.5:19,cf.5:20). The spirit of God dwells in us and drives us on, but we must allow ourselves to be impelled by him and mortify the (sinful) works of the body (Rom.8:11,cf.8:13). We live in the Spirit, now we must walk in the Spirit (Gal.5:25). We have died with Christ and now we must mortify our members upon the earth (Col.3:3,cf.3:5). Our 'old man' has been crucified with Christ (Rom.6:6), but we must in turn put off the old man and put on the new (Eph.4:22-24;Col:3.9ff.).[28]

His conclusion is that religion and morality are brought into the closest possible relationship; faith imperatively demands proof in moral action. This, he claims, is more than providing morality with a religious motivation; it is giving it a super-natural foundation.[29]

The objection to this is that to regard the religious truth as the foundation of an ethical position is to misconceive the purpose of the sacred writer. From the fact that this kind of appeal to faith is made one cannot conclude that the imperative is derived from the indicative. One cannot conclude, just because the writer linked his exhortation with a faith-consideration, that he is giving a moral rule based on faith.[30] Schüller alleges that Ratzinger's position on the link of faith and ethics fails completely to take account of this. His own position is quite clear. He maintains that there is no new ethical imperative in the Bible that is not available to secular morality and that one must not presume that Jesus or Paul or John or the other writers were communicating to their hearers an ethical demand that they were not already aware of. After all, Paul's thesis was that the Romans knew the law in their hearts. What the biblical writer was doing, Schüller says, was trying to exhort his hearers to do the good which they already knew. So his final position is that everywhere in the Old or New Testament where ethics is related to gospel one has an instance of paraenesis, not of normative ethics.[31] He challenges Ratzinger to show how faith leads to moral insights about marriage, the family, promise-keeping, etc.[32]

This is important because Roman Catholic theology has often based moral positions on faith-considerations, e.g. it regards the symbol of Christ and his church in Ephesians 5 as proof of its position on indissolubility.[33] More widely, it is important because it also raises the question of what exactly is being claimed for the moral teaching of the Bible, for example when a moral topic is introduced by biblical reference: we saw this problem in the early writings of Häring. Is it a source of ethical information? Or is it a source of faith-obedience? Is it a further clarification and illustration of insights that are already substantially available to the non-Christian? Is it, as Schüller and others maintain, a source of encouragement and exhortation? It makes a considerable difference to one's methodology whether the Bible is seen as offering us moral directives derived from faith or offering exhortation. Paraenesis gives no new ethical insights. It has the effect that the persons addressed find themselves confronted with familiar ethical positions: they experience the demand to conversion, to do penance, to change their lives — because they are reminded of the fact that God has loved them, or that Christ has died for them, or that they are temples of the Holy Spirit, or that their bodies are members of Christ, etc. In paraenesis what is important is the efficacy of the appeal, i.e. whether one moves the reader or listener to change his or her ways and live up to his or her obligations. In normative ethics what is important is the cogency and the clarity of the argument.

79

It is clearly necessary to keep this distinction between normative ethics and paraenesis in mind in one's use of the Bible. But can one accept Schüller's blanket statement that every instance of the union of faith and ethics is an instance of paraenesis rather than of normative ethics? Is it the case that Paul or the other writers are never teaching morals, i.e. never opening to their hearers a way of life that accords with being Christian but always exhorting them to do what they already know? This I find hard to accept. I wonder about:

> For it has been granted to you that for the sake of Christ you should not only believe in him, but also suffer for his sake.... Do nothing from selfishness or conceit, but in humility count others better than yourselves. Let each of you look not only to his own interests, but also to the interests of others. Have that mind among yourselves, which you have in Christ Jesus, who, though he was in the form of God, did not count equality with God a thing to be grasped, but emptied himself, taking the form of a servant... (Phil.1:29ff.)

or,

> Therefore, I tell you do not be anxious for your life, what you shall eat, nor for your body what you shall put on. For life is more than food and the body more than clothing.... But if God so clothes the grass which is alive in the field today and tomorrow is thrown into the oven, how much more will he clothe you, o men of little faith. And do not seek what you are to eat and what you are to drink, nor be of anxious mind. For all the nations of the world seek these things; and your Father knows that you need them. Instead, seek his kingdom ... (Lk.12:22ff.)

or,

> Go, sell what you have and give to the poor, and you will have treasure in heaven and come, follow me.... 'How hard it will be for those who have riches to enter the kingdom of God' (Mark,10:21ff.)

or,

> And there are eunuchs who have made themselves eunuchs for the sake of the kingdom of heaven. (Matt.19:12).

> The unmarried man is anxious about the affairs of the Lord, how to please the Lord; but the married man is anxious about worldly affairs, how to please his wife. (1 Cor.7:33).

or,

> Let no one seek his own good, but the good of his neighbour.
> (1 Cor.10:24).

or,

> ... we, though many, are one body in Christ and individually
> members one of another ... love one another with brotherly
> affection.... Bless those who persecute you ... do not be
> haughty but associate with the lowly; never be conceited ...
> Do not overcome by evil but overcome evil with good.
> (Rom.12:2,5,10,14,16,21.)

> Be kind to one another, tenderhearted, forgiving one another
> as God in Christ forgave you. (Eph.4:32)

> For you know the grace of Our Lord Jesus Christ, that though
> he was rich, yet for your sake he became poor, so that by his
> poverty you might become rich. (2 Cor.8:8)

> By this we know love, that he laid down his life for us; and we
> ought to lay down our lives for the brethren. (1 Jn.3:16).

or,

> Do not resist one who is evil. But if one strikes you on the right
> cheek, turn the other also. (Matt.5:38).

Such statements must, of course, be interpreted according to
their genre and their setting — but that is not the point just at
the moment. They may belong more to values, attitudes and
ideals than to moral rules. Their place in Christian moral life
may depend on how one defines morality and moral content —
and that is something that must await the next chapter. But it
does seem to me to be arguable that they are not just paraenetic
but are proposing a moral stance that is seen as related to a
particular faith-vision. This should emerge more clearly in the
following chapters. While, therefore, the distinction between
normative ethics and paraenesis is important, the very general
statement of Schüller appears to me to be too sweeping.

Another serious difficulty of which moralists gradually
became aware is that one cannot easily refer to biblical ethics or
to the morality of the bible. The Scripture scholar, de la
Potterie, rightly pointed out to the Italian moralists in their 1972
meeting that there is a tension between different types of New
Testament ethics and that one cannot say that any one type is
the distinctive New Testament ethic.[34] There are different

theologies among the biblical writers and different conceptions of morality related to them. Has the Law been superseded (Rom.7:4) or is it the case that not a jot or tittle of it is to pass away (Matt.5:17-19)? How is the Christian to understand morality: is it faith that is crucial to salvation for us as it was for Abraham (Gal.3; Rom.4:3) or are we to learn from James that works justify (James 2:20ff.)? Is the Christian commanded to love the wide world and the whole of humanity or is the Christian to love the brethren who are taken out of the world (John 13:34; 17:9)? To take a very obvious example, both the motive of action and its content are sometimes related to the fact that 'the appointed time has grown very short' so that 'from now on let those who have wives live as though they had none' (1 Cor.7:29). At other times Christians are encouraged to settle down and be good citizens, obeying the state and paying their taxes, since the state is the will of God (Rom.13:1ff.). Likewise, the call to discipleship and to suffering in Mark is dominated by the ideas of watching and waiting (Mark 13:29; 8:34) while in Luke it is a call to endurance and to bring forth fruit in patience (Luke 8:15; 21:13).[35] The biblical scholar will explain why the New Testament writers have different and shifting theological viewpoints. But that only goes a small part of the way to solving the problem of the moralist.

Even in the accounts of the conduct of Jesus himself there are difficulties that are not easy to reconcile. He counsels non-resistance to evil but resists it himself in the cleansing of the temple. He counsels meekness and patience but mercilessly condemns the Scribes and Pharisees. We too easily assume that the gospel accounts give us a clear and obvious model to imitate. But the moral life of Jesus as we find it is more complex than that and leaves us with some questions. It comes as a further shock to us to discover that some have found part of his conduct and preaching cruel, harsh and unloving.[36]

Hanging over all of this is the wider question of whether we can reach the ethical teaching or practice of Jesus. It is true that one does not need this in order to claim that there is a revealed morality: God can make his will known through the faith of the early church and its stories about Jesus. But if the sayings and conduct of Jesus are to have a special cogency, if discipleship or following of the biblical Christ is uniquely the Christian way — as many from Paul down have suggested and especially many of

82

our renewal authors[37] — the question of reaching the ethic of Jesus is a critical one. We know that when the evangelists attribute a teaching or conduct to Jesus, it is to one who is the object of faith they attribute it, one who is now the Lord. Their faith — their different individual conceptions of that faith and their different purposes — could not fail to colour the tradition of his words and deeds and it refracts into different theologies. This makes it difficult to affirm that at any particular point we reach the precise teaching of Jesus. Even if one could, one is always aware of the nagging question of the extent to which the ethic of Jesus himself was related to his world-view and to his knowledge. The debate about the presuppositions of the Sermon on the Mount is a case in point.

All of this makes any facile appeal to the Bible look naive. In spite of that, however, it may well be that the consistency of the early church's ethics is more striking than its diversity. This does seem to me to be the case. Generations have been convinced that the New Testament suggests a form and shape of moral life and that one can speak of a moral outlook that is characteristically Christian or in accordance with the Bible. This may relate not so much to moral rules but to the more general level of attitudes, dispositions and intentions.[38] It is impossible to avoid the conclusion that the way of life expected of the early Christian included love, consideration of others and forgetfulness of self. It included a readiness to serve others in humility and to suffer and forgive. It involved a readiness to strive for unity. It called for a relativising of worldly goods and success. There is an overall consistency of direction here which goes some distance to meeting the objection that there is no such thing as a biblical ethic or that it is, at best, a thing of shreds and patches.

These considerations may be very general but they have important and far-reaching implications for behaviour. One may put the matter in perspective by saying that there are values, purposes, dispositions and intentions in human life that are certainly not recommended by the Bible and that are clearly antithetical to its outlook. How these general considerations will be cashed in terms of concrete behaviour, whether they will stand up to other objections to biblical ethics, whether they yield a behaviour or content that is specifically Christian, whether this behaviour will differ from one age to another, are all further questions. The only point that is being made at the moment is that there are biblical directives, albeit of a very general kind, that give a consistent and far-reaching vision of moral life, so that the legitimacy of appeal to the Bible cannot be entirely overcome on the grounds of the diversity of its morality. Biblical faith did call forth a moral style and behaviour in the early church. I shall argue in Chapter 5 that Christian faith still calls forth a typical way of life, and we shall consider how specific that way of life was in the early church, or is now.

Another problem is what used to be referred to as the peril of modernising Jesus. It has to do with the exegetical and hermeneutical problems of understanding what the Bible says and applying it in modern society. The first part of the problem is well put by Hughes: he hits off nicely the casualness of approach to the Bible which has bedevilled moral theology since the renewal:

> Theologians who would never dream of taking a literalist view of Genesis I, Jonah, or Mark 13, are still perfectly capable of being quite uncritical when it comes to New Testament ethics. . . . Fundamentalism, which in the end tries to deny that exegetical problems exist, still dies hard.[39]

What does the biblical text mean? The difficulty of interpreting the Sermon on the Mount is well known. The problem of the meaning of *me epi porneia* (Matt. 19:9) is always with us. The recent Roman Catholic *Declaration on Sexual Ethics* engages in very doubtful exegesis in its condemnation of homosexuality and masturbation.[40] Examples could be multiplied. But is this an insuperable problem? Is it such as to invalidate all recourse to the Bible? I think not. It is for this that the science of exegesis exists. It has made considerable progress. It is true that it ought to make us more cautious — one hopes that it will. It is true that difficulties remain and that some of them are in crucially important areas. But the science of exegesis should make us more confident rather than less. It enables us to make a more informed appeal to the Bible. Such an intelligent appeal hardly requires that we be 'entirely confident' that we have understood or that we can 'always guarantee to have properly understood the New Testament text' — as Hughes demands.[41] If one were to take this absolutely seriously, it would render not only biblical ethics but biblical faith impossible, since one faces the same exegetical problems there.

The second part of the objection has to do with hermeneutics, with how we are, today, to understand the biblical precepts and prohibitions. The fact that we use the same terms as the Bible does not mean that we refer to the same reality. It may well be that the human meaning and significance of institutions and relations have changed since biblical times. It may be that our increased understanding of psychology and anthropology demands a more nuanced approach to behaviour which the Bible condemned. Would Paul have condemned all homosexuality absolutely if he knew about it what we know today? Would Jesus have condemned divorce? Schillebeeckx makes much of the fact that the present cultural understanding and experience of marriage is quite different from that of Christ's time. In Christ's time it was not thought of primarily as an equal interpersonal relationship of love. It was thought of almost exclusively as an institution for the continuance of the tribe, in which woman's role was that of child-bearer and was inferior. So, he says, we are faced with the real historicity of the essence of marriage. The hermeneutical question for us is how we are to translate the early Christian message of the unchristian character of divorce, which was given in the New Testament in a specific social understanding of marriage, into today's situation, which has a different experience and understanding of marriage and a differently structured set of sexual relationships.[42] There is a further important strand to the objection as we shall see in a moment.

It is obvious that such objections apply most forcibly to biblical rules or precepts. If the Bible is held to contain a revelation of some rules, that means that it prescribes for certain areas of life a precise mode of behaviour for Christians in all ages. Roman Catholics have held that some of these rules are absolute. For example, the church has interpreted the biblical teaching to mean the absolute indissolubility of Christian marriage.[43] Absolute moral rules are notoriously difficult to sustain — by comparison with more general moral directives. The more one descends to particulars, as in rules, the more is one's moral directive subject to exceptions. Moreover, if the argument for biblical rules is supported by the claim that they are the expression of faith, it must be conceded that it is easier to establish a link between faith and a very general moral directive than between faith and a very precise moral rule. Nevertheless, as we have seen, there is strong support in Roman Catholic circles for the position that the Bible reveals God's law in the form of moral rules.

We have noted, however, that some *Glaubensethik* authors take the position that what is normative in biblical ethics is not rules but more general directives, such as attitudes, values, dispositions and intentions. They mention exhortations to have attitudes of humility, of trust, of joy, of confidence, to value poverty and detachment from riches, to have a readiness to forgive, to be willing to seek the rights of others and not one's own.[44] To say that such moral directions or orientations for life are revealed is to say that the Christian is directed by God to have such in his life, however they are to be realised from age to age, and to avoid the opposite. The position of those who suggest that one should interpret the directives of the Bible as 'ethical patterns' reduces also to saying that there is a particular moral thrust or orientation — a normative core — enshrined in the biblical ethic which must be preserved but may be differently expressed from age to age. So Blank says that precepts are not to be literally accepted but regarded as types which admit of a different interpretation today.[45] Kerber proposes that one can find the general moral thrust in the concrete biblical directive — one can find what Jesus desired for us — and can translate it from age to age.[46] It should be noted, though, that it was precisely this suggestion of biblical precepts as patterns or types rather than as clear directives that was regarded by Ratzinger as a betrayal of biblical ethics.

It is true that such open and general moral directives can more easily accommodate themselves to different circumstances and times than the precise directive that slaves should obey their masters or that wives should obey their husbands or that one should not leave one's wife and marry another or some of the prohibitions in the lists of vices which we have considered already. It is also true that they can be more easily linked to faith. But it seems to me that many of the same problems arise for them as for rules. Are they part of the revelation? May attitudes, values, dispositions and intentions not be culture-bound or bound by a particular theology just as much as rules? To what extent are the exhortations of 1 Cor.7.29 dependent on a belief in the imminent return of the Lord:

> ... let those who have wives live as though they had none, and those who mourn as though they were not mourning, and those who rejoice as though they were not rejoicing, and those who buy as though they had no goods, and those who deal with the world as though they had no dealing with it.

Here there are some general directives for the Christian: are they of permanent value? How is one to know? If there is a revealed morality how is the Christian or the church to discriminate between what is still valid and what is clearly not applicable to Christian life to-day?

The attempt to discriminate between the various biblical directives runs into what Fuchs and Schüller regard as a very decisive element of their objection. They clinch the point about hermeneutical and exegetical problems by pointing out that we have, in fact, dropped some of the directives of Paul, notably those concerning the role of women and the position of slaves. In doing so we acknowledge that, whatever about there being a link between faith and ethics, Paul's faith was not enough to liberate him from the cultural horizon of his time. By what process, they ask, do we discriminate — as we clearly must. Their answer is that we do so not by appeal to the New Testament (which gives us no help in the matter) but by independent appeal to our moral experience, to our unaided (i.e. not aided by faith) reason.[47] In effect, we abandon the Bible as a guide. It ceases to be authoritative for us as a source of moral directives. 'It is thus wholly misleading', says Hughes, 'to suggest that our own moral reasoning must itself be based on revelation as it is transmitted by the New Testament texts.'[48] We must always subject the bible to the criticism of our reason, otherwise we can never be sure of its validity. So he finds appeal to the Bible viciously circular.[49]

This is a serious objection to any form of biblical directive. But is it as decisive as the authors think? The basic element in the objection is that one must step outside the biblical ethic in order to judge it. But is this correct? It is true that the Christian community can stick too rigidly to the biblical precept. But, like any other community, it may be open to development. It may seek to deepen and purify its insights. In doing so it does not shed its tradition or step outside it. It tests it against experience. If the community's faith is a living thing, if it admits of development, if

87

it has filtered out some elements of the faith of past ages, even of the biblical age, may the same process not take place with the community's moral tradition? What is most important to remember is that it is not an unbiblical person, a non-believer who tests the biblical ethic against his or her present-day experience but one who lives in the tradition of the Bible with its perspectives and values.

It is one who approaches the Bible with a pre-understanding that is already inwardly Christian, whose world-view is shaped by the great Christian stories. He or she does not shed this so as to enter into dialogue with the past. For example, the Christian brings to his attempt to understand the value of the Sermon on the Mount for today the Christian stories about the providence and forgiveness of God, about a future life with God, about the death-resurrection of Jesus Christ. Without such a background it is difficult to appreciate the thrust of the Sermon.[50]

When the Christian tries to enter into the faith of an earlier age and its moral life he may find moral teaching which he will reject because he is aware of the presuppositions and questions which occasioned it and which he sees to be no longer valid. But there may also be moral directives which he knows to have been influenced by faith considerations and which he finds no good reason to reject. This is more likely to be true of the more general moral directives — such as the command to love and forgive others to the end. This is so because of the open texture of such directives and attitudes. They are more likely to be of enduring value. But even here we must discriminate. The fact that such general directives and attitudes appear in the Bible is not *a priori* a reason for regarding them as answers to our present experience. As we have seen, some are born out of theological positions that we recognise today to have been mistaken. e.g. belief in an imminent eschatology. It is no easy solution to say, as some of the *Glaubensethik* have said, that such are paradigms or that they contain a kernel of truth. It is not possible to regard the kernel as a precise content that can be extracted from its expression and from the questions that gave rise to it. There is required a dialogue between present and past that is entirely aware of the presuppositions of both. But, that said, it is to be recognised that there is a link between the functioning of faith-ethos and ethic in the first and the twentieth centuries. There is a commonness of faith, of world-view seeking expression in daily life. Because there is, the apostolic community's attempt to express its faith in daily life has a significance for us. It does not make sense to take seriously the faith of that community and to discard completely its attempt to live that faith. It appears to me, then, that one cannot dismiss the very possibility that it could have normative significance for today. One must find a way between this extreme and the other which would say that because a moral directive appears in the Bible this is a priori a reason for regarding it in its precise statement as a valid directive for to-day. One must rather continue the Christian tradition of patiently examining both the faith and the morals of the Bible. One does this in accordance with a developing understanding of hermeneutics. But one does it from within the tradition.

So the community's discernment process is not one which logically involves making 'pure rationality' the criterion — if that means a rationality untouched by the Bible. That would mean that one must jettison the Bible as a source. Hughes says that Christianity requires a moral reflection that is 'epistemologically prior to our appeal to revelation' so that 'an independent morality is an essential tool in interpreting Christian tradition'.[51] This admits of different interpretations. A general moral awareness is necessary before a particular moral position or code can be appropriated. But if Hughes's position is that Christian moral experience and tradition must be answerable to 'an independent morality' in all its details, this appears to me to be incorrect. Such a position refuses to allow that faith considerations can have any effect on moral content. That this is not entirely satisfactory I shall argue more fully later.

The issue of a revealed morality involves a sharp division between our two shcools of thought and it obviously has serious implications for the doing of Christian ethics. If there is no revealed morality or if appeal to it is impossible, then much of the Christian tradition has been employing a method of moral argument that is invalid. But has the case been proven? A great lack in the debate has been some discussion of the key term, i.e. revelation. What does one mean by a revealed morality? It appears to be assumed by the authors on both sides that we have an agreed position about that. One might, first of all, question the implication that revelation is to be identified with the Bible. But what one particularly misses is an acknowledgment that our approach to the text of the Bible and the kind of authority which we give to it will be affected by our notion of revelation.

Until the middle years of this century Roman Catholic theology was dominated by Vatican I's theology of revelation.[52] Its central idea of revelation was that it is a matter of truth-propositions. Revelation, it said, besides confirming natural truths gives access to truths that are outside the possibility of the human intellect's knowledge if left to itself. It reveals truths about God and his purposes to us in order to guide us to our destiny. Such truths, it said, came to the human race by a special insight or inspiration to an individual prophet or sacred writer and were committed to writing in the Bible. The line of communication was God — the inspired writer — the Bible — the community. The intellectual content of such truths was to be accepted on the authority of God and not because they are intrinsically evident. So a contrast was set up between revelation and human experience, between faith and reason, between the authority of God and intrinsic reasons.

The indications are that in the debate about Christian morality both sides are still operating with this notion of revelation. The idea of revealed moral truths, fixed in their expression and valid for all time because communicated by God and found in the Bible, is prominent in the *Glaubensethik* thinking But the objections set up by the writers of the autonomy school also require such a notion of revelation. They object to a 'morality from beyond'. They regard a revealed morality as carrying the implication of being unintelligible. They make a sharp contrast between revelation and human experience. But such objections are valid only against the outdated revelation-theology of Vatican I. The odd thing is that what divides the parties is also what unites them.

How would the debate look if some of the elements of a modern theology of revelation were attended to? Much has been happening in this area in Roman Catholicism but it has not infiltrated moral theology. To talk about revelation, it is now widely agreed, is not to talk about truths passively received by an individual and passed on to the community for its acceptance on the authority of God. It is to talk about the fact that God reveals himself in human history, that within human communities and their traditions he enables his spiritual creatures to enter into an awareness of him. It is an awareness that is subject to the limitations of its time. It is variously

90

described as predominantly insight, understanding, experience, faith.[53] It is now more readily agreed that it is not confined to the Judaeo-Christian tradition: it occurs in all religious traditions and even outside of what are formally regarded as religions. It occurs in everyday events as well as in altogether special occurences such as the 'event' of Jesus, who is the high point of God's self-communication and of the response of faith. So that the contrast between Christian and non-Christian is not one between natural knowledge and revelation: human beings do not exist in a natural situation. What occurs in Judaeo-Christianity is not something of a different order from what occurs elsewhere. What is special to Christianity is greater clarity, fullness, certainty.[54] But if this is so, it is not because Jesus delivered himself of a set of fully articulated divine truths of a religious or moral kind which the apostles were to remember and hand on to us. What we have in the New Testament is the apostolic community's interpretation of Jesus Christ and of the implications of life in Christ and we know how gradually this was arrived at. It is a faith-experience that is caught in the Bible in a variety of ways for a variety of concerns. This is indeed our privileged access to God. And yet we know that what we have in the Bible is a faith and therefore a revelation that bears the marks of the questions, the presuppositions and the world-view of those who were actively involved in receiving it.

Our moral theologians are interested in the authority of the biblical text: in doing so they must take account of such considerations. In this new perspective there will be some reconciliation of opposites. On the one hand, there will have to be some modification of the view that the Christian revelation gives us immutable norms which are authoritative for all times and places: to hold this as an *a priori* position is to ignore how revelation occurs. On the other, it must be acknowledged that in such a perspective too much cannot be made of the objection that a revealed morality necessarily involves a 'morality from beyond'. Nor can the same strong contrast be maintained between a revealed morality and human moral experience. In particular, there is no good reason for the suggestion that a revealed morality will be unintelligible and destructive of human responsibility. The religious community arrived at its understanding of itself and its life through reflection on human events including the presence to it of Jesus Christ in his human and risen life. To say that some aspects of its morality are to be regarded as revealed does not necessarily involve one in saying that they come from outside human experience or that they are foreign to general moral experience.

These considerations take some of the sting from the general objection of the autonomy school to the very idea of a revealed morality. They do not, however, minimise the particular difficulty of recourse to the Bible for moral guidance. Even if one allows that the very notion of a revealed morality is defensible the major problem remains. It is the authority to be given to the apostolic community's perception of moral life. If one takes seriously the fact that any divine message is subject to the limitations of time, place and culture can one attach permanent value to any moral statement of the apostolic community and, if so, in what sense — as precept, general ideal, paradigm?

The issue shades into a wider one that would take us outside the scope of this work. That is the controverted area of authority — whether it be the authority of church leaders or of the *sensus fidelium*. Much will depend on how this authority in the community is understood, on how it is thought to function and with what dependence on the methods of patient scientific enquiry. The fact of authority does not obviate the necessity to take seriously the problems considered here about a revealed morality: authority is subject to such considerations. Judgments about the validity of biblical directives cannot be conjured up from nowhere: they must be informed judgments. Official Roman Catholic statements and some of the *Glaubensethik* authors only grudgingly recognise the real problems here. The document *Sexual Ethics*, for example, asserts that divine revelation 'manifests the existence of immutable laws' which are identical for all human beings, and simply dismisses any suggestion that the 'precepts of Sacred Scripture are to be regarded only as given expressions of a form of particular culture at a certain moment of history'.[55] There is a tendency here to stress authority at the expense of the evidence: one can even find the tension of the two lines of thought within Vatican II.[56]

The issue of the identity of Christian ethics does not stand or fall on the question of revealed moral directives. But the *Glaubensethik* has tenaciously clung to the claim that there are such revealed directives. This would appear to be partly because it sees it as crucial to the defence of some traditional Roman

Catholic moral positions, especially in sexual ethics, and partly because it sees it as the best support for its conviction that Christians do have a special morality over which the church has competence and which is not entirely subject to the normal rigours of philosophical proof.[57] For example, teaching which is said to be based on natural law 'illumined and enriched by divine revelation' is not entirley answerable to philosophical analysis.

In summary, the problem of a revealed morality may be put like this. We acknowledge that the Bible is the source of our distinctive faith and that such faith may well be folly to the Greeks. Faith implies a way of life and the Bible does contain moral directives. Are they — the rules, attitudes, values, dispositions and intentions of the Bible — to be accepted as revealed and normative even if they too are folly to the Greeks. The *Galubensethik* maintains that, at the very least, one must begin with an acceptance of them and jettison them only when one absolutely has to. It is not convinced that the objections are such as to impugn the validity of all the moral directives of the Bible: it regards them as in possession until the community's filtering-out process decides otherwise, as it has done in the past.

But can the various objections be met? From the discussion it will have emerged that no one objection, in itself, appears to vitiate appeal to the bible as a normative source. But their cumulative effect is powerful. Any moral directive will have to negotiate all the tests and it is only with difficulty that it will come through unscathed. Recourse to a revealed morality may not be utterly invalidated but there are serious problems about asserting that a particular directive is normative for today. The suggestion of the *Glaubensethik* that some of the biblical precepts can be shown to be bound to the common faith of the first and twentieth centuries is obviously meant to provide some sort of interpretative key. It is true that the dynamic of ethos and ethic is important but we have seen its limitations. It cannot be put forward as a justification for regarding the particular form in which faith found expression in action in the first century as authoritative for all time. It does not do away with the need for a careful hermeneutic.

It may well be that the *Galubensethik* case for a specific Christian morality has concentrated too much on the normative use of the Bible as if that were the sole significance of the Bible for morality. Perhaps this is an indication of the poverty of the Roman Catholic tradition in biblical ethics. A broader theological approach needs to be pursued: so far, it has only had its beginnings. Likewise, the autonomy school has concentrated too much on exposing the difficulty of direct appeal to the Bible as a normative source — as if that finally disposed of the question of a specific ethical content and vindicated the autonomy view on the identity of Christian morality. It, too, must reckon with a broader theological approach. What the possibilities are for such an approach I consider in the following chapters.

4

Key Concepts:
'Morality', 'Content', 'Motive'

If the Bible is thought of as a revelation of morality, then those actions and intentions which violate the revealed directives are judged to be wrong. If it is thought of as a revelation of faith, rather than of morality, then its bearing on morality will be a much looser affair. One will think of it as providing a theologically warranted framework which will inform moral life.[1] Given the complexity of both faith and morality, one might expect this relationship to operate in a wide variety of ways. This chapter and the following one examine the thesis — and the denial of the thesis — that the faith of the Christian community bears on moral discernment in such a way that moral judgments are, sometimes at least, dependent on or derived from or inferred from or in some way entailed by such faith. They consider whether there are ever occasions when a person might give a reason for the justification of his moral stance that is so bound to his Christian religion that a non-Christian could not share the judgment.

Faith may enter into a variety of relationships with morals: some of them we have already seen. It may have a causal relationship with morals. That is, faith may be the source or explanation of one's present moral positions but not necessarily their justification. There may be a psychological relationship, as we shall see later in this chapter: faith may enable or motivate one to live one's morality. There may be an ontological relationship — that is, moral goodness or value may be thought to demand acceptance of some ultimate good or value: moral obligation may be thought to point to some more fundamental ground of obligation. I shall give that some thought in the final chapter. But what I am primarily concerned with here is whether Christian morality is epistemologically dependent on

95

faith, i.e. whether some Christian moral positions cannot be intelligibly arrived at or supported without the framework of faith. It would be a mistake to reduce the whole question of the identity of Christian ethics to this and perhaps too much of the energy of recent Roman Catholic ethics has gone into it. But it has become a central question and it is undeniably important.

The autonomy school, which it allows a causal, psychological or ontological relationship, denies an epistemological dependence: Schüller, as we saw, challenges the *Glaubensethik* to produce a single instance in which a moral position is derived from a theological one. Christianity, it says, gives specific motivation and context to morality but not specific content. This means that, in its view, the content of Christian morality is detachable from Christian faith and that, whatever else may be said about the ethics of Christianity, it has no substantive uniqueness.

Against this the *Glaubensethik* maintains that there is epistemological dependence, i.e. that there is behaviour demanded of the Christian which can be justified only by appeal to Christian belief. There are values, it says, such as poverty, virginity, renunciation of power, humility, modesty.[2] There are demands to receive the Eucharist, do penance, preach the gospel.[3] There is the New Testament's new vision of marriage, of the world, of hope.[4] There are the attitudes of joy, thankfulness, prayer, indifference to the world.[5] There is not just the individual elements of morality but the 'overall conception into which the Christian's quest and aspiration are directed by faith', 'the spiritual structure of Christianity'.[6] There is the life of lived faith, hope and love.[7] There is the vision or perspective of Christian morality, its spirit and disposition, its open-ended character (*Zielgebote*).[8]

So there is a major difference of opinion. Some of it, at least, is due to a difference in understanding key concepts. Or perhaps to a failure to examine them. Whether or not there is specific content to Christian morality, and not just specific motivation, depends, in part, on how one defines the terms, 'morality', 'content', 'motivation'. So I consider this trio of words. They are obviously interrelated. The extent of the content of Christian morality depends on the extent of morality. And, as we shall see, the extent of content depends also on the extent of motivation.

Each of these concepts would be, in itself, matter for several major studies. I try to confine the discussion to our central concern about the identity of Christian ethics. To begin with, there is the broad issue of the range of the moral. How much of human activity does one include in moral life? There will be considerable difference of opinion about that. It has been a widespread practice to limit morality to decision and choice. But is that the limit of our interest in the person as a moral person? Should we not include in the data of morality one's inner life, in the sense of one's personal vision and attitudes, one's 'moral nature', the configuration of one's thought. When we assess somebody, when we say on hearing of the death of another, for example, that he was a good man we are not just considering his solution to certain practical problems but his stable dispositions, his character, his moral vision. This, it is true, issues in performance but is regarded here as something separable from performance.[9]

We ought to take seriously too the suggestion that many sensitive people see morality not as a matter of rule-obedience but as the realising of a pattern of life or the following of a pilgrimage. The form which morality will take for many — what will constitute their vision and be the guide of their pilgrimage — will be not so much rules as fables and stories. It has been remarked that it is in imaginative literature, rather than in any abstract fashion, that what is good in human life is concretely represented.[10] Some moral truths are complex and subtle and they may be more successfully represented in such stories than in any moral maxim. Iris Murdoch mentions the woman who broke the alabaster box of precious ointment, for instance.[11] There is moral vision here, but it cannot easily be put into a moral maxim or rule. The same can be said of some of the sayings of Christ, for example, that about the grain of wheat falling into the ground or it being more blessed to give than to receive. There are two distinct points here. One can be interested in stories and fables as preliminaries to choice, as justifying and explaining choice. That is a separate issue and it will soon concern us greatly. Here I am suggesting that such elements in themselves may constitute some part of the data of morals — although one must resist the temptation to force all thought patterns into the domain of morality.

What, then, of Christian vision? One can think of beliefs,

stories and symbols that give to the Christian a configuration of thought and imagination that would, on such an understanding, qualify as the data of morals. One thinks of such basic constituents of Christian consciousness as belief in a deity, in creation and its goodness. One thinks of Christian stories about the goodness of God, about his acceptance of the world and his love for each individual. One thinks of the Christian's awareness of sinfulness, his trust in God's providence and God's forgiveness, his hope of final union with God in the world to come. This Christian imagination, this Christian *Gestalt* engenders attitudes and dispositions and leads to behaviour in such an elusive and delicate way that one must ask if it can be excluded from the domain of the moral. It is hardly absent when the Christian makes his judgment — what he takes in the main to be a moral judgment — on the good man or woman. The *Glaubensethik* authors do not discuss or perhaps even advert to the problem of the range of the moral. But some of their claims for the specificity of Christian morality seem to fall into the category of vision: Häring even uses the expression.[12] Ratzinger refers to Christianity's new overall conception (*'in der neuen Gesamtgestalt'*) or spiritual structure (*'in der geistigen Gestalt des Christlichen'*).[13] There is difference of opinion with the autonomy school here: what should be adverted is that the real point of difference is whether vision is to be allowed as part of morality.

There are other, closely-related, considerations about the nature of morality and of moral judgment which are important for our subject. In the literature on morality there is a traditional distinction between right action and good action and between judgments of moral rightness and judgments of moral goodness. We can make two kinds of judgment about actions. We judge them to be right and we judge them to be good. The former judgment refers (depending on one's moral theory) to the act's intrinsic nature or to its consequences or generally to what the act does. The latter refers to facts about the agent's character, motivation, intentionality, interests. On the first acount, to ask what one is to do is only to ask what act to do, not what motive to act from. On the other account, what one is to do includes reference to motive, disposition, etc. — in general to what comes under the rubric of virtue.

Moral philosophy has mainly concerned itself with rightness, with an ethic of duty or obligation. Moral theology has not attended greatly to the distinction and has used the terms 'moral rightness' and 'moral goodness' interchangeably. But whatever about the terminology, one has the impression that the point of view of the autonomy school especially has reference more to moral rightness than to moral goodness. It is an interesting fact, however, that in recent times many moral philosophers, convinced that concentration on rightness misses some of the most important elements of moral life, have devoted attention to moral goodness. Specifically they have sought to rehabilitate the category of virtue, something that had long been unfashionable in moral philosophy.[14] The debate about the extent and implications of an ethic of virtue is many-sided and we will have to return to it. For the moment I wish only to suggest that there are lessons here for the theologian and to point to some emphases which a concern with virtue will set in relief.

(a) The moralist who is interested in giving prominence to considerations of virtue will stress the importance not only of what is done but of how it is done — as Aristotle did. ('But the doer is just or temperate not because he does such things but when he does them in the way of just and temperate persons'.)[15] This will include the intention in doing, the reason or motive in doing, the disposition out of which one acts, the desires with which one acts, even the facility with which one acts. (b) Intention is the most obvious candidate for consideration in a judgment of moral goodness. The importance of it is widely recognised. But in some instances the disposition out of which something is done is as much part of the virtue as the intention or action — as in the case of generosity, for example.[16] Apparently similar actions and similar actional traits may spring from qualitatively unrelated dispositions: what looks like an act of generosity may spring from self-aggrandisement and would not therefore count as generosity. In order to qualify as an act of generosity it must in some way spring from a disposition of generosity. (c) There seem to be instances in which virtue lies precisely in inner willing or in having a particular feeling. One thinks of gratitude or perhaps of humility. Being grateful *is* the having of a specific feeling. Worth seems to attach to the disposition itself and not just to the fact that it is the source of right action — though indeed it may be the source of right action.[17]

Such considerations should interest theologians. They will be found to be relevant at a number of points in this work. They very obviously apply to our next concern which is the meaning of 'content'. Here I am concerned about the wider concept of morality: when we refer to the identity of Christian morality, what is our understanding of morality? The more morality is thought of in terms of duty, the more difficult it is to establish that there is a Christian morality. But if morality is a matter of virtue and character, if attitudes and innermost desires are important to it and not only observable acts, there is greater room for the claim that there is a specifically Christian morality. The insight of the early church that the Christian should live his life in joy (2 Cor.9:7; Heb. 10:34), in thankfulness (Acts 5:41; Col.3:17), in humility (John 13:14-15; Phil.2:3) and without anxiety (Matt.6:25; 1 Pet.5:7) may not lead to an observable difference of behaviour but may refer to attitudes and dispositions that are part of Christian virtue (Phil.4:4-7).

One cannot hope to resolve the problem of what is to count as the field of the moral. We must, indeed, be on our guard against allowing everything in a person's outlook — or even every value system or action-guide which he or she has — to count as morality. But anyone familiar with the well-worn ground of the debate on the definition of morality will agree that the frontiers are, to say the least, not very clearly defined.[18] Our consideration of vision and of virtue suggests that in the issue of specificity much will depend on the understanding of terms. The discussion should advert to the fact that differences may result not so much from, or not only from, disagreement about what Christianity adds to morality but from disagreement about what is to count as morality. Sometimes, in the discussion, there is vague reference, on both sides, to Christian attitudes, to values, to the Christian view of the person. Auer, for example, in maintaining the position of non-specificity, says that there are new values given by Christianity but no new norms and, therefore, no new content of morality.[19] Schürmann and Stoeckle, on the other hand, point to the new values of joy, humility and modesty as evidence of specificity. But nowhere does one find any advertence to the critical question whether these are to count as part of the institution of morality. Until it is acknowledged that crucial to the question of the specificity of Christian ethics is agreement about — or at least thought about — what aspects of behaviour are to count as moral, the talking at cross-purposes will continue.

100

There is talking at cross-purposes also on another issue that has to do with the range of the moral. That is the issue of the status of acts directed to God. The *Glaubensethik* finds specificity in acts of faith, hope and love, in acts of prayer and penance and in the celebration of the Eucharist. The question is whether such acts are to be regarded as moral acts. Traditionally, Roman Catholic theology has regarded them as moral acts. Specifically, acts of love of God and of religion were treated as part of morality. As Maritain put it, 'Christian morality is a morality of beatitude, but first and foremost it is a morality of the divine Good supremely loved'.[20] The traditional teaching was that the good is that which perfects and that the fundamental moral stance is love of the good. For the Christian the fundamental moral stance was regarded as love of God with the whole of one's heart, soul, mind and strength: indeed, as Gilleman put it, following Aquinas, all moral goodness is a mediation of such love of God. The moral theologian taught that there is required not just a basic orientation of love towards God but acts of love: Noldin mentions complacency and joy in the glory of God, desire for his glorification in the world, sorrow for sin, obedience to his command, etc.[21] In like fashion, Aquinas regarded the virtue of religion, with its acts of worship and sacrifice, as a moral virtue, part of the virtue of justice.[22] He is followed by many modern theologians. Häring refers to religion, with its acts of prayer, worship and Eucharist, as the most eminent of the moral virtues.[23]

Much of this would be regarded as highly debatable both by philosophers and by theologians, especially those in other traditions. Many Christians find it odd to refer to such activities as morality. Some would regard love of God as faith rather than agape and would regard prayer not as the content of ethics but as a presupposition of it.[24] Barth sums up neatly what the problem is about:

> Alongside work there is also prayer; alongside practical love for one's brother there is also divine service in the narrower sense; alongside activity in state and community there is also that in the congregation; alongside the other sciences there is also theology. And obviously all these and similar activities are to be regarded also as a command and a duty, as a matter of human action.[25]

The question, however, is to what area of human activity prayer, divine service, etc. are to be assigned.

Religions and cultures typically have a host of action-guides or duties. But not all religious or cultural action-guides are necessarily moral action-guides and so the search for the definition of the moral goes on. The most extreme example of this in the religious sphere is Kierkegaard's notion of the 'teleological suspension of the ethical', in favour of the religious obedience of the 'knight of faith'.[26] But most religions are familiar with ceremonial prescriptions, rules for sacrifice, for prayer-life, even taboos, which regulate conduct but which could only doubtfully be regarded as pertaining to morality.

This does teach us that, when we discuss the identity of Christian morality, we need some agreement about what is to count as morality. Many philosophers want to drive a wedge between morality and religion. There is a widely accepted view about the definition of morality which requires that normative judgments, if they are to qualify as moral, must meet a material social criterion pertaining to the distribution or promotion of non-moral good or evil among sentient being.[27] Such a view could only with difficulty accommodate religious considerations. It could only include acts directed towards God either by including God among such sentient beings and adopting a process approach to God, who experiences benefit or harm from such acts, or by concentrating on the effect on the doer of acts directed to God.

The relevance of all of this to our discussion is that some of the authors of the autonomy school have recently been limiting the area of the moral by fastening on this distinction between religion and morality. The result is that there has been no meeting of minds with the *Glaubensethik* about the issue of the identity of Christian ethics. It is obvious that if acts directed towards God are regarded as part of morality — particularly in conjunction with the extension of morality to include vision — one has to take the claims of the *Glaubensethik* about specificity more seriously. Fuchs and others began by simply excluding acts directed to God from their field of interest. They were interested only in inner-worldly morality.[28] This was understandable since their emphasis was on the possibility of dialogue and communication with non-Christians in matters of morality. They have gone on, however, to solve the problem of acts directed towards God by adopting a sharp religion-morality distinction. There are many attitudes and activities, they say, which belong rather to religion than to morality but which provide motivation for moral life. Thus Fuchs says that acts of cult, prayer, contemplation, faith, hope and love belong to the area of religion but provide moral motivation.[29] Böckle says that directives about baptism, Eucharist or penance do not belong to morality in the strict sense but to religion.[30] (Fuchs even extends the net to describe virginity and sacrifice of life as religious behaviour. But I will deal with that in another context.)

So, once again, disagreement about the identity of Christian morality is revealed as disagreement not only about the particular contribution which Christianity makes but about the range and extension of the notion of morality. One can raise the question whether the neat distinction of morality and religion that is sought by the philosopher is possible within the religious view of life — or desirable. Religious and moral discourse seem to overlap. There is considerable overlap in such ideas as holiness, saintliness, righteousness, sin, atonement, perfection, beatitude. Gustafson is right to query whether, within the Jewish and Christian communities, the concept of morality does not evade the precise definition and usage that philosophers seek.[31] Perhaps the best that can be claimed for different accounts of morality in different cultures and religions is some kind of family resemblance. What is clear, at any rate, is that on some definitions of morality the claim for specificity of content for Christian morality is more easily sustained than on the narrower definition favoured by most philosophers.

So the general debate about Christian morality suffers from obscurity about the notion of morality. It suffers further from confusion regarding the notions of content and motivation. It is obvious that the range of morality will, to some degree, determine the range of the content of morality. But here I am concerned with the sharp distinction which we have seen the autonomous school make between content and motivation. It says that the content of Christian and non-Christian morality is the same: what is different is the motivation. The Christian has a different motivation for being moral but he is not required to do anything different. The unasked question here is the meaning of content. Although it is a central thesis for the autonomous ethic, none of the authors has explained the meaning of the term. On a certain definition of content it is possible to maintain the thesis. But our question must be whether it is a satisfactory definition.

The way into the issue seems to be through an examination of the use of 'motivation': 'motivation' and 'content' are used as correlative terms. It is a well-known fact that this is a philosophical minefield. Anyone who has tried to explore the area will very likely agree with Anscombe's sentiments that we need an account at least of what a human action is at all and how its description as 'doing such and such' is affected by its motive and by the intention or intentions in it.[32] And with Kenny's remark that the question of what it is to do something because of something is still an unsolved problem.[33] However, some stand must be taken and some attempt made to sort out the most obvious sources of confusion.

The reason why it is such a difficult area is that at any moment in any person's waking and conscious life there is always a set of possible true answers to the question, 'What is he doing?'. When we ask the further question, 'Why did he do it?', the question is capable of being asked and answered in a variety of different ways and the different concepts refer to the different concerns in asking the question. We sometimes go on to ask still another question like, 'What made him (or drove or possessed him) to do it?' We are looking for reasons. A motive is a reason for acting. But motives are particular kinds of reasons, or reasons under a particular aspect. All motives are reasons, but not all reasons are motives. We are interested in moral reasons and one may have a moral reason for doing something without thereby having a motive for it. (This, of course, is a sharply debated area between externalists and internalists.)[34] I take it that one has a moral reason for something, if doing that something corresponds to one's moral theory. Thus, for a utilitarian, the fact that an action is adjudged to be the action that produces more good than any other action open to the agent at the time, is a moral reason. But reasons for action can be independent of motives.

When one speaks of motive, one is referring to the reason why someone wants or desires to do something. One may have a reason for acting and not want to act. The fact that one does not desire to do what is right does not change the fact that one has a moral obligation: it means only that one has no motivation, at least concurrently. So we distinguish reasons and motives. Or we could distinguish reasons for regarding an action as right or justified and reasons for acting. Perhaps it helps to see that we likewise distinguish intention and motive. The intention is what a man means to do, his concrete purpose. The motive is the aspect under which he sees something as desirable. Anscombe suggests that to give a motive is to say something like: 'See the action in this light.'[35]

So the function of motive statements is to explain behaviour, to show it to be rational, in the sense of clarifying the logic of the situation, by clarifying the desirability (attractiveness, good), which the agent sees in what he does. Motive-statements do this by revealing how it was that the agent saw some good, or why it was he saw some good or what the particular kind of good it was that he saw. This means that motive says something about the character of the agent and his desires. (By this I do not rule out that one can act out of generosity, for example, in a particular instance, but one usually exhibits a certain pattern in one's wants and desires.) For example, if we ask why the belief that a certain action would ease his or her neighbour's burden was a motive for one person and not for another, the answer is that the former was a considerate person and the latter was not. Easing the burden of another was seen as desirable and good by one and not by the other. Moral reasons can be motives. But whether showing a person a moral reason is giving him or her a motive depends on how his or her desires are affected — depends largely, in fact, on character.

It is important, therefore, that the language of reasons and motives should not be carelessly used. One distinguishes justifying reasons and motives — which are explanatory or what Hutcheson called 'exciting' reasons.[36] A justifying reason refers to a consideration which entitles one to say that to act thus is to act morally. A motive or exciting reason does not. 'I should' and 'I shall' are logically distinct: it is not logically absurd to say 'I should but I shall not'. (Indeed, 'should' like 'ought' may be used in two different senses. But, if so, one is a moral use and the other a motivational use, so that the question, 'Why should I?' may be looking either for a moral or a motivational answer.) It is true that the good person will want to do what is right. For him or her there will be a coincidence of moral and motivational reasons: to give him or her a moral reason is to give a motive. It is true that one who is not totally depraved will have some disposition to act in the way morally prescribed — so that a

105

justifying reason may have some element of motive in it for him or her. But human beings may, sometimes at least, lack the motivation to do what they apprehend to be morally right.

It appears that this distinction has not been kept in mind by the authors of the autonomy position. 'Motivation' is a key idea for them — Christianity gives specific Christian motivation, they say, but not content — but there is great confusion in their use of the concept. There are some considerations mentioned by them under the rubric of motive which are really justifying reasons for moral judgment. These need to be sorted out. Thus to say, as Fuchs often says, that Christianity gives one a motive for virginity is not accurate. Motive has to do with desire. There is something more fundamental involved. Christianity may indeed give the desire for virginity. But, basically, it gives one the reason why virginity is a morally good choice. Without the considerations arising from Christian belief, it might not be an intelligible choice. The belief determines the facts. It determines what it is that is judged to be morally good. The same applies to other such judgments mentioned by Fuchs — regarding poverty, self-sacrifice, non-resistance.

Fuchs is clearly unhappy here. At one stage, he says that virginity could be understood and accepted 'only by someone who conceives the human situation in accordance with a complete Christian anthropology'.[37] At another, he says that to sacrifice one's life, to practise self-abnegation, to remain unmarried for high motives are morally intelligible positions without Christianity but that Christianity gives them a special motive.[38] At another, he says that these pertain rather to religious than to moral behaviour.[39] The fact is that Fuchs needs more than the concept of motivation here. In this context, religious belief is not just motivation but the ground of the judgments.

The same is true of Auer's position. Commenting on the Sermon on the Mount, he says that Jesus does not give new principles or norms but rather portrays the character of the man who has subjected himself to the kingdom. In such a man, he says, there develop moral attitudes. He becomes poor in spirit. He becomes like a child. He renounces power. He forfeits self-interest. He watches and prays. All of this Auer gives as an example of new motivation.[40] It is hard to accept this. What is in question is not — or not simply — motivation. The new beliefs of the Christian may indeed help him or her to lead a particular kind of life. But more fundamentally they have become the ground and justification for moral judgments. It is in virtue of such beliefs that one arrives at and can make sense of judgments about poverty, humility, self-abnegation.

'Content', I take it, refers to the moral characterisation of an act, i.e. how the act is to be described (from the moral point of view). Fuchs and Auer seem to have taken the view that acts which are physically similar but which have different motivations are to be regarded, from the point of view of content of the act, as similar. I think they need to look more closely at this. Acts are in part specified by reasons and intentions, or by what Fuchs and Auer call motives. These enter into and determine what the agent does — and on any showing should be regarded as the content of the act. Roman Catholic morality has traditionally recognised that for an act to be morally good the agent must to some extent recognise and seek it as such. Thus to give a meal to a poor person has the appearance of goodness. But if one does it solely for self-aggrandisement or in order to humiliate the person, how does one describe the act? Is it an act of charity or almsgiving? That seems not to be the right description of what is done, or the content of the act: it would appear that the description of an action contains assumptions about the agent's intentions. This is even clearer in the case of what are called indifferent acts — and among them one might include choosing not to marry, to be poor, to bear suffering. Here, especially, the reason why the choice is made determines the characterisation of the act as a moral act and must be said to determine the content.

So acts which look alike will bear different descriptions and you may consent to an act under one description and not under another. So we acknowledge that the statement that a person knows that he is doing X does not imply that, concerning everything which is included in his doing X, he knows that he is doing that thing.[41] To use Kneale's example, Oedipus chose to kill the haughty stranger who ordered him to give way on the narrow road from Delphi to Phocis, but he did not choose to kill his father, although the haughty stranger was in fact his father.[42]

What then is to be made of the claim that Christian and non-Christian morality have identity of content and that Christianity only influences the motive? Fuchs and Auer have to

107

ask themselves whether what they call motive — which they banish to the periphery of their morality — is not sometimes the reason why an act is judged to be for the Christian the morally right act; so that this reason determines what the act is and how it is to be described. Is what the Christian and the non-Christian intend to do, in the instances considered above, the same act with a different motive or is it a different act? Is the content of the act the same if the observable act is the same? *What* is being done is sometimes discovered by asking why it is done. It may well be here that Christian considerations enter: if so, they are more central to morality than the autonomy school allows. They may have to recognise that in some instances — perhaps some few instances — what they call Christian motives for an act really enter into and specify the content of the moral act.

'Motive' is sometimes used by the advocates of autonomy when what is in question is the giving of further or more convincing Christian reasons for moral judgments that are already accessible to non-Christians. Auer refers to the 'explosive and stimulating power' which Christian awareness of the worth and community of all people before God has given to moral understanding and to the development of consciousness about the place of women and slaves.[43] He says that while love of enemies is found outside of Christianity, it is only seen in its purity when one finds its source and binding character in the love of God for each man.[44] Fuchs refers to the 'further dimension' which Christianity gives to insight into the worth of the neighbour. Christian motivation and intentionality, he says, penetrate the content and give it a more profound and Christian value.[45] It is more correct to say that what is happening here is that some of the realities of faith enable one to see the ground of moral judgment more easily or more fully and securely. Insight into the value of the individual may be available to all. The Christian has a further perspective on the worth of each one and greater reason for arriving at his or her judgment about how each should be respected. (We shall meet this again in the chapter on *agape*.) If my reading of what is taking place is correct, we are not dealing with a case of motivation or the stimulating of moral activity but of justifying reasons or moral grounding.

'Motive' is also used by the school of autonomy in situations where what is in question is not motivation but the realisation that one should reach for ideals in moral life. I shall consider this point in more detail in Chapter 6. For the moment, let us say that Christianity does not accept a morality of mere duty: it proposes something that goes far beyond that. If, therefore, we are saying that the insight into the value of the other must not be limited to avoidance of harm but must extend a considerable distance in positive regard, we are not talking about mere motivation but we are justifying moral demand. Auer gives several examples of this sort of judgment in Christianity but regards them all as motivation.

> 'Since. in the inbreak of the kingdom, God's nature and his relationship with men is experienced, the imitation of God can be regarded as a moral motivation. If God is such that he makes his sun shine on the good and the bad, the Christian who enters into this movement of love can and must do likewise.'

On the love of enemies he goes on to say:

> 'The ethic of Jesus is fully theocentric. In the nature of God as the Father in heaven is the law of the perfect love of neighbour alone grounded.'[46]

What is involved here is the determination of the moral response. It is difficult for human beings to determine its extent. The Christian allows belief in Christ or in the Father to fill out his or her understanding. What is in question, therefore, is not the arousing of desire to implement a moral judgment already arrived at; it is not motivation but understanding of the moral demand. The same must be said about Böckle's remarks that faith in Christ's death and resurrection inspires one to a way of life that is not 'normal', and about his remarks that consideration of the new relationship in which one stands towards God gives a new perspective on such things as marital fidelity.[47] There may, of course, be motivation or inspiration here. But, if there is understanding of the grounds or the reasons for a moral demand, there is much more than motivation.

There is also genuine or pure motivation in Christian ethics. Much of the material which we have discussed can serve as motivation to do what one knows to be morally required. About this there is no argument among the authors. The Bible is a powerful example of the rich store of motives available to

Christians: much of its moral teaching comes in this form and the motives appear in many guises. Some of those mentioned by our authors are the love and forgiveness of the Father and of Christ, the fact that the kingdom has been inaugurated, the fact that one has experienced the freedom of Christ, the fact that one's body is a temple of the Spirit, the fact that we are all the Body of Christ, the desire to share in the work of creation, of redemption, of the bringing about of the kingdom.[48] I have already considered that much of Paul's teaching exhibits an indicative-imperative structure. It takes the form, 'You have been loved/saved/baptised/freed from sin/risen with Christ, therefore. . . .' This is motivation. It is calculated to make the Christian want or desire or be willing to live the life that he or she knows is required of him or her. It may not all be technically motive-statement: it does not always explicitly state the motive; sometimes it contains it implicitly. (In response to the question, 'Why did A injure B?', a motive is sufficiently expressed either by, 'Out of revenge' or 'B ruined his family'. Both kinds of logic appear among Christian motives.)

In the chapter on the use of the Bible we referred to this material as mainly paraenesis and said that the *Glaubensethik* failed to see that paraenesis does not purport to provide substantive ethics or to ground ethical positions but to provide encouragement, i.e. motivation. At that point I disputed the large claim of the autonomous ethic, especially that of Schüller, that Paul never intends to provide any new ethical insight or to teach ethics but only intends to exhort his listeners to live the moral insights of which they are already aware. In this chapter I have been making the related point that Christian beliefs which the autonomous school invariably regards as paraenesis or motivation are sometimes necessary to the grounding of a moral position and part of the content of the moral act.

Auer many times uses the terms, 'inspiration' and 'stimulation'. Are these distinct concepts from motivation? It seems not. They emerge because of the woolly use of 'motivation'. 'Inspiration' is the same as pure motivation, i.e. motivation which arouses the desire to do what one knows is morallly required. The whole point about motivation is that one is stimulated or inspired to do the morally good.

There is one further distinction to be made about motive which throws some light on the logic of Christian ethics. Are there not some motives arising from Christianity that are properly moral and others that are more properly religious? Belief in God, faith in Christ, provide the context in which we can be opened up to moral value. They perform a critical function in our lives. They help us to be aware of the negativities of our lives, of our selfishness, our moral laziness, our indifference. They can open us up to moral beauty and moral possibility, to generosity of spirit, to the realisation that the ultimate truth for us in our relations with our fellow humans is to be found in the example of the Father and of Christ. We know that the assimilation of moral attitudes often takes place through contact with morally impressive people. One thinks of Bergson:

> Why is it, then, that saints have their imitators, and why do the great moral leaders draw the masses after them? They ask nothing, and yet they receive. They have no need to exhort; their mere existence suffices...complete and perfect morality has the effect of an appeal.... Only those who have come into touch with a great moral personality have fully realised the nature of this appeal.[49]

There is taking place here a type of moral formation. Moral values are making their appeal. One is being helped *both* to see and to want what one comes to know that one should want. We all struggle with the gap between having justifying reasons for an act and wanting to do it. We have seen that whether a justifying reason will exercise appeal, i.e., whether it will be also a motive, depends on our character and desires. It is what lies behind and in between actions and prompts them that is important and it is this area which should be purified.[50]

If so, it would seem that religion offers one possibility here. Our Christian story is of one who proclaimed God's love and forgiveness for the least and the most forgotten and whose life was the incarnation of that, of one who received his life as a gift and who was prepared to lose it in the cause of goodness and truth. It is of one whose life broke through the barriers of prejudice and privilege and through limited views of goodness, success and failure, one whose view of success and failure was rooted in his union with his Father and who was faithful to his vison in what was humanly a failure. Discipleship, reflection on Christ's life, can shape our consciousness, can order our values and modify our desires. It can help us to assimilate our desires to his. It can

111

help us both to appreciate and to want considerateness, fidelity, justice, forgiveness, peace, even self-forgetfulness and self-renunciation. It can bring about a coincidence of justifying and explanatory reasons.

More commonly, perhaps, the Christian will have religious motives for being moral. A great variety of motive is possible here — Auer, for example, mentions several.[51] One can be just or truthful or keep promises or help others out of obedience to God, or out of love or out of thankfulness, or in order to forward the work of creation and redemption, or to bring about the kingdom which God desires, or for the sake of reward, or for a variety of other reasons. The result is a greater readiness to do what is known to be right. But the motive is no longer moral but religious. What closes the gap between justifying reason and desire is not any greater appreciation of justice or truth or fidelity or of the claim of the other. One appears to be moved to the act by some additional, non-moral motive. One wants to love God or please him or do his will, or perhaps, even, to obtain religious reward and avoid punishment. This is what moves one. How exactly a moralist will judge this act will depend, to some extent, on his theory of morality. Clearly, one is helped to do one's duty. But is this all that matters? Does it matter why one does it? D'Arcy's distinction of different kinds of motive-statement — although he is not concerned with religious motivation — is useful here. In one kind, 'What I want is simply and solely the natural outcome of X, which I want simply for its own sake,' — I do it because of its intrinsic attractiveness to me. In another kind, what I want is indeed the natural outcome or accompaniment of the action: 'But I want it, not because of its intrinsic attractiveness, but because of its being made worth while by some extrinsic circumstance.'[52] I take it that the act of the first person is that of one whom the tradition would describe as virtuous. Not so the second. The second does his or her duty but not for a reason that implies any greater love of what is morally good. We are back to the virtue-obligation controversy. At the limit, the act of the second person may be simply a matter of obedience: it may simply be a matter of the prudence of submitting to superior force. It was this kind of approach that prompted the remark of Nowell-Smith — echoed by many others — that religious morality is infantile.[53] It can be, of course, but it need not be. However this does say something to

112

us about the need to be careful about the different kinds of religious motive. It is possible to use religious motivation in order to achieve moral conformity, without any concern for the moral quality of the act — for an appreciation of justifying reasons. As we said, much depends here on one's theory of moral action. Some moralists, at least, would require that for an act to be judged morally good, it is a necessary condition that the agent to some extent recognise and seek it as such.[54] Those who are engaged in religious morality should remember this. We saw earlier that many moralists are not happy with a morality of duty, still less with a morality of obedience to authority. Indeed, it was precisely the desire to show that obedience-morality, or theological-positivism, or Christ-positivism, as they called it, was not a necessary part of Christian morality that moved the autonomy school to insist on the rationality of all moral norms and the autonomy of the moral demand.

One has, therefore, to enter reservations about certain kinds of religious motivation. But it would be ridiculous to reduce all religious motivation to obedience. Far from being an obstacle, religious motives are likely to enrich and enhance morality. The religious person can have religious *and* moral reasons for being moral: there is no need for any diminution of moral awareness. Indeed, as we saw, religious considerations may communicate and deepen moral appreciation, as well as communicating a readiness to do what is seen to be morally required.

In this chapter I have tried to deal with the terms involved in the claim that there is no specific content to Christian morality but only specific motivation. I have suggested that questions have to be asked about the range or extent of the notions of 'morality' and of 'content'. The latter depends much on how the notion of reasons in morality is understood: there are grounds for thinking that there is some confusion in the authors between justifying reasons, which belong to content, and explanatory or exciting reasons, which are properly motives. Finally, I have tried to distinguish different kinds of motive which are found in Christian moral experience. What conclusions can be drawn from this about our general theme? Two things should be noted. First, there is the now familiar conclusion that debate about the identity of Christian ethics is vitiated by confusion about terminology. On a narrow definition of morality or of content, it will obviously be more difficult to show any substantive unique-

113

ness in Christian morals. On a broader definition — one which would include in content some of what the autonomy school insists on referring to as external motivation — it may not be so difficult. Second, the importance of Christian motivation should be taken more seriously. As I remarked earlier, one has the impression that too much energy has gone into the issue of specificity of content — important though it may be. The issue of the identity of Christian ethics appears to have been reduced to this. There are other issues. The discovery of the right moral response, i.e. the finding of true norms, is only part of ethics. Perhaps a more fundamental problem for ethical life is the doing.[55] We are unable to respond as we know a Christian should. Like Paul (Rom.7:24), we can ask how we are to find the power to act ethically. How can we achieve and communicate a readiness to be moral in general or on particular issues? Paul's indicative-imperative structure was an attempt to do this. So to harness and delineate Christian motivation is an important task for ethics.

To say that it is only paraenesis is to undervalue the need of Christian motivation. Paul sees the power of Christian faith. One has the impression that for him faith and doing, the coming of the kingdom and responsibility for the kingdom, are almost inseparable. These two elements, the mystical and the ethical, are close fellows in any religion. Belief in God tends to express itself not just mystically but in deed. Who God is for us tends to appear in our deeds: if he is a God who cares for human life that ought to appear in our deeds, if we are to be consistent. It may even be that an ethic which has detached itself from a religious base can, in the last resort, have no meaningful effect. Awareness of God provides the strength to carry on working for others and for the world even in the face of apparent failure. It gives us confidence that what is impossible for us is possible for God.

5

The Moral Subject

The distinctions which I have argued for in the last chapter do two things. They show that the answer to the question about the specificity of Christian morality requires sharper definition of terms. They also raise the wider question of the adequacy of the notion of morality with which modern Roman Catholic theology, and especially the autonomy school, has worked. This chapter takes the matter further. The point of the distinctions will, it is hoped, be more fully seen. But the main argument of the chapter will be that we need a richer notion of moral agent than has been traditionally employed and that if we do employ such a notion it will cast interesting light on the question of whether there is a specific Christian morality.

Let us pick up the question from Chapter 4 again. Does the faith of the Christian community require or in some way entail moral judgments that non-Christians do not regard as required. The answer of the *Glaubensethik* authors is 'Yes': their concern is to defend specificity of content; their cry is *Handeln aus dem Glauben*, i.e. morality arising out of faith.[1] The answer of the autonomy movement is that, whatever relationships faith may enter into with ethics, they are not such as to impinge on the content of ethics. Faith, in this view, is seen as surrounding morality with interpretation, meaning and motivation, while leaving actual judgment intact.

It seems to me that neither position is entirely satisfactory. The *Glaubensethik* puts forward a variety of considerations as proof of its position — a Christian spirit and intention in morality, a Christian vision of the person and of the world, Christian attitudes of joy, thankfulness, modesty, humility, prayer and indifference to the world, Christian values of poverty, virginity and renunciation of power. It was not clear to

115

us in our treatment of the *Glaubensethik* authors how they arrived at these considerations — in particular it was not clear whether or not they were to be received as revealed moral directives and accepted on the authority of the Bible. Neither was there any serious attempt to meet the objection of the autonomy school that such considerations, as they stand, are not part of morality and cannot be shown to lead to distinctive behaviour. It seems to me, however, that if a more dynamic approach is taken to the moral agent and to the process of moral discernment, many of these considerations can be seen to be values, attitudes and dispositions that derive from the Christian's basic metaphysical stance and that lead to choices that may be called distinctively Christian.

The adherents of the autonomy school, on the other hand, have a very static view of the moral agent. They have considered whether there is a layer of moral directives in Scripture to be added to what we can learn without revelation. Or, at best, they have thought of the moral agent as working with two distinct sources, faith and reason, and as putting together what came from two distinct lines of information. One must at least ask whether this is how life is, whether this is how the moral agent operates.

What is at issue here is the question of the effect of religious commitment on moral judgment. Religious commitment goes deep. It gives basic meaning to life. It determines one's metaphysical stance. As Wach says, the fundamental themes in any statement of faith are the nature of the ultimate reality, the nature of the cosmos and the world, the nature of man. Or as he puts it speaking specifically of myth (and our religious faith contains our basic myths)

> The kinds of question which myth attempts to answer are: why are we here; where do we come from; for what purpose; why do we act in this way; why do we die?[2]

So religious faith is likely to have something to say about origins and destiny. It is likely to shape one's view of the nature of the human person, to have convictions about salvation, beatitude, wholeness, perfection, to suggest attitudes to the world, to matter, to success and failure. It determines, to some extent, one's meanings, what one sees in the world, what are the facts of life, and what among them are the most prominent and relevant

116

facts. It does this in a highly complex and subtle way. Because religious faith is communicated and received not just in abstract formulations of belief but in stories, myths and symbols which deeply pervade a person's consciousness.

One would expect, then, that the question of the content of Christian morality would be a question of considerable depth. The persistence of the relationship between religion and morality is well documented. The story of religions has been that the mystical, or more specifically religious, element — the faith element — does not seem to have been able to exist without the ethical, so that religions without an ethical dimension are rare.[3] *Prima facie*, it seems odd that this religious element, which so deeply shapes our consciousness would never have anything to say about patterns of living and never impinge on moral judgments. There are possibilities here that need to be examined. Too much concentration on Christian morality as a given — the will of God mediated through the unique insights of the apostolic community — and too little attention to the dynamic of moral discernment have resulted in only slight interest in the significance of the Christian's total religious consciousness for moral judgment. If there is a specific content to Christian morality, it seems to me that it is best understood as an instance of the bearing of metaphysical or religious stance on the understanding of patterns of existence.

What is being suggested is that we need to look at the 'I' who judges and acts. We need to do more work on why particular people make particular judgments. Judgments are not made in a vacuum. They are made by people who see things in a particular way, because they are particular sorts of people. My perception, my evaluative description of the field of action, and the responsibility which I believe I have in a situation all depend on the sort of person I am. And that, in turn, will depend on my beliefs, my loyalties, the myths and stories and symbols that shape my consciousness.

The autonomy school makes a sharp distinction between beliefs, attitudes and judgments of behaviour. What is distinctive of Christianity, it says, is its religious message. It has distinctive beliefs and it may have distinctive moral attitudes. But it does not require distinctive moral behaviour. One wonders if the sharp distinction can be sustained. Beliefs found attitudes. Attitudes involve objects: they are expressed in directed behaviour, that is, behaviour of a consistent kind directed towards some object or class of objects. Dispositions such as humility, pride and truthfulness are attitudes in so far as I am humble *towards* some definite person or group, proud *of* something definite and truthful *in relation* to someone. As Scruton puts it, a typical manifestation of the belief that Jews are shrewd and mercenary might be suspicion, reluctance to engage in financial dealings, a desire not to be under obligation and so on. Together these might amount to a durable pattern of judgment and behaviour directed in the appropriate way towards Jews.[4] Is it not arguable that Christian beliefs and attitudes operate in the same way? As we saw in the last chapter, there are some who would simply include attitudes and values in the definition of morality. But, even if this is not agreed, do the values and attitudes of Christianity not lead to judgments about behaviour? Can they be left standing apart from behaviour? Are Christian beliefs and their related attitudes such that they do not, in any way, affect how one is to live? Are they such that the humanist has exactly the same thing to say about how one is to live? Is Christian belief so unrelated to life?

At the moment, these are but questions. The point that is being made is that theologians are not in a position to answer them one way or another until they take more serious account of the nature of moral discernment and of the total integrated consciousness — religious and moral — out of which it is done. A remark of Ricoeur is relevant:

> Values are the very substance of the life of a people. This is found expressed in practical mores which represent some sort of inertia, the statics of values. Under this thick skin of practical mores we find traditions, which are the living memory of a civilisation. Finally, at a deeper level we find what is perhaps the very kernel of the phenomenon of civilisation — a collection of images and symbols by which a human group expresses its adaptations to reality, to other groups and to history.... One could speak in this sense of the ethico-mythical kernel, the kernel both moral and imaginative which embodies the ultimate creaturely power of a group.... Each historical group in this sense has an ethos, an ethical singularity, which is the power of creation linked to a tradition, to a memory, to an archaic rooting.[5]

Berger makes the same point — that at the root of our laws, customs, economic mechanisms and structures are the controlling key images of the person, of reality, and of society.[6]

All of this is suggesting that more attention should be paid to the total background out of which judgments and choices are made. It is, once again, saying something about the importance of character and virtue in morality and about the influence of character not just on decision but on judgment, not just on doing but on seeing. One can think of religion as forming or having the potential to form a particular kind of character, to communicate values, to evoke certain kinds of awareness and sensibility, which issue in moral judgments of a qualitatively different kind from others. In recent Roman Catholic moral theology, much has been made of the importance of starting from experience, as an antidote to heteronomy.[7] But one must ask: what experience? Is it naked moral experience? Or is it the moral experience of the person of faith? Some authors have suggested that one should start from moral experience and, when full weight has been given to that, one should move on to a theological consideration of that experience. That may be a good pedagogical method for an understanding of morality — too many Christians still see it as derived from religion. But it is open to misinterpretation. We must insist that it is the whole person who does morality, out of a particular world-view, with a particular set of beliefs, a particular story of reality. The Christian clings to his world view because he believes that it is the one that comes nearest to the truth. So he has every reason for taking account of it in his moral judgment. Moral experience is not detachable from it. To try to detach it is not to be objective but to mediate moral experience through some other world-view.

This, then, is — or ought to be — the context of the contemporary debate about the identity of Christian ethics. What is being pointed to is the complexity and subtlety of moral reasoning and the fact that it is done, not by some impersonal rationality, but by one whose world-view is formed, to a notable extent, by religious considerations. The question for Christian moralists is: will a self-awareness formed by Christian faith shape one's loyalties, colour one's preferences, order one's values and so affect one's judgment of moral situations? Will belief in God — in his creation and lordship, his goodness, forgiveness and fidelity — affect moral judgment? Will the story of Jesus —

119

his trust in his Father, his sense of life as gift, his life of simplicity, his relativising of this world and its goods and successes, his *kenosis*, his death and resurrection — will this lead the believer to a particular way of life? (In what way are faith and life-style united in the life of Jesus himself?) Will the value of union with God and considerations of eternity be factors in earthly choice: will a realisation of finiteness and sinfulness enter into discernment; will hope of enabling grace count in determining moral responsibility?

Such questions might seem to point in the direction of a specific Christian ethic. But the autonomy school replies that they make no difference to the content of ethics. We have seen in the last chapter how much depends on the understanding of the terms 'morality', 'motive', 'content' and I expressed reservations about the way in which this school understands the moral act. For the moment, however, let us try to bracket the issue of definition as best as we can and examine the elements of Christian faith which have been, or can be, put forward as most likely to lead to specificity of content. The challenge facing the *Glaubensethik* authors is to show how faith translates into behaviour, to show that one whose self-awareness includes Christian beliefs and stories cannot but have, if he or she is to be consistent, certain attitudes which, in turn, lead to judgments about appropriate moral behaviour.

It is certainly difficult to show that one can deduce a particular and specific moral rule from a particular theological truth. But there are some indications of a more hopeful approach in the suggestions of such as Demmer and Simpson, who, rather than take their stand on an explicit deduction from a belief to a moral judgment, have been insisting that we look at the way in which nature and grace, faith and reason compenetrate one another and form a unity of consciousness which affects the whole of the Christian's thought and action. This corresponds more to the point I have been making about the possible influence of one's metaphysical-religious stance on moral discernment. It is the line that I shall explore for most of this chapter. (I shall give some thought towards the end of the chapter to the implications of liberation theology for moral methodology.)

The authors mentioned argue for some kind of immediacy of perception of the moral demand. Demmer says that one does not argue as in a syllogism but that the concrete decision lies in the lap of the Christian's interpretative self-awareness.[8] Simpson has deliberately chosen the notion of self-awareness rather than that of self-understanding: he says that, if pressed about some moral action he has performed, a Christian's final appeal can only be to 'the person he is', to what he has to do in order to be 'true to himself'.[9] Mackey, too, has important suggestions, which could be developed here, in his concept of picture-ideals. Between the most general values and the most concrete precepts there are in human consciousness, he says, pictures of situations worth realising: they form part of a person's general *Weltanschauung*, his picture of how one ought to be in the world. Such picture-ideals do not immediately yield detailed codes of law and convention but they do exercise a genuine influence.[10] The question is whether specifically Christian religious beliefs have influenced specific moral ideals: the answer seems to be that they have. (Mackey's most telling contribution is his contrast of a dualist or apocalyptic world-view, which leads to moral positions of detachment and withdrawal from the world, with the world-view of Jesus, for whom the world was God's world and was good. So that Jesus, he says, and those who share his faith can preach a life-style of the most immediate commitment to one's fellow human beings in this world.) Rahner proposes that there is a 'human and Christian "instinct" in the moral field', 'a synthesising element which cannot itself be reflected upon in isolation'.[11] When he applies this to the question of genetic manipulation, he says that the moral faith-instinct is aware of its right and obligation to reject such manipulation, even without going through (or being able to go through) an adequate process of reflection.

With this general approach I am in agreement if what is meant is that the Christian is to be sensitive to the wide variety of considerations which arise from faith, which are part of his consciousness and which are relevant to moral decision. In making a moral judgment a Christian may have choices that are intelligible and compelling for him but that may not be so for the secular moralist. But my view is that it should be possible for the Christian to go a considerable distance in explaining his decision. My inclination is to try to rid moral judgments of mystery. It is too easy (for the individual and for the churches) to appeal to faith-instinct or to the Spirit to justify moral positions.

121

Christian intuitionism can hardly be any more acceptable to the moralist than any other form of intuitionism. There are facts here that are public facts for the Christian. Several of them may be relevant to a particular situation. They may be delicately related to one another or may reinforce one another. They may enter very subtly into discernment — moral discernment requires imagination and sensitivity.[12] But, however subtle and delicate the process of judgment, it should be possible for the Christian to indicate the factors (the beliefs, myths, stories, symbols, loyalties, commitments) that seem to be operative in the decision. It may well be that this is a second moment in the discernment. That is, one may not arrive at the judgment by the weighing of these factors but more directly, as the authors suggest. But, on reflection, it should be possible to indicate the faith-elements that are relevant and that seem to point the decision in a particular direction.

There is a sense in which there must be a Christian morality because, if Christianity or any other religion is to be consistent, it must have a morality that is consonant with its world-view or picture ideals. But to what extent is this at variance with or to what extent does it cut across the humanist world-view in its judgment of inner-worldly activity? Can the Christian world-view simply incorporate or assume into itself the humanist world-view or, at most, add something to it while leaving it intact? The view of the autonomy school seems to be that, as far as inner-worldly moral activity is concerned, it can do so. The old scholastic dictum was that grace builds on nature, while leaving nature intact. Does Christian awareness, while admittedly different from other religious or humanist awareness, have such a view of the order of inner-worldly reality that, on some kind of analogy, it can leave the humanist moral vision intact and assume it into itself? Or do the concrete conclusions which follow from Christian awareness necessarily cut across the humanist position? It should be noticed that Mackey's suggestions draw the contrast more successfully between different religious approaches than between Christian and humanist approaches.[13] Perhaps it is the case that, in the end, Christian awareness about human life and about the world are not so distinctive as to lead to conclusions about behaviour that are significantly different from those of the humanist.

Certainly, it is striking how difficult theologians find it to translate Christian faith convincingly into substantively unique behaviour. Nevertheless, I believe that one must put a question mark against the autonomy thesis that there is no content to Christian morality that is not available to humanists. It seems to me that it is possible to show that there are some pieces of behaviour that are intelligible to and seen as a moral demand by Christians but not by upright and thinking humanists. They may not be many. It may be argued that, if there are some, they are not very important and do not substantially weaken the autonomy case. It may also be, as we shall see, that they relate more to the hightly personal, vocational areas of choice rather than to general norms. But if there are any, it suggests that the autonomy thesis is too bland and that to the question whether faith yields specific moral judgments, a positive answer must, in some instances, be given. I would like now to explore some of those instances as examples of the interplay of world-view and moral judgment. The immediate issue is that of specificity. But behind it is the more general question of methodology in Christian ethics.

For many moral systems the notion of welfare or well-being and the related notions of flourishing, perfection, good, harm, happiness and need are key notions. The question must be asked whether the Christian understanding of welfare or flourishing does not differ from that of the non-Christian. If so, does it not affect the content of moral judgment? For the Christian, to know God, to believe in the friendship of God and human beings, to accept that union with God here and in the life to come is our fulfilment and perfection, is likely to have a bearing on judgment about our own welfare and that of others. It has been argued by the autonomy school that such union with God is simply the context or final significance of Christian morality and does not affect the content of inner-worldly choice. But is that right? It seems to me that the fact that union with God is the most important component of welfare or happiness will affect choice both for oneself and for one's service of others. One's own flourishing will mean preserving that relationship above all: this will relativise some goods that a non-believer might regard as important and highlight some which he would regard as un-important. It will mean that choices which will lead to a weakening of one's sense of the relationship or which will endanger it will be regarded as morally undesirable. Williams,

123

commenting on Luther's rejection of happiness in favour of suffering and the Cross remarks that it only shows that Luther placed man's well-being elsewhere, in eventual reconciliation with God: so, he says, happiness is still the point.[14] That is true, but happiness of a different order may affect choice here. It is an interesting fact that, while theologians of the autonomy school do not find any significance for moral choice in the religious dimension, some philosophers do. Warnock says:

> I suspect that religious views differ from humanist views not by denying the essential moral relevance of human benefit or harm but rather by incorporating very different beliefs as to what really is good or bad for human beings. The religious believer finds in a supernatural order a whole extra dimension of pre-eminently important gains and losses, benefits and harms; his difference with the non-believer is not on the question whether these are of moral significance, but simply on the question whether they are real or chimerical.[15]

It is true that there will be considerable overlap between Christian and secular morality. But secular notions of welfare will have to be regarded by Christians as falling short of the truth, because they omit religious considerations. This is not just a matter of supererogation or ideal but of basic need or good. Neither is it a matter of the addition of extra elements of welfare. There may be important differences of judgment. It is not just that religious welfare is to be chosen in addition to secular welfare or that we are to be aware that we do not live on bread alone. There may be acute and pressing problems of choice. There may be situations in which one has to abandon some worthwhile project — something that at one level is developing and fulfilling — for fear, as the Scriptures have it, of losing one's soul. Demmer is right to make the point that for the Christian the justification of one's life is supra-historical and that what might appear to others as a limitation on development may be regarded by the Christian as creative self-development.[16] All kinds of people, of course, will differ about what is and what is not development: the point I am making is that Christians as a class have a scale of values which humanists do not have and which may lead to distinctive choices.

The same considerations arise about service of others. If religion is regarded as a basic value, concern for others will mean, among other things, concern for the religious dimension of their lives. One can see the point of the remark of Barth that the first service of others is witness, because, as he says, the most urgent need of the neighbour is God himself.[17] Anyone who thinks that these are not pressing problems has only to look at the considerable debate in recent mission theory about the relationship between evangelisation and development,[18] or at the literature on the relationship between secular history and salvation history.[19]

One is not saying that others, besides Christians, do not have to sacrifice present laughter for future joy. They do. The prudent person takes the long-term view. Much secular morality is concerned that a person so conduct himself that he achieve what he really desires. Lawrence is often quoted about the tension between our little needs and our greater needs:

> There is a little morality which concerns persons and the little needs of man; and this, alas, is the morality we live by. But there is a deeper morality, which concerns all womanhood, all manhood, and nations and races and classes of men. This greater morality . . . is often in conflict with the little morality of the little needs.[20]

This is true. For all people personal limitation may lead to enrichment or flourishing. But for Christians as a class there is an enlarged reality in which there are values and meanings that do not exist for the non-Christian and which relativise secular notions of welfare, success and failure. And they do this for Christians in judgments both about what they themselves should seek and what they should be concerned to seek for others.

It is some such approach, I feel, which gives meaning to the recurring remark that the Cross or the death-resurrection of Jesus Christ are factors which modify Christian moral choice. There is, in the Christian consciousness, an awareness of death-resurrection, which was first realised in the person of Jesus, but which is taken to express the situation of every human person. Many of our authors (von Balthasar, Stoeckle, Simpson, Demmer) find in it a distinctive element of Christian moral life. One takes them to mean that a Christian may well come to a situation in his or her individual life which bears analogies to Christ's fidelity to his mission and Christ's refusal to engage in violence, even at the price of being unjustly put to death. It may be a situation of non-resistance, of suffering in silence, of not vindicating oneself, of enduring injustice, of self-sacrifice. The individual Christian may well decide that goodness requires of him that he comport himself in this way. His choice is intelligible to him because of the stories, myths and beliefs that make up his consciousness. It may not be easy to trace the precise entailment involved. But it seems clear enough that entering into it and disposing the Christian to his judgment are a belief in God's providence and in the significance of Christ's death-resurrection, an assessment of success and failure that is wider than the humanist's, a hope of final fulfilment in the hereafter, a conviction of the value of union with God. They all enter into the judgment of what piece of behaviour is the right one in the circumstances.[21]

One can make sense, then, of the remark that the true moral response both of individuals and of Christian communities involves a readiness to bear the Cross. It must be so, partly because of the Christian's understanding of flourishing, and largely because we live in a world that has a considerable admixture of injustice, inequality, evil, sin. Justice will not always be done, rights will not be allowed, the conditions that make for humanisation will not be fulfilled, fair opportunities will not be forthcoming, goodness will not be rewarded, evil will often succeed. The life and death of Jesus show his followers the kind of moral judgments with which one is faced in such a world.

It could be argued that it is such a combination of belief in the providence of God and in the creative value of suffering and self-sacrifice in terms of closer union with God — exemplified in the life of Jesus and which made his own choices right and intelligible for him — that is at work in the Christian tradition of non-violence. It is an unwillingness to engage in the logic of self-defence (who gets whom first). It is also an unwillingness to engage in the logic of impartiality or equality: it is a refusal to demand even what one is minimally entitled to. It is, nonetheless, a choice, a decision in the light of one's total world of values that non-violence is the better thing.

Religious moralists may adopt different moral systems. They may be teleologists or deontologists, they may adopt an ethic of duty or an ethic of virtue, they may build their theories on the idea of perfection or on other-regard. But there are issues that recur for them — concepts of human good, of welfare, of flourishing, notions of rights, of fairness, of impartiality, problems of response to injustice, violence and evil. My point here has been that the Christian who allows the full range of his faith to be operative in these areas may well find himself accepting as his moral responsibility a piece of behaviour that the humanist does not consider to be morally required and that the humanist, according to his calculus, does not see as a reasonable decision.

Are there other areas of conduct on which Christian belief can be seen to impinge? We have already met suggestions that Christians have a positive attitude to the world — which has implications for morality. But that is not the whole story. There are attitudes which derive from faith and which are summed up in the biblical injunctions to be in the world but not of it (cf. Jn. 15.19; 17.16) or not to be anxious for tomorrow (cf. Matt. 6.34). They are not taken literally by Christians but neither are they empty of content. They say something about the horizon of our evaluations, about concern for the God-dimension in our lives, about the relative importance of human success, about providence. They say that a Christian sense of values should lead to a particular kind of behaviour. One should so conduct oneself in human affairs as not to forget divine things. One should not be so seduced by the physical as to lose sight of the metaphysical, as to allow the faith-dimension to become dimmed. One should, if needs be, sacrifice human development to progress in divine things. One should remember that immersion in human development is not only not the whole of a person's destiny but may even lead him or her to forget the true end of life. Kierkegaard's remark is strong but most Christians will recognise some truth and some expression of the Christian attitude to the world in his words:

> Every man is God's servant; therefore he dare not belong to anyone in love unless in the same love he belongs to God, and he dare not possess anyone in love unless he and the other belong to God in this same love; a man dare not belong to another human being as if the other were everything to him; a man dare not permit another to belong to him in such a way that he is everything to the other.[22]

Religious vision here does lead not just to attitudes but to

127

concrete action. A friend of mine recently gave away his car and what little luxuries he possessed. It was not an act of almsgiving. That was not the way he saw it (and therefore not the act which he did). In fact, he did not give to the poor. It was a piece of conduct that was meant to accentuate religious value in his life and that was, presumably, related to some wider notion of wholeness, flourishing and personal creativity. On such an understanding it was not just a religious but a moral act.

Poverty is a variation on this. It has to do with thought of God and union with God, with preserving one's vision of the relative importance of spiritual values, with freedom for religious things. All of this relates to Christianity's vision of the meaning of the person and to its way of measuring human perfection. Much of human morality is based on concepts of interests and desires. It is concerned about the best arrangement among people who are striving for a share of scarce goods. It is concerned with fairness and impartiality, with one's right to a fair share of the cake. While attention to fairness or impartiality might be regarded as the normal, acceptable and justifiable moral stance for the secular moralist, the spirit of the Gospel has been interpreted by Christians as recommending a way of life that is quite at variance with this. They understand it as saying that concern for the total meaning of one's life implies a certain kind of poverty in the pursuit of one's interests, desires and rights and that the way of radical poverty — of leaving all for the sake of the kingdom — may be, at least for some, an intelligible moral choice. When taken in conjunction with other elements of the Christian outlook the moral advice of Paul, 'Let no one seek his own good, but the good of his neighbour' (1 Cor. 10:24) makes moral sense.

A further variation is trust in God. It is engendered by Christian belief in God's providence. Can it — can the injunction, '... do not be anxious about your life ... look at the birds of the air' (Matt. 6:25,26) — be shown to have implications for moral choice? Coupled with a belief in the enabling grace of God, it may well be a factor in one's life-project, in the plans one makes. It appears to have been a factor in the courage with which some Christians have undertaken difficult tasks. It has enabled some to undertake a life that a secular calculation might have regarded as imprudent or as not providing sufficiently for the future. The point is not so much that one is encouraged to do what one knows to be morally good but that trust in God and his

128

enabling grace is one of the facts of the situation which one reads: this may lead one to judge a particular course of action — which appears folly to the secular moralist — as the best course or even as the one morally demanded.

The point of talking about Christian self-awareness is that these different attitudes compenetrate one another. Certainly the last three mentioned — detachment, poverty, trust — do so. They form a notable part of the Christian consciousness.[23] Some of the *Glaubensethik* authors tentatively mention humility as a further Christian attitude. One can see that there is a cluster of beliefs — belief in God as creator and sustainer, as holy, good, perfect, as one's last end, as giver of all good things — which engender attitudes of reverence, humility and thankfulness. They engender, too, a sense of equality and of the preciousness of the individual. Some of these Christian themes confirm or deepen the moral stance that may be taken by the non-Christian. But some point to a distinctive moral stance. The believer knows that the human person is not the most important being in the universe and that he must not comport himself as if he were. He knows that all are subject to the reign of God, that all life must be seen as stewardship, that all history is in God's hands, that the ultimate judgment on human events is not bounded by this world, that even failure can be entrusted to God. He knows that:

> None of us lives for himself only, none of us dies for himself only; if we live it is for the Lord that we live, and if we die, it is for the Lord that we die. Whether we live or die, then, we belong to the Lord. For Christ died and rose to life in order to be the Lord of the living and of the dead. (Rom.14:7-9).

It is arguable that these attitudes do not remain without an effect on behaviour but that they dictate how one regards oneself and how one regulates one's relations with others. There is a meaning and content to modest and humble behaviour that is not, in any sense, pejorative but that is only a sign that one has come to appreciate one's place in the universe in the light of one's belief in God. It can be argued that it is a distinctive bearing that is not simply the courtesy of the gentleman. The Christian can make something of the advice:

> There must be no room for rivalry and personal vanity

129

among you, but you must humbly reckon others better than yourselves. Look to each other's interest and not merely to your own. Let your bearing towards one another arise out of your life in Christ Jesus. For the divine nature was his from the first; yet he did not think to snatch at equality with God . . . (Phil. 2:3ff.)

Simpson claims that the Christian's awareness that our destiny must not be identified with the present life can give our moral judgments a distinctive content in cases of intense suffering: in particular, he says, such a consideration rules out the option of suicide.[24] (The question of suicide will arise again in Chapter 6.) It should be acknowledged, however, that the humanist may not see suffering as completely meaningless. Let us accept that he may see it as a growth-point — even terminal suffering. If both Christian and humanist see it as a recognition of the value of life or as the truly humanising and fulfilling response it is not easy to detect the difference in the moral act. But if the Christian understands suffering as bringing him closer to Christ, which for him is the way of fulfilment and flourishing, is there not some nuance of difference in the act? And what if, like Paul, he rejoices in it because he completes 'what is lacking in Christ's afflictions for the sake of his body, that is, the church' (Col. 1.24)?

There is also in Christianity, from earliest times, a firm tradition of virginity. The *Glaubensethik* authors all assert that it is part of specific Christian morality. We have seen that some of the advocates of an autonomous ethic do not quite know what to do with it and suggest that it be regarded as part of religion, not of morality. But it does seem to be a choice that has moral implications for one's behaviour — for one's own flourishing and for one's relationship with others. There are analogies with it in non-Christian life. But we shall have to look at the notion of analogy and ask whether in analogous situations one is talking about the same moral act? Augustine says that it is not their virginity that we extol in virgins but their consecration.[25] Virginity as a sign of transcendence, virginity for the sake of the kingdom — 'The unmarried or celibate woman cares for the Lord's business: her aim is to be dedicated to him in body and in spirit' (1 Cor. 7:34) — is inexplicable without Christian belief. Without this background, it might even seem to be a rejection of

130

human flourishing. It requires that the boundaries of understanding be extended by faith.

These are some of the directions in which the question of the identity of Christian ethics might be pursued. The list is not meant to be exhaustive: I am only testing the thesis that a Christian self-awareness will yield a specific content. If we except virginity, which belongs to the highly vocational element of morality, I think it can be argued that choices on the lines indicated in this chapter are part of the fabric of Christian life. The general thrusts which I have considered may not fall under the rubric of material norms — they are more general than that — but they do issue in concrete behaviour. To reduce morality to the observance of norms or moral theology to the elaboration of norms is greatly to impoverish both. There are different levels of moral perception and of moral discourse and not much of life can be caught in material norms, particularly negative norms. Morality is a matter also of creative responsibility in the light of one's vision (in this instance one's Christian vision) and, further, of highly personal vocational choices. I shall say something in the next chapter about the relation of norms, creative choices and vocation. Here I only wish to say that, in my view, all these levels belong to morality and must be considered as part of the relation of faith and ethics: the question of specificity or of the content of Christian morality cannot be limited to questions about norms.

There hangs over the discussion a question — who are we talking about, what Christian(s), at what period of history? A Christian may not pursue the implications of faith into either judgment or action: he or she may not be sufficiently alive to faith or sufficiently interested in the moral point of view. A church may for a variety of reasons be blind to the implications of faith — it may be inhibited by its organisational structure from pursuing certain moral values or it may be limited by its prejudices or caught in its cultural horizons — as the apostolic church was in relation to the place of women and of slaves. It may well be that a Christian community in a particular time and place is less open to some of the great movements of the spirit for liberty and equality, for example, than are secular philosophies. However this hardly takes from the question of the logic of faith in the moral area. If Christians, or Christian churches, are to be fully alive to their moral call they have to

131

make their moral pilgrimage in fidelity to their story: if they do, they will find themselves in their concrete choices moving in the directions suggested in this chapter.

The attempt to delineate a specific Christian morality is not, one hopes, some kind of chauvinism. It should be the calm attempt to discover the implications of faith for behaviour. There is no doubt that there will be a large area of agreement between Christians and non-Christians. But today we often hear talk about the need for Christian values in society. Does this refer only to religious duties? Or is it the case that belief should leave its impact on social life? Is this solely a matter of motivation to do what everybody knows to be good — if so, reference to *Christian* values is misplaced.

The immediate reply of the autonomous ethic to the probings of this chapter will be either (a) that the conduct proposed as specific Christian conduct belongs to the religious rather than to the moral area of life, or (b) that it is conduct already accepted by non-Christians. I have already considered that it is a matter of dispute in Christian ethics whether acts directed to God, such as prayer, are to be included in the institution of morality. That will affect the issue of content. But much of the conduct envisaged in this chapter does not fall easily or entirely into the category of acts directed to God. Choices about welfare, development, suffering, non-resistance, self-sacrifice, virginity, humility, detachment, poverty, rights and injustice all have some reference to social life. It might be argued that some of them pertain also to the area of religion. But even these will appear as part of morality in moral systems for which the notion of perfection and the notion that good moral choices are choices that lead to perfection are key structural elements. If union with God and awareness of God are part of human perfection or welfare one can see how choices that encourage and develop that may be regarded as moral choices. From this point of view choices about poverty, detachment, virginity and asceticism fall under the rubric of the moral. Perhaps religious morality extends the area of the moral or at least extends the world of considerations that affects judgment about behaviour. One can see the wisdom of the remark that the concept of morality in religious morality may evade the precise definition and usage which philosophers seek, and that stipulative definitions of religion and morality which make them exclusive of each other

132

may not fit the complexities of historically developed theological ethics or the experience of the commingling of religious and moral consciousness.[26]

About the second objection of the autonomy movement — that non-Christians reach the same judgments of moral content — the point made in the last chapter will, one hopes, have become clearer. (a) If one includes vision in morality one finds in the material discussed in this chapter support for the claim that there is a specific content. There is involved in much of what we have discussed a vision, an evaluation of life, a configuration of thought about living that can be claimed to be specific. (b) If virtue is a prime category, if the performance of acts not simply out of duty but in the way of the virtuous person is important, if attitudes and innermost desires are part of moral action, then one can point to specific elements which should be of interest to the moralist. A Christian may live and act with a sense of humility before God and others, with a joy and gratitude for forgivenness, with a reverence for creation, with a sense of stewardship, with hope in God's promises, with confidence in his lordship. This is a recognisably Christian style of life but perhaps only for those who have eyes to see it — to see the why and the how. An advocate of autonomy may contend that he observes nothing different from the life of the humanist. But it can be argued that what is done is done differently. (c) If one does not allow vision, attitude and disposition as part of morality but insists on a narrow definition of moral content, there may still be specifically Christian choices. But whether some of the choices which we have looked at in this chapter are to be understood as specifically Christian or not depends on how one understands the notions of moral act, intention and motive. I have expressed the view that the autonomy school confuses justifying and explanatory reasons and that it is mistaken in making such a sharp distinction between act and motive. The reason why something is judged to be morally desirable is not just a motive: it determines what moral act is being performed. If this is right there would appear to be instances of moral choice — such as choices of poverty, detachment, virginity — which will qualify as distinctive Christian content.

One may say that analogous choices are made by non-Christians. But to say this may be question-begging. 'Analogous' presumably means that others who do not have the

Christian's reasons for a particular choice — the reasons which justify the choice for him — still manage to do the same (external?) act. The question that has been raised in the last chapter is whether and in what sense that is analogous. From the moral point of view can two actions be said in any serious sense to be analogous if, although they appear to the observer to be the same, they are justified as moral choices (not just motivated) from entirely different reasons. Does it matter at all to the moralist and to his conception of what is done why one chooses poverty, detachment, asceticism, missionary life? Is a hippy who chooses a simple life-style doing the same thing as St Francis? Does it matter to the moral characterisation of an art that one sometimes makes choices precisely for the sake of developing or preserving nearness to God, of 'saving one's soul'? Does it matter why one chooses a life-style of celibacy — for the sake of the kingdom or in order to write a book or out of fear of sex or out of unwillingness to engage in family life? This points up the importance of reasons for choosing and the difficulty of talk about analogy. One could think of the closer analogy of the person who chooses a life of celibacy in order to look after a sick relative but the question must still be asked whether it is the same moral act.

A related question is this. Is identity of morality proven if non-believers sometimes do (even exceptionally) what is proposed as consonant with Christian faith-vision? Must it not be shown that in the same set of circumstances the logic of Christian faith is no different from the logic of secular morality? If a particular moral choice is a general expectation of Christianity then it is not sufficient to say that it is not unknown in or is sometimes found in secular literature. For example, self-sacrificing love or a certain kind of humility are found in secular literature — *dulce et decorum est pro patria mori*. But to say that something that is regarded by our tradition as a clear demand of Christian life and that is a constant of Christian preaching and proclamation, such as humility, detachment, the relativising of worldly success, is sometimes found among non-believers is hardly to demonstrate identity of content. This will, I hope, emerge more clearly in the next chapter. Such considerations again point to the difficulty of pinning down precisely the issues in the debate.

Two other objections may be raised against the thesis that faith leads to distinctive moral positions. Some authors make the point that Christian morality has no distinctive duties but, rather, new derivative duties from basic ones already accepted by the humanist.[27] Thus, for example, one who believes in the goodness of God or of Christ has a duty of gratitude. But all sorts of people are recognised to have different duties of gratitude, depending on their condition in life: a Christian claim about duties of gratitude to God or to Christ would be nothing new. This objection is not destructive of the claim that there may, in some instances, be a specific Christian moral position. First, what we are interested in and have tried to pursue is whether Christians, as a class, should have particular moral positions. Second, the objection will not meet the distinctive moral positions outlined above — suffering, non-resistance, virginity, humility, etc. Third, if one were to say that there are no new duties because Christian and humanist morality share concepts of welfare, flourishing, etc., this would hardly be a very interesting remark, because it can be shown that their concepts of welfare and flourishing will, in some instance, lead them to a quite different understanding of responsible moral choice. And that, presumably, is the point at issue.

Another feature which might give pause to anyone pressing the claims of a Christian morality is the ability of Christian writers to come to quite opposite conclusions in their attempt to draw out the moral implications of faith. It is interesting to note that in the area of medical risk and experimentation, two outstanding Protestant moralists find themselves on opposite sides — for theological reasons. Gustafson recounts that, in discussing interventions in the evolutionary process with scientists, he found that he was less anxious about the destructive possibilities than were the scientists. They agreed that what made the crucial difference — what, therefore, dictated whether such procedures were seen as acceptable or not — was religious belief. The theologian's belief in the goodness of the ultimate power, his trust in providence and his hopefulness that out of tragic mistakes could come subsequent benefits seemed to justify a more courageous policy of intervention.[28] Paul Ramsey, on the other hand, insists that we have to contrast biblical or Christian eschatology with genetic eschatology and observe how practical proposals may change their hue when shifted from one ultimate philosophy of history to the other. One who intends the world as a Christian, he says, will find *more* elements in the nature of man which are deserving of respect and which should be withheld from human handling or trespass.[29]

This, however, is not decisive against the suggestion that one's theological beliefs influence moral judgments: it merely points up the difficulty. Christians can and do differ about what Christian faith means. Within one faith there is the possibility of stressing or giving prominence to different elements. It can still be argued that a methodology of Christian moral judgment will always be some kind of interpretation of what it means to act in faithfulness to Christian faith and commitment. However, this does underline a point made earlier, that there can be no facile recourse to faith-instinct in justifying moral judgments. An expression such as 'in the light of revelation' must not become a *deus ex machina* to justify any desired conclusion: it must be possible to indicate the particular Christian considerations which lead one in the direction of particular concrete judgments. It is possible, of course, that theological beliefs give rise to a clash of values: that occurs obviously in the area just mentioned. But dealing with a clash of values is nothing new for the moralist.

It is obvious that the theological use of Scripture or the general bearing of faith on morals, which we have been considering, is quite different from the normative use considered in the third chapter. It approximates more to the suggestion of Vatican II that human realities should be considered 'in the light of the gospel'. The movement known as liberation theology is a different version of the attempt to interpret human realities in the light of the gospel. It involves such a fundamental displacement of theological *loci* that it might be nearer the truth to say that it is an attempt to interpret the gospel in the light of human realities: it is the most radical version yet of the claim that God reveals himself in human history. It has not been explicitly developed by moralists and the point has often been made that it is more interested in theology than in ethics. But to some extent it appears to imply a moral methodology and moral judgment and from that point of view it concerns us.

For this movement theology grows out of the situation — and it is a very special situation. Whereas much of European theology is addressed to the non-believer, South American theology sees itself as responding to the non-person, the one who is oppressed socially, economically and politically. The first act

136

of Christians in this situation, it is argued, must be solidarity with the oppressed and commitment to the struggle to deliver them from bondage. It is out of and in response to the questions and problems of such people that all theologising is to be done. Praxis therefore enjoys a normative value: theology is to be inductive, a second act which follows on commitment to a praxis that is not only political but is subversive of the existing order. So Gutiérrez can say that the task of liberation theology is

> To reconsider the great themes of the Christian life within the radically changed perspective . . . born of the experience of shared efforts to abolish the current unjust situation and to build a different society, freer and more human.[30]

The point of departure for such a reconsideration he sees as 'the questions posed by the social praxis in the process of liberation as well as by the participation of the Christian community in this process'.[31] It is this actual historical situation and one's commitment to it, it is said, that enable one to know who God is and the meaning of God's activity in history.

The theologians of liberation maintain that what the Christian comes to know in this situation is that God is a liberator and that he has a bias towards the poor; that Christ is to liberate us from sin, which is the root of all oppression and injustice; that the salvation which Christ offers is total and integral salvation and that the promises of God and the kingdom of God intend also earthly and social realities. The situation has enabled the Christian to re-interpret the gospel message and to disengage it from all interpretations whereby it was made to sanction existing oppression and injustice. This interpretation, it is said, should have a dialectical effect on praxis: it underpins it and throws light on it. The struggle for liberation, then, is seen as a sign of the continuing liberating activity of God: one who had come to know such a God through the struggle must be engaged with him in the struggle.[32]

That is, obviously, the merest sketch of a considerable literature. But this is no place for a full-scale discussion of liberation theology. What is important for us is its implications for a methodology of Christian ethics within Roman Catholicism. We have to ask ourselves what manner of discernment is at work here. The attempt to read what is going on in the world in the light of God's action in history and thereby to derive some guidance for action is nothing new in Christian theology. The question 'What does God do?', rather than, 'What does God command?' is one strand of the traditional approach to Christian ethics, although almost exclusively found in the Protestant churches. So too is the search for a central theme that will serve as a hermeneutical key to human action — what liberation theology has found in the theme of liberation.

There are general problems about liberation theology that need not concern us. But in line with the main interest of this book we have to ask whether the contribution of liberation theology is simply a matter of motivation for the race's age-old struggle against oppression and injustice. Does it perhaps also give what the autonomy school calls a Christian context or interpretation to what the upright humanist knows to be morally required?

It is a well-attested theme of the biblical tradition that faith works through love. Liberation theology has given a fresh and powerful impetus to that. It has also helped to highlight several related themes: that salvation is not just personal and spiritual but social and institutional; that bringing about liberation from oppressive situations is bringing about God's kingdom; that in the Christian tradition God is father of the poor. All of this is exceedingly welcome.

But does it enable the Christian to know what to do: does it, through its interpretation of revelation, give a specific and concrete Christian insight into what is morally required, what God is requiring and enabling us to do? The moralist will have two questions about this. By understanding liberation as the power and action of God in the world the movement gives a theological legitimation to liberation activity. The question is: how much is being legitimated? One does not need to be a Christian to recognise that situations of inhumanity must be changed, that there is a moral demand to bring about a world in which all people can live humanly. One might want to claim only that there is theological warrant for the general work of justice and of deliverance from oppression. Or is there warrant for the choice of socialism against capitalism? Is there warrant for saying that every movement that improves the condition of the oppressed, whatever its means, is the bringing about of the kingdom and deserves to be supported? Is it to be accepted that in cases of established violence we may be morally required to

138

use the force that is necessary to remove such? Does Christianity commit one to accepting both the Marxist analysis of society and the Marxist solution? Can praxis be absolutely normative? Ellacuria seems to claim biblical warrant for revolutionary violence.[33] Segundo and many others insist that there is a biblical warrant for the choice of socialism against capitalism.[34] Is all of this the logic of faith? Is it the case that Christian faith allows no other choice, that the moral duty of Christians as a class is clear?

The second question concerns the general problem of the choice of a specific biblical theme. In making the theme of liberation central and applying it to social and political movements, is liberation theology faithful to the totality of Christian faith or is it arbitrarily selecting one element of faith? If biblical symbols and events are authoritative, if they are, in some way, revelatory of God and his purposes, what criteria do we have for the selection of such symbols and themes? There have been examples of appeal to contrary themes for the interpretation of situations, leading to contrary views of what God was demanding of his people. It is well known that in the nineteenth century Dutch Calvinists in South Africa appealed to the conquest of the land of Canaan to support their expansion into the lands of the black tribes. The exodus theme, on the other hand, was used by the oppressed to lend biblical authority to liberation movements. Is the biblical theme of liberation being used by the South American theologians merely to confirm a moral stance that is taken for, and justified by other, non-Christian reasons? (If it is, this *interpretation* of good moral choice, which has been arrived at independently, may yet be a valid and important part of Christian life.) Or is it a help towards arriving at the judgment of how one should act — the key concern of the moralist? One has to ask, in particular, if a situation of oppression is to be interpreted by a Christian exclusively and necessarily in terms of a liberator-God, with a consequent bias towards action and, perhaps, revolution, or if it is to be sometimes judged in terms of the death-resurrection of Christ, with a bias towards resignation and suffering? Is there any master-theme, any theological reason, which would enable one to choose between themes and to determine clearly what God is requiring and enabling us to do?

It might be argued that when faced with the problem of the

choice of biblical theme or symbol one should try to find a theme more basic in the Judaeo-Christian tradition than the variety of themes and symbols with which one is confronted. It has been suggested that the primary Judaeo-Christian experience is that God's action is gracious and beneficent: it is, therefore, the humanising thing in any situation which will reveal what God is requiring and enabling us to do; that will be the criterion of choice among symbols.[35] Thus, it would be argued in the example given above about South Africa that liberation is more consistent with the Christian experience of God than is conquest and suppression: so the exodus theme, rather than the Canaan conquest theme, gives the clue to what the Christian should do in the situation. But one wonders if the symbol has not suffered the death of its qualification. Are we now saying only that the Bible validates activity that is humanising? The choice between liberation and conquest may be relatively easy. But one sees the problem if one asks about the choice between violent revolutionary action and resigned suffering. Which action is humanising? The choice is not always easy and perhaps not even the same for all.

To say that one is morally required to commit oneself to activity that is humanising is to say something to which many secular moralists would subscribe. The appeal to the Bible is not then throwing any extra or special light on moral choice. The theologian may well be right in saying that socialism or revolutionary violence in a particular situation is the morally right choice but he will have to argue it in terms of 'humanisation' or some other ethical calculus and not by appeal simply to the biblical theme of liberation. But if there is anything in what I have been saying in the earlier part of this chapter, the Christian ethicist will also have to allow several other Christian themes to bear on his choice. I have said something about the manner in which considerations of personal union with God, of self-sacrifice and suffering, of patience in the face of failure and injustice, may enter into the notion of Christian flourishing: they cannot be left out in an assessment of humanisation. It is this total Christian vision which is to enter into ethical choice. In this Christian vision a person who has managed to retain love in a situation of oppression, who has forgiven enemies, who is unwilling to shed blood for the sake of deliverance, who is tranquil in spite of the failure of efforts to achieve justice, must be said to

140

have reached a large measure of liberation and may even have achieved it more significantly than those who reach political, social and economic freedom but without such values — as will be argued more fully later in this book. Such elements are not ignored by liberation theology. But it may be that there has been impatience with them in the very necessary attempt to understand revelation realistically in situations of dire oppression and distress.

If liberation theology is put forward as an instance of Christian ethical methodology — and one must insist that this does not appear to be its major preoccupation — then it must face up to the — not new — problems which this raises. What I have said in the last few paragraphs may look like nit-picking. There is no doubt that faith in a God who seeks justice for the poor commits one to struggle for liberation and humanisation. Nor can there be much argument about the point, often made, that it is only those who are involved in the situation who can appreciate fully the dimensions of the moral choice. But I am interested in liberation theology not just as validating a general commitment to justice but in relation to precise and detailed moral choice. To settle on one Christian theme as a key to action and to apply it unilaterally to every movement against oppression would be to sell Christianity short. In a world of evil there are no simple solutions to the question of what God is requiring of us. However naïve it might appear for an outsider to say it from the comfort of the developed world, it must be said that the death of Jesus may have something to teach us about God's activity in the world; and the Sermon on the Mount has something to say about ethical choice in the face of evil. In seeking to allow faith to bear on discernment or in seeking to come to the meaning of faith out of the realities of a tragic situation, we must try to be open to the fullness and richness of our tradition.

The whole thrust of this chapter has been that, when account is taken of the way in which one's religious world-view bears on moral judgment, a case can be made — even on a narrow definition of morality — for a specifically Christian content to morality: the result would be that the identity of Christian morality cannot be limited to context and motivation. But all of this may be in vain because there are those who would maintain that it is illegitimate in morals to allow beliefs to exercise such an

141

influence. What they accept as belonging to morality is only what any 'rational' man would accept. Particular interests or a particular vision of life are regarded as extraneous elements which militate against the pure rationality of the moral enterprise. The aim of such a view is to reach some kind of consensus in morals, but perhaps it is a consensus reached at too high a price. A quotation from Frankena carries the attack:

> If morality is dependent on religion, then we cannot hope to solve our problems or resolve our differences of opinion about them, unless and insofar as we can achieve agreement and certainty in religion (not a lively hope): but if it is not entirely dependent on religion, then we can expect to solve at least some of them by the use of empirical and historical enquiries of a public, available and testable kind (enquiries that are improving in quality and scope).[36]

The statement is mild enough but the implications of it for religious morality are considerable. Frankena's concern is to establish the independence of moral discourse from all the relativities of human interests and commitments save one — the interest of being rational. In particular, any reflection on morality that finds justification or warrant for moral values or principles, which are themselves grounded in religion, is unacceptable. The implied value-judgment is that religious reasons for policies must be viewed with suspicion.

The implications of such a view for one of the key concepts we have considered in this section — that of welfare — can be seen from some remarks of Little and Twiss. They contend that the concept of human welfare has a relatively fixed core, 'which includes such "objective"conditions as physical survival, bodily and psychic health, security from arbitrary violence, and the like'.[37] They argue that, when a religious action-guide calls for the violation of this core, on grounds that the other's welfare is really different from this — and I have suggested that in the Christian view welfare cannot be limited to this and could conceivably relativise this — the religious action-guide cannot be regarded as moral. Dworkin would also suggest that if religious beliefs contradict basic assumptions about human welfare, their related moral positions should be disqualified as moral.[38]

Frankena's position introduces a bifurcation into the life of

142

the religious person. He seems to hold that there are moral duties and religious duties but that the twain never meet. His key point — that not all normative or value systems or ways of life are to be regarded as part of morality and that not everything that is certified as a duty or virtue within the rules of a religion is thereby certified as a moral duty or virtue — is a fair and important point. But to say that there can be no interaction between religious outlook and moral judgment is another matter. It involves a very narrow conception of what is meant by 'rational'; and requires an arbitrary and unreal limitation of consciousness.[39]

It will be objected that the inclusion of background beliefs leaves open the way to relativism in morals. Some of this is unavoidable. The exclusion of background beliefs also leads to relativism: the adoption of an anti-metaphysical view of the world is itself an option and one that cannot be conclusively shown to be the right one. Background beliefs and the manner in which they bear on moral judgment can be subject to analysis: one can examine the rationality of the process; this offers, at least, the possibility of understanding, if not of agreement. It will also be objected that, if background beliefs are allowed to influence judgment, there is no possibility of public policy: this is one of the fears of the autonomy school. But this is not necessarily so. Even if one can defend the claim for a specific Christian morality, the claim must not be overplayed. There is still considerable overlap between religious and secular ethics. Where there is difference due to different vision, it may, as we shall see, relate to the more personal, rather than to the more public, aspects of morality. Morality may then be thought of as a union of widely-agreed elements and of the inevitable nuances contributed by different cultural and religious beliefs — including the adoption of philosophical stances.

One must ask further if it is possible to discuss morality in the detached, impersonal manner required by Frankena? It depends on one's understanding of morality. If, for example, one's understanding includes such notions as harm, welfare, flourishing, perfection, etc., then morality cannot be easily engaged in without reference to one's background, vision, world-view. As Mitchell says, our conception of people's interests is normally related to our conception of human excellence where this includes but is not restricted to moral

143

excellence.[40] Conceptions of human excellence can hardly be reduced to a flat 'rational' consensus, without any consideration of the religious value-system that, on Frankena's admission may be more profound and significant for the individual than his moral experience. Hampshire has the relevant remark about virtues and vices:

> To show that these vices are vices, and unconditionally to be avoided, would take one back to the criteria for the assessment of persons as persons, and therefore to the whole way of life that one aspires to as the best way of life.[41]

This seems, in the end, to be also the burden of Hare's remark that, if pressed to justify a decision completely, we have to give a complete specification of the way of life of which it is a part and that the nearest attempt to give such a specification is found in the great religions.[42] One's overall vision, then, seems to be inextricably linked to one's justification of moral positions that depend in any way on notions of welfare, well-being, good, flourishing, etc.

One final objection needs to be mentioned. The claim for a specific Christian morality seems to have most justification in the very personal areas, such as poverty, detachment, self-sacrifice, virginity, suffering. Is the Christian who assents to such judgments prepared to universalise them? Universalisation is widely — if not universally — regarded as of the essence of moral valuation. If poverty, virginity, non-violence are a moral call on some individuals, are they not a call on all? If they are morally good for one, are they not good for all, or at least for all in the same circumstances? This is an issue that must be faced both by the advocates of a specific Christian ethic and by those who reject such. The *Glaubensethik* must take a stand on the issue of universalisability. The autonomy school, if it maintains that there is no difference in content between Christian and secular ethics, must say whether it attaches the same status to such ideals as the secular ethic. This issue arises acutely with regard to *agape* and I leave over its treatment to the next chapter. There I will say that I think it is an objection that can be met.

These last two objections again underline the fact that there is no agreement about the definition of morality and that this greatly affects our central concern. If a principle is a moral principle, by definition, only if it is obligatory on all persons, or if it can be justified only on grounds on which all persons could agree, or if any reflection on morality that finds justification in religious belief is, by definition, not ethical reflection, then there is no possibility of pointing to a specific Christian content of morality. But one is justified in asking whether such a narrow, 'rational' approach to morality is warranted or even possible.

There is not, as far as I can see, any good reason why Christianity should feel any compulsion to prove specificity in morals: there are more important issues for the churches. The desire of the autonomy movement to present a responsible and credible morality and to engage in dialogue with the non-believer are indeed worthy objectives. Yet the movement appears to overreach itself in the interests of dialogue. In spite of the qualifications which it enters, its position amounts in essence to saying that the Christian can ignore everything that comes from Christian faith as he or she faces a moral question.

What has issued from our explorations into the bearing of faith on ethics does not yield a compelling proof of specificity. Yet it seems to me that enough has emerged to suggest that the autonomy claim is too rigidly stated and does not account for the whole of Christian moral life. A person's religious outlook does affect how he or she sees the world. This affects moral judgment in such a way that there may be occasions when a person will give a reason for a moral judgment which is bound to his or her religious belief and which non-religious thinkers would not find compelling. There may be moral actions which are mandatory for religious persons for reasons which derive from their religion and not for reasons on which all persons could presumably agree. Christian moralists need to bear that in mind as they approach their subject. Individual Christians need to be aware of it in their efforts to discern the particularities of the moral demand in the complexities of their lives. That will mean an openness of thought and imagination to the great shaping Christian stories and a readiness to allow moral vision and moral demand to be influenced by them.

145

6

The Issue of the Specificity of *Agape*

Section 1
AGAPE AND SECULAR ETHICS

A major point of disagreement in the debate about the identity of Christian ethics is the question of the specificity of agape. The Christian tradition says that Christians are to love others with a love of agape. That love for others is to be characteristic of Christian life and central to it is not disputed: the *Glaubensethik* and autonomy schools agree on this. What is disputed is whether the demand of agape is specific to Christianity. To say that it is specific is to say that it is dependent on christian faith and that it cannot be reached by one who does not share that faith. It is to attach considerable significance to the adjectives 'Christian' and 'theological' in the expressions 'Christian love', 'theological charity'.

Many of the *Glaubensethik* authors, as we saw, claim that it is precisely agape that gives its specific identity to Christian morality. They do not agree among themselves on what exact element of agape renders it specific. Stoeckle and von Balthasar say that the foundation of agape depends on the realisation that God has loved us.[1] De la Potterie, Remy and Giavini find the newness in the nuance 'to love as Christ loved'.[2] Gründel and Delhaye see the demand to love unto death, in the likeness of Christ, as unique.[3] Rigali and von Balthasar say that Christian love is devoid of any element of selfishness and demands more than is demanded by any other kind of love.[4] Ermecke says that one loves others not for themselves or because of human prerogatives but as members of Christ: for him there is no true love of self or of others without Christianity.[5] Gilleman

146

maintains that the Christian and the non-believer do not see the neighbour in the same light: the Christian loves others in their relation to Christ.[6] An editorial in *La Civiltà Cattolica*, not so many years ago, even claimed that non-Christians cannot practise genuine love and self-sacrifice.[7] The advocates of an autonomous ethic, on the other hand acknowledge the centrality of agape in Christian ethics but do not see it as any different from the central element in many secular systems of ethics. Fuchs makes the point that non-Christians regard love, 'a non-egoistic attitude to the neighbour and a non-egoistic gift of self' as *the* moral value.[8] Auer goes to a lot of trouble to prove that the details of the teaching of Jesus about love are found scattered in Jewish and extra-biblical sources, so that there is nothing original about them.[9] Schüller explicitly rejects the idea that agape — even love of enemies — depends on Christian revelation: he regards it as fundamentally intelligible to reason.[10]

The question of agape, then, is an important one in the current debate. Some of the *Glaubensethik* authors find it incomprehensible that one would not recognise its altogether unique character.[11] But so much depends on what one means by agape and why one chooses it as a moral position. However loud the claim that is made or however important the notion to the Christian tradition, the fact is, as several philosophers have pointed out, that it is very difficult to discover what is meant by the term.[12] The *Glaubensethik* authors do not give us much help. Although they see agape as a very obvious case of faith producing a specific morality, they do not tell us what they mean by agape, or how it gets into their moral theory (is it a divine command?), or what kind of piece of morality it is (is it a principle or a virtue?). So we have not much to go on. This cannot become a book on agape but an attempt must be made to assess the significance of the debate and to uncover what it is that prevents agreement on what might seem to be a relatively straightforward matter — whether what is demanded by agape is also demanded by secular morality. What could a claim to specificity mean? Keeping in mind the (rather scant) suggestions of our authors, I will try in this chapter to examine various structural elements of the doctrine as it has been received in the Christian tradition and to test possible meanings of the claim. It would seem to be a fair test of specificity to confront the tradition

147

with some of the best-known positions of moral philosophy relating to the welfare of others.

Before proceeding there are two questions which we must bracket. One concerns the meaning of welfare. If agape refers in some way to welfare — as most people would think it does — will the Christian understanding of welfare give a specific content to agape? I considered that issue in the last chapter: it seems to me that on this score there will be a specific Christian understanding of the expression of agape. But this is not a consideration which I find in the *Glaubensethik*: its thinking seems to be that there is a fundamental specificity about the very principle of agape. The other question refers to the fact that agape seems to require a very high ideal of love: both schools refer to the example of Christ who laid down his life in love. Is this what is specific about agape? This takes us into the area which some secular moralists refer to as the area of supererogation and which some theologians refer to as the area of the counsels: both the *Glaubensethik* and the autonomy movement have problems with this. I propose to take this as a separate issue in the next section of this chapter.

Our basic problem is to discover what the authors mean by theological agape. It appears to me that an examination requires that we consider first the biblical reference or the source of the teaching. Within that biblical reference we need to tease out the moral justification of agape, i.e. to ask why one should adopt the biblical teaching. We then need to consider the form in which agape is expressed: is it a duty or a virtue, in-principled or consequentialist? All of that will affect the confrontation with secular morality and the issue of specificity.

We refer rather freely to the biblical teaching on agape. But the biblical teaching is various. The exact source of our teaching may determine the form of our concept of agape and this, in turn, will have implications for the question of specificity. The most obvious source is the double commandment in Matthew 22:39, Mark 12:31, Luke 10:27 (cf. Matt. 5:34, 19:19 and John 13:34). But the belief that agape should characterise the Christian life does not depend on a command of Jesus. Nor is New Testament teaching on agape necessarily tied to the actual incidence of the word 'agape'. In Paul it is the whole kerygma that forms the basis of the demand (cf.Rom. 3:21, 2 Cor. 4:4, 5.14, Gal. 4:4). Agape answers to the very nature of God in his

148

redemptive activity. It arises out of the gift of the Spirit: it is a fruit of the Spirit. For Paul the realisation that one should love the other arises from gratitude for God's grace, rather than from a command of God or of Christ: love, expecially forgiving love, should be the attitude of one who has been forgiven by God (cf. Col. 3:13). The same dynamic appears in John in what Cullmann calls 'the catechism of the ethics of the New Testament'.[13] Love, John says, is of God. He has first loved us and we ought to love one another (1 John 4:4): Christ has laid down his life for us and we ought to lay down our lives for one another (1 John 3:16). The same themes appear in the Synoptics. The Father is generous and merciful, his concern is sovereign, unmotivated and spontaneous. He shows kindness to those who despise him. This spontaneous love (Matt. 5:45, Luke 6:35) is the theological basis for agape, and especially for love of enemies: the Christian should love as the Father loves, without expecting a return, giving blessing for cursing and praying for his persecutors (Matt. 5:44, Luke 6:27, 35). This is a mere sketch of the New Testament teaching on agape. But it is enough to show us that one needs to be precise when one refers to biblical agape. When the *Glaubensethik* makes its claim that agape is revealed and specific, we simply do not know to what biblical source it is referring.

Before going further, we must refer to an ambiguous statement that is often found. That is the statement that the specific character of Christian agape is that one must love 'as Jesus loved'. This is altogether too vague for serious debate. It may mean many different things. It could refer to the meaning of agape as a formal principle. It could refer to Jesus' understanding of the content of the welfare of others. Or it could refer to the extent of his love, i.e. to the fact that one should be prepared to sacrifice one's life for the other. More broadly, it could refer to the religious context of his love. So it will not do for the *Glaubensethik* to assert that Christian ethics is unique because one ought to love as Jesus loved. It must cash the expression in other terms. Only then can one deal with the claim.

What is the theologian to make of this material? We have already discussed the possibility of a revealed morality and have seen the difficulties which such a notion must face. The autonomy school would presumably press these difficulties against a revealed agape. Two points, however, can be made in

149

support of a *prima facie* case for a revealed morality of agape. It is a persistent demand right through the different New Testament writings: indeed, even cautious scholars are prepared to grant that it very probably goes back in some form to Jesus himself. Second, if agape is a revealed moral directive it is presumably a very general directive and is therefore less likely to be affected by cultural conditions than some other directives which we have considered. However, that is to jump ahead. Questions must be asked here about justification, about why one should adopt agape as a moral stance. Is it because God has commanded it, because it is a moral precept? If not, is it that the stance of agape follows as a necessary demand of biblical faith? This latter position would mean that the judgment that agape is the right moral stance is deduced from or implied in or in some way entailed by what one learns through the revelation about God and his purposes or about the meaning of the human person. One's position here will have significance for the claim of specificity.

What was said in the third chapter about the distinction between paraenesis and normative ethics and in the fourth chapter about the distinction between motivation and justification is important here. Much of the biblical material on agape may motivate me to live a moral life. The love of God may confront me with my own selfishness. The fact that God loves me may enable me to love others. The fact that God's will is a kingdom of peace and reconciliation may give me additional religious reasons for trying to love others. None of this, however, will support a claim of specificity. To claim that Christian agape is a specific piece of morality — the claim of the *Glaubensethik* — is to claim that the fundamental demand of agape arises for us from the revelation and is not understood without it. What one is looking for is the justification of a moral position. We should, therefore, be careful of commonly used statements that are more likely to be paraenetic than justificatory, such as 'God loves us, therefore we ought to love one another', 'We should love all others for love of God', 'We should love all others as children of God'.[14]

Genuine justification will take the form of saying that we are commanded by God (who is perfectly good) to live a life of agape or that we adopt it because we know from revelation that it characterises the life of the good God or of Jesus who is the model

150

of moral life. Or else, justification will take the form of saying that what we come to know about the human person in the revelation, i.e. the particular appraisal which the revelation makes possible, is such as to require the special moral response of agape. Either way, the claim that agape is a specific Christian position commits one to saying that what we are commanded, or what we seek to imitate, or what we discern to be the true response to others, is something that cannot be known to those outside of Christian revelation.

But if we have a revealed morality of agape what is so special or specific about such a way of life? What about it is closed to non-believers? I will tease out possible positions. The relatively late advent of Roman Catholic moral theology to a theology of agape has meant that little analysis has been done — there seems to me to be a much richer Protestant tradition. However, we can set out different strands of a theology of agape and see how the hints of position which we have from our Roman Catholic authors relate to them. It could be argued — as some Protestant theologians have formally argued — that what is special is that one is talking about agape only if one is talking about love as pure bestowal, i.e. as love independent of the worth of the other, either his generic worth as a human being or his particular worth. Agape, they say, must be spontaneous and unmotivated: it must be pure agent-commitment; it is not based on the merits of others nor is it derived from any conception of treating all people as their personhood intrinsically deserves. It has nothing to do with the kind of love that depends on the recognition of a valuable quality in its object. The agape of the Christian, in this view, will be genuine only if it conforms to the spontaneous love of God.[15] This bestowal-love, as against appraisal-love, is what the Christian discovers in God and is commanded to have in his or her life. This is revealed as the basic moral stance which Christians should have and it is known only to them.

The apparently opposed position sees agape as appraisal. We are commanded to love agapeically but the reason for the command is that the human person is worthy of agape. Or we discover from the revelation that he or she is worthy precisely of the love of agape. (The distinction between bestowal and appraisal may not be as sharp as is sometimes suggested. If God has bestowed his love in an unmotivated way, this gives grounds for appraisal). If an agape of appraisal is to be specific the

151

grounds for it must be religious or revelational. That means that the worth of the other is understood as worth only in relation to God. The person is understood as having a status which has been conferred by God in unmerited grace. He or she has irreducible value but not as an anthropological datum apart from the divinely elected events: what claims our regard is not simply our neighbour but God in our neighbour and our neighbour in God.[16] This status is known only in Jesus Christ: only the Christian can respond to it.

One might hold for a strict dichotomy between judgments based on faith and judgments based on natural moral experience. But it is possible for the theologian to hold a mixed position, i.e., to regard religious and non-religious experience of the claim of the other as continuous. He or she will see non-religious moral experience as partial, as giving only a limited understanding of the reasons for agape and a limited appreciation of the appropriate response to the other: he or she will see faith as a fulfilment and complete revelation of justifying reasons and as the key to the total response. That may be the thinking behind statements of the *Glaubensethik*, which we will consider later, that Christians have a greater respect for the person or a greater respect for life than non-Christians; that for Christians human life is less expendable; that Christians more easily extend love to the less fortunate or doubtfully human; that Christians have more compelling reasons for loving others.

There are, then, different positions on the meaning and justification of agape as a moral stance. Any claim about the specificity of agape should make clear which position is being espoused. The problem with recent Roman Catholic moral theology is that, while it frequently makes the claim, there is little serious attempt to analyse the grounds of the claim. For example, there is no formal consideration of the viewpoints just mentioned. However, there are some clues about positions. Stoeckle says that it is in the experience of God's love that we discover the duty to love:[17] that does seem to mean that for him the whole case of agape, its very foundation, depends on revelation. Von Balthasar warns that the love of Christians is not to be confused with human fraternity: no Christian ethic, he says, can prescind from the word of God; its demands derive from the fact that the Father is perfect and merciful. Neither in the Old nor in the New Testament, he says, is morality an expression of intersubjectivity: it is not based on the person but its motive is the profound revelation of the sanctity of God who is faithful to his covenant.[18] This, too, grounds agape on God. For Rigali the centre of a true supernatural morality is charity, and the law of charity is revealed by Christ. Charity for him is a form of divine command, a piece of revealed morality. But what is revealed he does not say. His main conclusion is that the Christian cannot be satisfied with the demand of the natural law: the point seems to be, therefore, the extent of agape.[19] Gründel (and Stoeckle at times) sees revelation as giving more compelling reasons for neighbour-love, which broaden the extension of agape beyond what might be arrived at by natural morality: that looks like a form of mixed appraisal.[20]

What we have here are sketchy remarks. It should be obvious from our discussion so far — and what immediately follows will underline this — that the issue of the specificity of agape cannot be discussed without a sharper *prise de position* about its meaning and justification. At the level of the foundation of agape or the grounds for it, one who identifies it with bestowal is in a stronger position to make the claim for specificity. A morality of sheer bestowal in the likeness of God, without any consideration of even the generic worth of the person, is not very likely to find a counterpart among secular ethics — at least not in all particulars. On the other hand, such a morality has some explaining to do about how it would regard traditional moralities of appraisal — whether secular or religious — with their insistence on the value-claim of the person. Is the whole tradition of human rights, with its base in the value of the person to be regarded by theological charity as mistaken or inadequate: can theology accommodate it? It is hard to accept von Balthasar's dismissal of non-Christian love or his claim that wherever it is found it exists only as some spark of Christian revelation. A theological morality of appraisal, on the other hand, will find a counterpart among secular systems: moralities based on respect for the person, or on the claim of the person to equal regard, or on benevolence, are widely found. The question will be whether and in what way they fall short of agape. The advocate of specificity will claim that because they lack the dimension of appraisal given by revelation, they are not the same as agape: he will deny their cogency or assert that they

153

are limited in the range or depth of their concern. Whether he can succeed in this claim we have yet to see.

Whether agape is considered as bestowal or appraisal, it might well be asked what difference the Christian element makes to its practice. Does it give the practice of agape different content? The question brings us to the third level in our consideration of the meaning of agape — to the ethical form or category which the theologian gives to agape. He cannot remain with a theory of agape as bestowal or as appraisal. He must say what that means in active Christian moral life. Christian thinkers have found it difficult to know how to characterise the law of love: they have called it not only a commandment or law but also a norm, a standard, a principle, an ideal, a virtue.[21] The point for us here is that the autonomy school may well ask how the *Glaubensethik* understands agape as a moral theory. It will say that considerations of agape as bestowal or as Christian appraisal, which are adduced by some as proof of specificity, do not prove the claim. Whatever the reasons for the adoption of agape as a way of life, it will say, agape is centrally about action, about attending to one's neighbour. The fact that one understands agape as bestowal, for example, does not mean that one judges differently about what is to be done from the philosopher who bases his judgment about the other on impartiality, respect or benevolence. Whatever the genesis of one's agape stance, it will say, one does not *do* anything different from the secular moralist. So that the bearing of faith on ethics, even in the area of agape, is seen by it as peripheral and contextual, rather than as a matter of substantive content.

The autonomy school may well point out that there are systems of secular ethics that claim to approximate to agape and in fact do so. Schüller claims that agape is identical with the morality of the golden rule, something that is found outside of and prior to the teaching of Jesus and that is widely adopted by secular moralists.[22] What more do theologians claim for agape than is required by the golden rule? Some Christians do regard the rule as found in Matthew 7:12 and Luke 6:31 as illustrative of the commandment of love. Others regard it as enshrining a reciprocity or retribution ethic, a kind of measured justice: they see it as antithetical to agape.[23] But is it and, if so, in what respect? There are, of course, different interpretations of the rule and it has to be recognised that some of them make logical room for principles of substance that are not easily reconcilable with traditional agape. But in its developed form it requires of us that we put ourselves in the place of the other with his or her mental and physical qualities, interests, resources and status, desires, needs and wishes. We must then ask ourselves if we could accept a particular maxim as a directive which would guide the behaviour of others towards us.[24] It requires, therefore, a considerable sympathy with the other and a willingness to be as concerned about the other's feelings as one would wish others to be concerned about one's own. There remain problems — should one do to the other what one believes is best for him or her or what the other wishes for himself or herself? — but they are problems that arise equally for almost any conceivable version of agape.

What more is added by theological appraisal? What difference will it make? It might well be difficult to point to a difference. One suspects that the *Glaubensethik* might want to say that the secular moralist would confine the demand of the golden rule to duty and would be slow to press the higher demands of other-regard. That, as we shall see, is important. But it is not as decisive against the golden rule as theological agapists might think. It takes us into the area of ideals and super-erogation where the position of agapists themselves is far from clear. One suspects also that the defender of a specific agape would want to say something about the reasons why one adopts the choice of agape and why one adopts the golden rule. That, too, is important. It has cropped up for us a number of times already. I shall say something about its relevance and about its application to agape at the end of this section.

If some see an exact equivalence between agape and the golden rule, others find the equivalence between agape and a morality of respect for persons. By respect one presumably means a positive concern for the welfare of the other, independent of the kind of person he or she may be, an active sympathy, a duty to be concerned about his or her welfare for no other reason that that he or she is a person and thus has intrinsic worth. There are those who consider that however agape entered our spiritual tradition it is capable of sustaining the absence and surviving the loss of the theistic faith that is so often appealed to in justification of it: agape, they say, rests on our purely natural capacity for other-concern.[25] Some philosophers who base their moral theory on respect for persons claim that it gives 'in secular or humanistic terms a view of morality which is characteristically expounded by Judaeo-Christian thinkers' and that it is the same as the Christian concept of agape.[26]

Is there any difference here between philosophy and theology?[27] Is the autonomy movement right to say that philosophical ethics arrives at a stance towards the other that in practice is the same as what is claimed for agape — Donegan says that Kant's statement of the categorical imperative, 'so act that you treat humanity, whether in yourself or in others, always as an end and never as a means' is the best interpretation of the New Testament demand of neighbour-love.[28] (It should be noted that Kant held that the imperative was not met by refraining from injuring others: one must further the ends of others and treat them as one's own.)[29] Or can the *Glaubensethik* find something specific in agape, something that grounds positions that are closed to secular ethics? Can it demonstrate ways in which living agape means doing something different from living a life of respect for the other?

Some *Glaubensethik* authors simply and straightforwardly deny that rational reasons for respect for the person are compelling: Stoeckle and Rotter assert, in particular, that I can only love myself if I see myself as a child of God.[30] Such assertions appear to fly in the face of the facts. The advocates of a philosophical ethic based on the claim of the other and on the respect due to the other find their reasons sufficient. Their tradition is a very persistent and honourable one in the history of ethics. They can point to an impressive history of acknowledgments and declarations of human rights that do not depend on a religious vision. In the face of this, to say that theological insight is required to base the claim of the other is not very convincing. Nor is it easy to see why respect for self or for one's own life requires a religious reason. Stoeckle and Rotter also assert that only Christianity provides an argument against suicide. What is this theological argument? How does one show that the wrongness of suicide follows from a Christian love of oneself and does *not* follow from a human respect for oneself?

It is certainly open to the religious moralist to claim that he understands others more fully. He sees them, in their full meaning, he will claim, as children of God, brothers and sisters in Christ, destined for eternal life with God, etc. In responding

156

to others, he will say, he is aware of the full meaning of those to whom he responds. This is true. But the question is whether this makes any difference to moral life. The autonomy school counters by saying that this new dimension does not significantly affect the moral foundation of other-regard and that it does not make a discernible difference in practice between agape and respect for the other — that, therefore, it does not make theological agape specifically different from a philosophical theory of respect for the person. Whether that is an adequate answer I will consider later.

A second move which the *Glaubensethik* has made has been to say, not that appraisal depends on Christian belief, but that the new understanding given by theology gives a new stringency to respect or regard for the other. Some have used the expression 'more compelling reasons'.[31] Here the argument is not that true regard for the other is impossible without religious vision. It is that there is continuity between the two, with the religious vision giving a greater strength to the demand for other-regard. It does seem plausible that a Christian's awareness of the relation of each one to God and of his or her value in the sight of God gives a new sense of the untouchableness and of the inalienable character of the person. It can give a more striking sense of his or her worth, a further sense of the dignity of each person. And, since it is this sense of the dignity and worth of the other that is the source of moral respect, it seems that one can make sense of the notion of more compelling'. One could say that, just as there can be growth in the human, non-religious understanding of the worth of the other and of the respect due to him or her so there can be growth beyond that to the religious understanding. This does not mean that the non-religious notion is not adequate. Nor does it mean, in itself, that the religious vision will issue in a different content of response. But it does say something about the stringency of the demand. And, perhaps, it also says something about the clarity of the demand to care for each human being, irrespective of his or her talents (or lack of them) limitations or idiosyncrasies. There is no reason to think that non-religious ethics will not respect each one. But it is arguable that a Christian, one of whose basic tenets is that each one is a child of God and that Christ died for each one, may, especially in situations of difficulty or of very severe handicap, arrive at an appreciation of the need for such respect and regard more easily or more quickly.

A related question is this: could it be that the range of regard for others is wider in religious agape than in non-Christian ethics? It is a highly practical question: it arises, for example, in the issue of abortion and in the treatment of the doubtfully human. To put the question another way: who qualifies for regard and respect? Do the doubtfully human qualify in Christian and not in non-Christian morality: is this a specific difference? Is it their Christian agape that obliges some Christians to take an absolute view of the sacredness of the foetus from even the first moment of conception? Some of the *Glaubensethik* authors hold this, e.g. Gründel.[32] There might seem to be a *prima facie* case for thinking so, based, perhaps, on some notion of 'more compelling'. This is a mistake. We must make sure that the terms of the comparison, here as elsewhere, are fair. Both agape and philosophical respect are concerned about the worth of the human person. For both of them it is the quality of human person that is the distinguishing feature. By that I mean that the object of regard is the human being, as distinct from rocks or trees or lower animals. The problem of determining who is a human being is no easier for Christian than for secular morality. If the entity in question is a human being, then God has care for him or her as such. The Christian will hold firmly to this. Equally, the philosopher will say that if it is a human being, it is due the respect given to human beings. The problem of determining who is a human being remains for both and is not solved by Christianity's attributing human personality more widely than is warranted — nor is it any part of agape's function to attribute it more widely than is warranted. Whether Christianity enables one to recognise the proper response in situations of difficulty more easily than it is recognised by non-Christians is a separate question — for example, in the case of the undeniably human who are seriously defective or limited. What I said earlier about more compelling reasons operates here: one's faith that this individual is a child of God may help when the observable characteristics do not easily claim or evoke a response. But as far as the range of regard for the other is concerned, Christian and non-Christian are in the same position.

It seems, then, that a philosophical ethic which centres itself on respect for the person can well challenge the *Glaubensethik* to say — whatever may be the source or genesis of its agape stance

— what it is in the practice of agape that is different from the practice of respect for the other. The autonomony school can sustain its objection that the identity of Christian ethics is not found in its specific content. About this one has three qualifications. (i) Our old question about the meaning of 'content' and about the way in which reasons and attitudes enter into the definition of a moral act is relevant here. (ii) If agape and respect imply concern for the welfare of the other, account must be taken of the Christian understanding of welfare. I have remarked that the *Glaubensethik* authors do not seem to relate their claim for specificity to this changed conception of welfare: as far as one can discern, the case seems to be that the principle of agape itself is different from anything found in secular morals. (iii) One can make sense of the notion of 'more compelling reasons' but this, in itself, does not make for the specificity of agape.

Are there other angles to the claim of the *Glaubensethik* which might mark off agape as specific? Gründel and Stoeckle say that religious agape protects the person better or that the person is less expendable in an agape system than in systems of secular ethics.[33] It seems to me, however, that everything depends on what form of secular ethics is the term of comparison and, in particular, on how one understands agape as a moral theory. We are back to the difficulty of determining what is meant by agape. If agape is in any way related to welfare or human good, it runs into all the problems of deciding whose good, how much good and how the greater good of the group relates to the good of the individual. If agape commits one to love of the other and if that implies seeking to bring about the good or welfare of the other, does it commit one to bring about as much human good or welfare as possible? Is it best understood in utilitarian terms?

Some moralists have simply identified the two. Mill did it, to begin with, and so do many present-day moralists.[34] One finds Christian theologians who have a frankly utilitarian understanding of agape. In a recent book O'Connell contemplates the possibility of dropping a bomb which will kill a million people because the greater good requires it.[35] But the movement is more widespread. Following disillusionment with the traditional natural law theory, many Roman Catholic moralists have turned to a method that is consequentialist. They seem to have slid into this unconsciously without an awareness of the problems that had for decades been raised about it in Anglo-American philosophy. They take the view that in trying to determine what act is right one should calculate the human or pre-moral good and evil consequences: they regard an act as justified if in the totality of consequences good outweighs evil.[36]

If agape is in any sense a matter of bringing about the good of others then agape in this perspective overlaps with utilitarianism and obviously runs into all the problems of utilitarianism. This should make one chary of claims made for agape. If agape is interpreted by some theologians in this way it must make one wonder about the undifferentiated claim of the *Glaubensethik* authors that agape protects the person better than forms of secular ethics. It can be seen that this claim depends on how one elaborates agape into a moral theory and the *Glaubensethik* authors have failed to declare their hand on that. If it is understood in the bland form of utilitarianism just described, then it will not be more protective of the person than secular ethics. It may be less so.

Perhaps, then, Christianity commits one to a deontological agape and away from utilitarianism. This is Häring's view.[37] So, too, Finnis regards utilitarianism as incompatible with Christianity.[38] The point is, presumably, that Christian vision gives to agape a care for others that will be elaborated in terms of personal goods or values that are inviolable and will not yield to any calculation of good consequences. Behind such an approach are theological beliefs about God's care for each person and also about God's providence. For Häring (as for Paul Ramsey) God's covenant with each individual becomes the norm of agape and gives it its particular form: agape has to do with keeping covenant with each.[39] Finnis's position owes much to the realisation that 'God is going to bring good out of all things and deeds and lives in this world'. The Christian 'is not to expect or calculate on a this-wordly success or a this-worldly consummation of that hope and work'.[40] This view is saying that it is from such a faith in God and in his love for each person that one learns how to love. Such love is to be non-teleological. Come what may, one must adhere to a principle of non-transgression of the individual.

A possible middle way is some form of mixed utilitarianism. I have not found any attempt to develop this among Roman Catholic theologians. But perhaps they might look at a philosopher like Frankena who identifies the law of love with 'what I have called the principle of benevolence, that is, of doing good, and to insist that it must be supplemented by the principle of distributive justice or equality'.[41] Or there is the Protestant theologian, Frederick Carney, who would add to beneficence and justice the principle of non-transgression — apparently for religious reasons.[42]

Is it the case that Christianity tends to favour a deontological interpretation of agape? Or, at least, a mixed utilitarianism in which some kind of non-transgression of the individual will play a part? We know that we are to love others, to wish them well and do them good. But does Christianity help us to make up our minds about one way of doing it rather than the other? When we move down from the heights of biblical agape and come to the level of agape as a moral theory we meet all the problems attaching to the deontology-utilitarianism debate. Does Christianity help us to solve this issue?

Obviously one does not have to be a Christian to be anti-utilitarian. Many philosophers find it an unacceptable theory, precisely because of their understanding of respect for the individual and for reasons that do not have anything to do with Christianity. Nor does one have to be a Christian to adopt a mixed utilitarian view, which would build in principles that would be protective of the person. So a deontological or mixed approach, in the interests of the person, can hardly be said to be specific to Christianity. Is it demanded by Christianity? In the last chapter I considered the influence of Christian awareness or world-view on discernment. It seems to me that Christianity, with the importance which it gives to each individual, with its belief in his/her preciousness and his/her individual destiny in God, with its over-riding trust in God and in his lordship, does suggest an ethical understanding that gives high priority to the non-transgression of the individual. It tends to support the view that deontological considerations should be built into agape.

When one brings agape face to face with secular ethics one finds some surprising answers. This last question was: is there something to agape which is protective of the person; is the person less expendable in an ethic of agape than in a secular ethic of respect or of benevolence; if so, is this something specific to agape? When one looks at the history of attempts to formulate a theory of agape, the answer can only be that it depends on how

161

agape is elaborated as a moral theory. An agape formulated in consequentialist terms will be less protective than a secular ethic of a deontological type — as we saw in the case of O'Connell. An agape formulated in deontological terms will be more protective than a secular ethic of a utilitarian type. Indeed, there is a greater affinity between some theological notions of agape and some versions of secular ethics than between different notions of agape within theology itself.

The question from the autonomy authors to the *Glaubensethik* was this: leaving aside the source of Christian agape, and leaving aside consideration of bestowal or Christian appraisal, does the Christian agapist do anything specifically different? We have hinted a few times in this chapter that one must ask, as we did in chapter four, whether the question is clear. What does 'doing' mean? This broadens the issue. The point is underlined when we note what a measure of agreement there is about content between agape and moral theories that explicitly repudiate agape as an ethical theory. Take, for example, the relevant writing of Mackie and Richards.[43] Morality is justified for them as an institution that furthers self-interest: the principles of morality will be those arrived at by the rational egoist; any altruism involved will be self-referential. Yet Mackie found it necessary to include most of the standard rules which one finds among agapists. Richards includes such principles as a principle of mutual aid, a principle of non-maleficence, a principle of consideration requiring people to make allowance in their own plans for the feelings and concerns of others by not arbitrarily annoying them. These he regards as principles of duty or obligation. He also includes such principles of supererogation as mutual respect, mutual love, civility and benevolence. An agapist might be hard put to it to say what else he or she would require. And yet, although there is considerable coincidence in the matter of content, there is considerable difference in moral stance. In agape systems the moral reason for doing an action is respect and concern for the other: in these other systems the moral reason is self-referential even if the system sometimes dictates altruistic activity.

The point here is to underline again the importance of one's understanding of content and of the moral act in any comparison of religious and secular ethics. Do vision and spirit count in morality? Is agape a matter of doing or of being: is it a matter of why one does an act as well as of what one does; is it the disposition with which one does an act of importance? What has emerged is that even an ethic which is antithetical in spirit can show a considerable similarity of content with agape if one adopts the very thin notion of content which seems to be advocated by the autonomy school. But most Christians, I think, would regard the reason for which one acts or the disposition from which one acts as an essential element of agape, as entering into its very definition. There is required some disposition of care or sympathy, of concern or benevolence.[44] A disposition to do one's duty towards the other would not be sufficient, if by duty is meant the mere performance of certain external acts, which provide for the well-being of the other. Most Christians, I believe, would feel that such is not New Testament agape. The dispositions mentioned, of course, are not foreign to secular ethics. But some secular systems that look like agape may differ here. Even the golden rule requirement that one be ready to treat all impartially and not claim privilege for oneself — whatever about the sympathy and sensitivity required to enter into the concerns of the other — may not coincide with agape: golden rule morality, while it requires unselfishness in order to implement it, may be more inspired by a concern for logic than for persons.

It is interesting that there has been some debate in recent years — although not among Roman Catholic theologians — on the very question of whether Christian agape can be satisfactorily understood at all in the category of an ethic of duty or of principle. The argument has been advanced that it can only be adequately understood as an ethic of virtue — that some of the classic cases of biblical agape, such as the Good Samaritan story, can only be understood as such. Again there will be arguments about what it means strictly to treat the ethic of love as an ethic of virtue. But it is certainly the case that the more one stresses attitudes, dispositions and innermost desires the more one opens the case for the claim that there is a specific Christian agape. This applies most obviously to a comparison of agape with self-referential theories. But perhaps it could be argued that some nuances of difference can be found even in a comparison of agape with theories of respect for the person or with a theory of benevolence. What the Christian tries to do may be to love in a spontaneous, unmotivated way, as God loves. Or one may love the other because one appraises him or her as someone cherished by God. I am not talking about motive but about what one tries to do. The *Glaubensethik* has not tried to work this out although some of its remarks lie in this direction. There may be some possibilities here for its claim but they seem to me to be rather slight.

The *Glaubensethik* has made the issue of agape central to the debate about the specificity of Christian ethics. But a claim for specificity would need to define more carefully what kind of life is being proposed to Christians in the name of agape — and why. At the very general level of the justification of agape as a moral stance, one can see differences between agape and secular theories of morality. At the more particular level of action it is more difficult. Certain versions of agape will show an overlap with certain versions of secular ethics. I have indicated that some versions of secular ethics may be more protective of the individual than some versions of theological agape, although this very protectiveness may be considered by other theologians as the distinctive feature of agape.

There is one other outstanding consideration. It may be a matter of some surprise that I have not yet considered the extent of agape. It is widely accepted that agape requires a very high degree of other-regard and it is clear from the remarks at the beginning of this section that some of the *Glaubensethik* authors see the specificity of agape not so much in its source or basis, not in its understanding of how other-regard is to be expressed, not in the vision one has of the other, but in the extent of love that it requires. Here the *Glaubensethik* is on firmer ground and the autonomy position has greater problems in sustaining its thesis that there is no difference in content between a Christian and a secular ethic. However, there are more problems here for both sides than appear on the surface. The issue of agape as an ideal is not at all clear. I treat it separately now in the general context of ideals in Christian moral life.

Section 2

AGAPE AND CHRISTIAN IDEALS

By the ideal of agape I mean the Christian tradition that one should love with a love that has no measure, love to the end, love with sacrifice of self, even to the point of laying down one's life for the other. Are ideals part of the content of Christian morality — and in what way? The autonomy school argues that Christian teaching on agape does not propose a different content from the secular ethic. But is there a question to be asked about the degree of response that each requires? Is the matter disposed of completely by the remarks of Curran:

> Non-Christians can and do arrive at the same ethical conclusions and also embrace and treasure even the loftiest of proximate motives, virtues and goals which Christians in the past have wrongly claimed for themselves. Certainly the Christian explicitly reflects on the imitation of Christ, but the proximate attitudes, values and goals that come from this are the same attitudes that other people can arrive at in other ways ... self-sacrificing love, freedom, hope, concern for the neighbour in need or even the realisation that one finds his life only in losing it.[45]

If non-Christians do reach this, do such moral attitudes and actions have the same status as they have in Christianity? The other side of the question can be put to the *Glaubensethik*. It regards the high ideal of agape as specific to Christianity. Does it regard the fullness of agape as obligatory or as a matter of super-erogation? Is it, to use traditional Roman Catholic terminology, a command or a counsel — or is that a legitimate way to put the question?

A further question remains over from the fifth chapter. That concerns stances such as poverty, a certain indifference to the world, hope in undertaking difficult tasks, joy in suffering, virginity. They arise out of faith: they are recommended in the New Testament. Some of them pertain to the more personal areas of life. Some of them admit of degrees. They, too, are often described as ideals. Is there a problem about declaring them part of Christian morality? The problem seems to be about whether they are regarded as obligatory by Christians. If so, are they universalisable — and how important is that consideration to their right to be regarded as part of the institution of morality?

We must ask again whether we are talking about theoretical possibilities or everyday realities. Is the autonomy movement saying that it is not impossible for a rare genius or a saint to arrive at and embrace such ideals, or is it saying that people generally can and do regard them as binding? How does the secular ethic regard them? An important issue for us will be not only whether they appear in it but what status they have. Because if they do not have the same status, it is hard to see how one can maintain a thesis of identity between Christian and secular morality. In particular, if the two arrive at the same ideals but one regards the ideal as a matter of moral obligation and the other as a matter of free choice, we seem to be faced with an important difference.

In fact, this is what we find. Most moral philosophy makes a distinction between a level that is regarded as a matter of duty or obligation and a level of ideal that, whatever status it may occupy in the total scheme of morality, does not have the same stringency. Take a few examples. Strawson distinguishes morality and ethics.[46] The former derives from the fact that some set of rules is a condition of the existence of a society — 'certain human interests are so fundamental and so general that they must be universally acknowledged in some form and to some degree in any conceivable moral community'. They will include the abstract virtue of justice, some form of obligation to mutual aid and to mutual abstention from injury and, in some form and in some degree, the virtue of honesty. The area of ethics is the area of ideals, such as 'self-obliterating devotion to duty or to the service of others', or even, simply, love of others. Here, he says, there are truths but no truth: in fact the best society is one in which there is variety of ideals. Any doctrine that the pattern of the ideal life should be the same for all he finds intolerable.

Hare is much in sympathy with Strawson's point of view, although he does not limit the sphere of the moral as Strawson does. There are different ways of being a good man, he says: it is impossible, and philosophers should not try, to find methods of argument which will settle disputes between upholders of different ideals in all cases.[47] Hart distinguishes the 'morality' of a society and moral ideals. The former is concerned with certain rules of conduct which any social organisation must contain if it is to be viable, the minimum content of natural law, as he sometimes calls it. Ideals are a matter of choice — such things as bravery, charity, benevolence, patience, chastity. They are a matter of private morality, which may govern a person's life but which he need not share with others or regard as a matter for censure of others. He agrees that they are analogous to morality but would say that the analogy is more a matter of form than of

166

content.[48] Urmson finds a most important difference between self-sacrificing life in the service of others, disinterested kindness, going the second mile and 'the rock-bottom duties which are duties for all and from every point of view': one must separate basic duties and higher flights of morality, the Ten Commandments and the Sermon on the Mount.[49]

There are obvious differences between the authors. What is entirely clear is that they all agree that the two areas of duty and ideal must be kept distinct, that ideals are a matter of personal choice, that they cannot be regarded as a matter of general obligation and that they do not have the same stringency as the area of duty, that they fall outside the bailiwick of those actions which one may legitimately demand from others and blame them for omitting. This position may not be universal in secular morality. But it is widely held and must be reckoned with. It is important to note that the authors do not confine the notion of ideal to heroic acts but include also favours of a very ordinary kind. I do not think, either, that they are simply concerned about what society can or cannot require, about a range of socially sanctionable obligations. What is in question — and it is here that Christianity will differ — is whether there is a morally good life that can be expected from all.

Running through all of this is the widely-held conviction that a moral rule, in order to qualify as such, must be universalisable. The consequence is this: if evangelical poverty or virginity or self-sacrificing love is held by the *Glaubensethik* to be part of morality, to be a moral call on some individuals, must it not be a call on all in the same circumstances? If it is the morally good choice for one, must it not be held to be the morally good choice for all in the same circumstances — a matter of obligation? Is the *Glaubensethik* prepared to see this through? Frankena, in particular, has engaged in debate with theologians on this point. He objects to regarding ideals as part of morality, taking the view that one is not making a moral judgment unless one is making a normative one and that one is not making a normative one unless one is willing to universalise it.[50]

The conclusion is this. Philosophical ethics generally recognises ideals but it gives them a special status. They are commendable but not obligatory and perhaps only analogously part of morality. For some philosophers the ideal begins at the point of not injuring others: for all, the higher reaches of love and the poverty of such as St Francis certainly fall into the category of ideal.

Our theological authors — of both the *Glaubensethik* and autonomy camps — assume on the other hand that the New Testament message of far-reaching and sacrificial love and the ideals proposed in the Sermon on the Mount and elsewhere in the Bible are part of the Christian ethic. They have different views on the originality of this teaching. The *Glaubensethik* accepts it as unique: some of its adherents regard the extent of agape as precisely its distinctive character. The autonomy movement says that the New Testament is merely maieutic, i.e., that it does not give us an ethic that is unavailable to the non-Christian but one that stretches a person's horizons to see what is *per se* accessible to him or her though he or she has great difficulty in recognising it. Auer and Fuchs, like Curran, often state that the ideals of the Sermon on the Mount are accessible to and attained by non-believers.[51] Schüller stresses that the whole meaning of agape, including love of enemies, is accessible to them.

At the moment, the point is that both sides accept high ethical ideals. They do this rather uncritically, especially when one considers the tradition in which they are writing. Whatever problems the question of ideals raises for Christian moralists generally, it raises additional problems for Roman Catholics. This is because (a) the teaching of the neo-Scholastics and of their whole tradition was that, in the order of love, the love of self is more important than and takes precedence over the love of others, and (b) the traditional teaching, as we saw, made a distinction between counsel and obligation. The manual position on self-love is stated by Noldin:

> In the second place one should love himself: for, according to the will of Christ, the love of oneself is to be the norm for the love of the neighbour. The norm is more important than what is measured by it: therefore, one adopts the axiom, 'The order of charity begins with oneself'. In the third place each one should love his neighbour according to the degree of one's connection with him.[52]

The last point was also a constant of the tradition — that one should love one's relatives more than others. Where do Roman Catholic theologians stand today? The remarks of the

Glaubensethik that the specificity of Christian love consists in loving with the sacrificial love of Christ and the statements of the autonomy group that the experience of the kingdom opens one to the heights of love all suggest that the neo-Scholastic position has been abandoned. One can only presume this: unfortunately, there is no formal discussion of the issue. Neither is there any attention to the problem of self-love and to the wide variety of possible positions on that.[53]

The second point relates to an important shift in Roman Catholic theology in the period we have been surveying. We saw that the neo-Scholastics made a clear distinction between command or obligation and counsel: counsels, they said, do not strictly belong to morality. It is worth quoting Noldin-Schmitt on the point.

> Counsels are actions which are good and better than their opposite but which are not prescribed by any law. . . . Besides actions which are commanded and forbidden by law, there are many others, which are neither commanded nor forbidden but allowed and one includes among the latter counsels, which are commended. God makes known his will in two ways, by commanding or by persuading and commending. Actions which are commanded are necessary to reach the end: counsels are not necessary but free and permitted, at the option of the individual. . . . Laws oblige all, counsels oblige only those who have bound themselves to them. Laws have their binding force from the divine will; counsels only from the will of the one who has bound himself.[54]

He notes that some have erred in holding that all good actions are demanded of us: in particular he rejects their use of the texts, 'You, therefore must be perfect as your heavenly Father is perfect' (Matt. 5:48) and 'You should love the Lord your God with your whole heart. . . . (Matt. 22:37).[55]

It is interesting to note that one of the complaints made against the renewal of moral theology was that it blurred the distinction between command and counsel. Take, for example, the following remarks of a well-known work of the fifties, which were especially directed against the renewal writing of Leclerq.

> But, if the obligation of seeking perfection is then explained in a way that, in practice, would exclude the objective

169

distinction between precepts and counsels, and would make of every 'ought' an obligation as unlimited as that of love itself, then we are in danger of distorting the law of charity. . . . The question of love, therefore, as the basis of morality must be treated with circumspection if we are to avoid errors and distortions which so easily occur in this slippery terrain. . . . Catholic morality, which distinguishes clearly between obligations imposed under pain of mortal sin or of venial sin, and those works of supererogation which are not of precept but of counsel. . . . The law of the gospel contains commandments which are of obligation, and counsels, which are not. . . . And while a morality of precepts without counsels is conceivable, a morality of counsels without precepts is not.[56]

Carpentier, a great advocate of the morality of charity, was also disturbed at the development. He found it necessary to reiterate the distinction between precept and counsel. He distinguishes between obligations under pain of sin, which attach to minimum objective norms of love, and perfection or counsel.[57] Even Fuchs, in an early article, pointed to the danger of allowing love to make excessive demands.[58] That is a reservation which he has long since left behind. For him, as for most Roman Catholic authors, the sharp distinction between precept and counsel has vanished — McDonagh says that it is no longer defended or defensible.[59]

However, a failure to tackle the problem head on makes it difficult to know where theologians stand today. The *Glaubensethik* regards the extent of Christian love — as the Father loved or as Christ loved — as distinguishing Christian from secular morality. The autonomy school maintains that the two are the same in content. On the part of the *Glaubensethik*, one would have liked some attempt to say whether it regards the heights of agape as obligatory, just as obligatory as, say, Urmson's 'rock-bottom duties'. One would have welcomed from the autonomy movement a clear statement on the status which it gives to the ideal of agape and how it regards the position of the philosophers on ideals. If the ideal of agape is an integral part of morality, can there be said to be identity between Christian and secular ethics? If, on the other hand, one ranks the ideal as the philosophers rank it, is one doing justice to

170

Christian morality? But if it *is* an integral part, is one who falls short of it deserving of moral condemnation: does one not need some such distinction as that between duty and ideal? (It may be that philosophical ethics is not entirely happy with the sharp distinction between duty and ideal. It can adopt it because generally it conceives of morality in terms of duty or obligation. But, as we saw, there are other, increasingly popular, ways of conceiving it. There is a further problem for one who adopts a strict utilitarian morality: he is committed to the duty of doing the act which brings about the greatest utility and this does not leave room for ideals.)

Theological ethics cannot hold the same position as philosophical ethics here — and that for two reasons.

(a) The general tradition of Christian ethics would not accept as an adequate statement of moral demand the rather jejune concept of moral duty proposed by some of the philosophers, e.g. Strawson or Hart. Christianity holds out the ideal of agape to all Christians.

(b) Christianity does not regard biblical ideals in the same light in which secular ethics regards ideals: ideals have a different status in the two systems. It does not regard a life of high agape as a matter of choice, as some philosophers do. It would not regard other ideals of life as equally valid and interchangeable with it. It would not agree that there is no ideal good life. It would not agree that, in this area there are truths but no truth. I think Christians generally would take the view that while all people may be reproached for the non-performance of duties, those in the community of believers may be intelligibly harder on themselves and may reproach one another for not going the second mile. I think they would strongly hold that the way of life to which Christians have been called goes beyond mere fundamental duties to one another.[60]

This appears to be true not only of agape but of other characteristic Christian stances such as those for which I argued in the fifth chapter — for example, a trust in the providence of God, a certain poverty of life, a humility before God and before others, a particular view of human flourishing, of success and failure, and an attitude to suffering — all of which the philosopher might regard as being in the area of the heroic. Such are consonant with the distinctive beliefs of Christians and some measure of them is required by genuine Christian discernment.

171

Because of its Christian story there is in the community a certain universalisability of expectation about them. This is how Christians see life. Such dispositions and behaviour possess a stringency for them that they may not possess for others.

The autonomy position comes under some strain here. It rightly acknowledges such ideals as demanded of Christians. To say that they are *per se* available to non-Christians is at least to fail to take account of the different status accorded to ideals in Christian and secular morality. The fact is that Christians accept moral positions as required of them which secular morality generally does not accept as required. This is, in reality, the force of what Mieth, Schüller and Fuchs refer to as the maieutic power of revelation — it is of greater significance than they allow. It is what is at work when Auer acknowledges that revelation gives an impulse to a high ethical ideal (*hochethische Impuls*), drawing Christians beyond the commandments to the pure model of love, which is found in God alone, and when he says that it is out of an acceptance of the kingdom of God that the beatitudes grow. What is happening here is not merely that one is moved or enabled to live a certain kind of life but also that one comes to an awareness, out of one's whole Christian vision, of the kind of life that is appropriate to the Christian. The Christian, Auer says, because of his acceptance of the kingdom, becomes poor in spirit, meek, merciful etc.[61] That must mean that, in the first instance, one recognises that one should become poor in spirit — because of what the kingdom means. That is also what is at work when Schüller says that the Christian's awareness that he has been forgiven his sins is the source of new possibilities (although it can also be a matter of motivation).[62] What is in question is the justification of a moral position. We have seen that Fuchs, presumably aware of the problem here, relegates such ideals to the area of religion rather than to morality.[63]

Apart from such general ideals the community recognises individual forms of life, such as radical poverty and virginity. They correspond more to individual possibilities, individual perception and invidividual faith in God's enabling grace. They are not expected of everybody. But it is recognised that individuals will see such as for them an apt and perhaps even a necessary way of reaching the moral wholeness to which they aspire. The fact that such a form of life is often referred to as a vocation or a calling is a pointer to its highly personal character. In the debate

172

about the specificity of Christian ethics Rigali strongly argues that this element — what he calls the Christian existentialist element — is something that the autonomy school has not taken cognisance of in its thesis that there is identity of content between Christian and secular.[64] Fuchs adverts to this claim of Rigali but insists again that what Rigali refers to belongs more to the area of religion than of morality.[65] That reply appears to me to be of doubtful validity.

The most serious consideration of this existentialist morality among Roman Catholics has come from Karl Rahner — though not in reference to the issue of specificity. Rahner asserts straightforwardly that there are two elements in the make-up of every human being, a common human nature and a unique and irreplaceable element and that to them correspond two elements of morality, universal norms and individual pre-scriptions — which 'cannot be called a mere application of a universal principle to one case'.[66] Rahner sets out to give a formal account of how one arrives at such particular judgments — to give general principles about them.[67] His epistemological account is much debated. Its distinction of choice into universal and particular elements is seen by some as artificial. Some also find its manner of discerning particular imperatives esoteric. But the conviction that there are judgments to be made about one's individual condition and possibilities in life, judgments which lead to a specific vocation or to a calling of a particularly demanding kind, is hardly controverted among Christians and is not dependent on any one epistemology.[68] The question to be asked here is how there can be judgments of this kind which are regarded as individual or personal. Are they not to be univer-salised? If one says that St Francis is a good man because of a particular life of evangelical virtue, must one not say that such a life is to be the criterion for others, or at least for others in similar circumstances?[69] How is the Christian to regard such personal choices as part of morality and yet refuse to universalise them? What answer is one to give to Frankena? For in the debate about the identity of Christian ethics the point to be remembered is that if such judgments qualify as morality the *Glaubensethik* case is strengthened and that of the autonomy movement again made more difficult.

Whether a willingness to universalise is a necessary condition of morality can be debated. There are instances where one is prepared to adopt a moral position but refrains from legislating the same conduct for others or where one will regard something as wrong for oneself which one does not condemn in others.[70] Are such stances not deserving of the name 'moral'? If the principle amounts to saying that similars are to be similarly understood, it should be remembered that in the area with which we are dealing it is difficult to arrive at similar situations: we are dealing with highly personal aspects of life. Being in exactly similar circumstances would involve having the same dispositions, the same potentialities, the same personal qualities, the same vision, the same hope in the enabling grace of God. It might indeed be very difficult for a neutral observer to say that 'exactly similar circumstances' are present. It might be very difficult for anyone to say that another is in the same circumstances as oneself. One may be able to account only for oneself and how one sees reality. So that, even if one holds to the principle, one may have doubts about its applicability or usefulness in the more personal areas of morality.[71] However, as I suggested earlier about Christian discernment in general, it should be possible to go a considerable distance in indicating the factors which suggest that the choice is a good moral choice. If the principle is regarded as a substantive moral principle, i.e. an option for fairness and impartiality, one must ask whether the point of impartiality is to demand that everyone else take on the obligations which one takes on oneself? Is the point of it not rather that morality forbids one to demand more from others than from oneself, but not vice versa?[72]

It would seem, then, that one must distinguish two kinds of ideal. There are the personal choices which an individual will regard as his or her personal calling or vocation. They are accepted by Christianity as commendable choices: there is no good reason why they should not be regarded as moral choices. But while they are regarded as good moral choices for the individual, there is no suggestion that they should be embraced by all Christians and there is no blame or reproach attaching to those who do not embrace them. If they are part of Christian morality, the autonomy school must say how it regards them.

There are also moral attitudes and actions that are expected of all Christians. They go beyond what the humanist regards as moral duty. At best, they would be consigned to the area of ideals and would be even excluded from the domain of morality by some philosophers. But the Christian community regards them as not only desirable but as pertaining to the general configuration of Christianity. I have given some examples above: they include a readiness to go the second mile and to take seriously the injunction of Paul, 'Let no one seek his own good, but the good of his neighbour' (1 Cor.10:24); they certainly go well beyond impartiality. If the Christian community is asked whether one should have done such, the answer must be, Yes. But it must be recognised that there are degrees in such stances. Does the community go on to say that one who fails to live up to the ideal is worthy of moral condemnation? Perhaps it will distinguish: in what circumstances will it say that one should give one's life for another? There are degrees of failure: the community is aware of the difficulty which the average Christian experiences in living up to what Christ exemplifies.

Much depends here on how one understands morality. Richards has the useful remark that secular moralists make a mistake which derives 'from the seductive assumption that, in moral contexts, the use of "ought" is everywhere interchangeable, without distortion of meaning, with "under a duty" or "obligation"'.[73] If one sees morality in terms of duty/non-duty, one can rather easily apportion moral blame. But if again we return to a notion of virtue, if we see morality on a scalar model, then all falling short of the perfection of Christian life is some moral imperfection, some failure. It seems that the Christian must see it in this light. There is only one perfect moral way for the Christian. That is the way lived by Christ, the fullness of agape. The Christian *ought* to live like this: all falling short of it is a falling short of the morality to which Christianity invites the believer and which it hopes for from him. But to fall short of ideals is not necessarily to be deserving of moral condemnation. Neither, however, should the point at which moral condemnation begins be identified with the point which the philosopher regards as rock-bottom duty. There is a sliding scale: moral blame is not easy to assess and may be a concept that does not coincide perfectly with the ideal of morality conceived as virtue.

The conclusion is this. It should be recognised — and not all of the *Glaubensethik* authors recognise it — that non-Christians do love to an extent that is not different from agape and that they have ideals that are analogous to Christian ideals. But while this is true, there is a stringency attaching to the ideal of agape and to other ideals in the Christian community that is not found in the broad philosophical tradition of secular morality. It is true that it is difficult to find agreement among Christians on the definition of agape, and philosophers are right to say that many theologians use the term without defining it. But what does seem to be widely agreed among Christians is that if love is related to care and concern for the other, Christians cannot be satisfied with an interpretation of it that stops at duty. Its only model of morality is Jesus. And to love as Jesus loved is to love in a way that goes far beyond not injuring others, that is not satisfied with merely acting impartially and fairly, that involves a concern that even forgets one's own claim or rights. That is part of Christian morality. So too are the other ideals derived from or, in some way, implied in faith: some are part of the general expectation of the community from its members; some are part of that morality which relates to the special capacities and vision of the individual. If this is so, then it would seem that the autonomy school must qualify its thesis that there is identity of content between Christian and humanist morality and must face the wider question: can Christian morality be successfully elaborated in terms of rules, or can this be adequately done only in terms of values and ideals which offer a dynamic and creative approach to individual situations?

7

Christian Context and
Moral Obligation

Discussion about the identity of Christian morality has been
almost entirely confined to the issue of content. It seemed to the
renewal movement and to the modern *Glaubensethik* that it was
crucial to the self-respect of Christian morality to prove
specificity of content. It was equally important to the autonomy
movement, with its concern to dialogue with non-believers and
to demonstrate to them that Christian morality did not diminish
the human person's moral responsibility, to show that there was
no distinctive content. I have said on a number of occasions
already that, while the question is important, it may have
absorbed too much of the energies of theologians. We should
take seriously the constant reference of the autonomy school to
what it calls the Christian context of morality. What this chiefly
means is that morality is to be situated in the overall scheme of
the Christian's personal relationship with God.

So the autonomy authors say that while the Christian is to
behave in the different areas of human life exactly like the non-
Christian, he or she must be aware of one's relation to the One
who creates, saves and brings about the fulfilment of the world.[1]
Or that he or she must relate moral life to the Father of our
salvation in Jesus Christ in faith, hope and love.[2] Or that he or
she must take up 'the natural ethical norms of life' into theologal
life.[3] Certainly, such suggestions provide a context. Morality is
related here to a variety of Christian themes. Several other
themes could be suggested: the depth and richness of Christian
faith allows of different ways of integrating moral experience.

Another approach to context stresses that Christianity
contains truths, stories and myths that are significant for
morality because they have something to say about the
possibility of the moral enterprise, or about the difficulty of it, or

177

about the final point of it. It is sometimes said that morality raises questions beyond itself, questions which pertain to the domain of religion. Religion, on the other hand, can provide for morality a world-view or climate which is favourable to it. There is considerable sympathy and harmony between questions and experiences innate to morality and those innate to religion. Certainly, Christianity favours and gives a value to the whole moral enterprise. It gives a hope in the face of the frequent futility of moral undertakings. It is a source of energy in the face of evil — the evil in the world and the evil in oneself. It confirms moral responsibility and one's attempts to achieve purpose and order in the universe. For many it has given an ultimate interpretation to the unconditionality of the moral demand and the inviolability of the person.[4]

Such talk of context has, unfortunately, been dismissed by Stoeckle as mere decoration.[5] This seems to me to be a serious mistake. How one sees one's moral life is important. The humanist sees it only as morality. The Christian must have recourse to another language to describe adequately how he or she sees it. The fact that he experiences and lives it as an expression of his personal union with God or as his discipleship with Christ is of great importance. We have seen in the last section that one's discipleship performs a critical function and is a source of enlightenment, that it leads one to recognise the appropriateness of high ethical ideals (although some of the authors persist in referring to this as the maieutic effect of revelation). But here we are more concerned with the fact that to live one's moral life in response to God and in union with Christ is to have a special awareness about one's morality and to give it a special significance. One's morality assumes a distinctive shape. It is a response to the action of God. It is called forth by discipleship and is an expression to it. The moral call has the further dimension of a personal call which beckons one on, encourages in failure and even makes sense of failure. All of this is part of the identity of Christian morality.

However, when one looks back to our point of departure, which was the neat structure of the neo-Scholastic, one has other questions which affect identity intimately and which one might expect to be dealt with under the rubric of context. Most of the statements which we have quoted are statements about the religious faith of Christians rather than statements about the precise relationship between faith and ethics. They point to the fact that the Christian is not just a moral being but one who lives a life of personal union with God and they quite properly affirm that this is the deepest truth and value for Christian life. But as far as the significance of morality for that life is concerned, they do little more than repeat the widely accepted fact that there is a relationship between faith and ethics. They do not throw much light on the nature of the relationship. Two major questions lurk here. The first is that of moral obligation: how is God thought to relate to autonomous moral obligation? The second is that of the relation of moral life and salvation: in what way is moral life significant for union with God here and hereafter — if it is significant for it at all? The neo-Scholastic had clear views on these two issues and they contributed much to his understanding of morality. They greatly affect one's concept both of morality and of God. They are important to the identity of Christian morality. Indeed, the God/morality/salvation model is a critical issue for contemporary Christian faith. It is very arguable that if people find the notion of God incredible it is particularly the ethical God with his panoply of laws, rewards and punishments that they find incredible.

This is an area, however, that has not received much attention from our authors. It is understandable that the present-day moralist would not treat the subject of morality and salvation/justification. The neo-Scholastic disposed of it in a sentence. But it is, of course, a very considerable area of theology and the moralist today regards it as the responsibility of the systematic theologian. It would take us outside our field and outside the group of moralists whom we are studying. So I feel justified in confining myself to some passing remarks. Moral obligation, on the other hand, is justifiably regarded as part of the moral theologian's bailiwick. About their positions on this we get some light from the authors and I will try to tease out their thought on the matter.

The neo-Scholastic had no problem about the context of morality. Noldin's statement of position is classic:

God constituted himself man's ultimate end; but by the very fact that he did so, he imposed on man an obligation of tending to the ultimate end. . . . The moral order instituted by God is the way by which man is to tend to his ultimate end and the means, by observance of which, he achieves it.[6]

179

This model of morality is held together by two key concepts — that of morality as the law of God and that of beatitude as a reward for good moral living. The renewal movement, as we saw, while it greatly changed the understanding of morality, persevered with the neo-Scholastic model: the model is compatible with a religious life of love as well as with one of fear. 'If you keep my commandments, you will abide in my love' (John 15:10): the keeping of the commandments which God had promulgated was seen as the way and the proof of love. So we saw that the authors managed to combine the new ideas of morality as the following of Christ or as the fruit of the new grace-life with the understanding that moral obligation derived from the law or will of God. That position has not changed with the present-day *Glaubensethik*.[7] Any moral system that depends heavily on a revealed morality is likely to have a strong notion of morality as the will of God.

Indeed Roman Catholicism has found it very difficult to do without the concept of morality as the will of God. But much depends on how it is understood and on the emphasis given to it. I referred in the first chapter to the long debate in Christian theology about the source of moral obligation, which reached its high point in the Suarez-Vasquez controversy. The neo-Scholastics adopted the position of Suarez — that moral obligation requires a command of God for its force and validity.[8] It is precisely this conception of morality that the autonomy movement rejects: it questions any suggestion that morality gets its justification or binding-force from any authoritative act, even from God. In contrast to the 'morality from above' it proposes a 'morality from below'. This is true both of the authors who stress identity of content with secular morality and of those, like Böckle, who are less interested in stressing that than in stressing that the human being must be the discoverer of his or her own moral norms. It is also true of theologians like Demmer and Simpson who argue for a distinctive content but refuse to accept that it is given 'by an authority external to human con-sciousness'.[9] The autonomy school says that the ethical order is a product of human reason and can be discovered and developed entirely by human beings (Auer)[10] the person gives himself his maxims of action: they are the creation of his reason (Böckle).[11] Morality arises from human nature, *etsi Deus non daretur* (Mieth).[12] It arises from the fact that each person is an end to himself/herself and it does not require the command or proclamation of anyone (Schüller).[13] So this school rejects every kind of 'theological positivism', 'revelation positivism', 'Christ positivism'.[14] Its position is (a) that the norms of morality are discovered by human reason, like the norms of logic, or aesthetics or psychology, (b) that they have what the authors call an inner rationality, i.e. that the reason why they are moral norms and binding is understood by human beings, (c) that, therefore, they do not require any external decree of God to be binding and that we do not need to be aware of such a decree to experience them as binding.

But the question can be asked whether morality can be left free-standing like that. Is an autonomous morality considered to be entirely its own justification? Does it require God for its legitimation? Is there any sense in which it can and should be referred to as the law or will of God? One sees the issue more clearly if one remembers that the movement for the autonomy of ethics in Roman Catholicism reflected a wider movement for secularisation and for an ethics for a world come of age. John Robinson, for example, also aimed to bring about 'a revolt in the field of ethics from supranaturalism to naturalism, from heteronomy to autonomy':[15] his proposal was that we should 'take our place alongside those who are deep in the search for meaning, "etsi Deus non daretur", even if God is not "there" '[16] Ricoeur had called for a demythologisation of current religious ideas in ethics: one should render to ethics, he said, the things that are ethical and not attempt to project ethical values into heaven. In particular, he said that if a link must be established between religion and ethics, it should not be via the concept of a so-called law or will of God.[17] Some of the Dutch advocates of autonomy reproached Roman Catholic theologians for clinging to the notion of morality as the will of God simply because it offered a device to make 'clear and tangible' the connection between the moral order and God.[18] Van Ouwerkerk said:

> We believe in a human and 'worldly' order which contains salvation and holiness. The actual connection between our goodness in this world and salvation is not obvious and does not fall within the perspective of eschatological fulfilment.[19]

The task for moral theology, as the Dutch saw it, was to accept the autonomy of morality and to concentrate on providing an interpretation of the relationship between this order discovered by human reason and eschatological salvation.[20] That meant, presumably, that one is to explore the relationship between the language and categories of autonomous moral awareness — good, bad, right, wrong, virtue, obligation — and the language and categories of Christian proclamation — salvation, grace, sin, damnation. But in doing so one was not to have recourse to the language of morality as the will or law of God.

We are obviously in a difficult and controversial area. The attempt to rethink the context of ethics raises profound questions. They are questions about the nature of God, about the relation of God to the world, and about the theological doctrine of justification. Robinson is right in saying that it is impossible to reassess one's doctrine of God, of how one understands the transcendent, without bringing one's view of morality into the same melting-pot.[21] The converse is also true: the Christian cannot discuss his view of morality without bringing his doctrine of God into question also. Can one maintain the autonomy of morals and be a Christian? Can one retain the idea of God and still uphold the autonomy of morals?

The autonomy position has been beset by enemies on every side. It has been accused by the *Glaubensethik* of weakening the Christian ethos and even of undermining Christianity with its talk of autonomy.[22] The *Glaubensethik* authors would only be confirmed in their worst fears if they noticed a remark from a quite different source. John Mackie said about the case for the autonomy of ethics:

> This seems to have the almost equally surprising consequence that moral distinctions do not depend on God any more than, say, arithmetical ones, hence that ethics is autonomous and can be studied and discussed without reference to religious beliefs, that we can simply close the theological frontiers of ethics.[23]

On the other hand, some of its advocates have been accused of abandoning the autonomy position under pressure and of scurrying back to a neo-Scholastic position which requires a command of God for genuine moral obligation. Schüller accuses Korff of this and remarks darkly that there are several modern theologians who make the same mistake.[24]

Both charges seem to be false. The autonomy school, in reply to the charge that it is undermining religion, says that what it is proposing is a theonomous autonomy,[25] a relational autonomy,[26] an autonomous morality within Christianity.[27] By this it means that, while morality is a human creation and the human being is his or her own lawgiver, the Christian cannot be content with this as a sufficient explanation of or foundation for moral obligation. Auer says that morality requires a final ground and foundation and that in faith we recognise this as the eternal law or reason of God.[28] Böckle says that the moral claim is theonomously justified, that it is in God that it finds its legitimation,[29] that it has its unconditional character by being founded on the eternal law.[30] Korff says that while, on the one hand, human reason is its own legislator, on the other hand God is the divine legislator, the ground and end of our normative activity: the unconditional demand of morality, he says, demands a metaphysical, theological explanation and it is God's 'Yes' to the world that gives a guarantee to the unconditional demand of human reason.[31]

The authors are walking a thin line here: can there be such a thing as 'theonomous autonomy' or 'relational autonomy'? After all the brave talk about autonomy, are they saying — or is any one of them saying — that moral experience is not of itself a sufficient source of moral obligation? And in what sense of not sufficient? Not sufficient to generate moral obligation? Or not sufficient as an explanation of itself, of its existence and nature? Is the argument here about ethics or about metaphysics? To say that for moral obligation to be moral obligation, to be binding or fully binding, one has, in the end, to appeal to the authority of God seems to be an abandonment of the thesis of autonomy. It would look like a failure of nerve and a reversion to the old neo-Scholastic position.

It is not easy to decide whether Schüller's strictures on Korff are justified or whether they could be extended to the other two authors, because it is not clear what they mean by saying that the moral demand requires a 'grounding' or 'foundation' or 'justification' or 'ratification' in God. Does it imply some version of 'fully binding' moral obligation after the manner of some of the neo-Scholastics? Böckle says that the ultimate basis of our moral obligation is found in God's radical claim imposed on us but that we must be careful how this is understood.[32] A page later, however, he himself understands it like this:

... our faith in God does not put an end to our duty to realize our freedom in this world, but rather justifies our giving of ourselves as free, rational creatures. We do not need to presuppose God in order to impose commandments or prohibitions, but we are convinced that a recognition of creation and a knowledge of our own state as creatures are the basis of our duty to exercise our freedom rationally. We also fear that without this — and therefore, in the last resort, without God — everything would be the same to the autonomous will.[33]

The 'basis of our duty' to act rationally — what does this imply? Or again, 'the transcendental justification of obligation'?[34] Or the remark that 'the claim to rational self-realization acquires an unconditioned character by being founded on the *lex aeterna*'?[35] Such remarks raise doubts. So do the remarks of Auer that a person cannot explain the unconditioned character of moral demand without going beyond himself,[36] and that a person is to dispose of his life in freedom but knows that he is called to that duty by the one who placed him in history.[37] The doubts open up the question of the extent to which the autonomy movement can banish the suspicion of the humanist that Christian morality is committed to heteronomy. The objection to heteronomy presumably extends not only to the content of moral obligation but also to its source. The autonomy movement may be able to convince the non-Christian that (a) the content of Christian morality is to be discovered by reason and not given by God, (b) that the content is not different from that discovered by some non-religious moral theories. But it must also decide (c) whether, on the one hand, it regards human reason as a sufficient source of moral obligation — and in what sense — or whether, on the other hand, it understands moral experience or moral responsibility as having the character of a claim or demand ultimately because it is validated or confirmed by God. This would reduce to saying that a moral demand is binding not because of its inherent rationality but because of the authority or will of God. It would give a context for morality and a link to God not greatly different from that of the neo-Scholastic.

The language of 'require', 'demand' and 'need' is strong language. But it admits of a different explanation from the above. It may be that what the authors want to say is not that morality requires an authoritative act of God to justify its claim on us but that all reality requires an explanation. They can be interpreted as saying that in the Christian view no one is autonomous, since God is his or her source, meaning and end. They may be giving expression to the traditional position of Christian metaphysics that innerworldly experiences raise questions beyond themselves; that, in particular, the experience of good and value contained in moral experience raises questions about the existence of an absolute good or value; and that the Christian knows God as that absolute good and value. In this view, ethics is not its own final explanation but has a reference beyond itself.

The non-religious person will deny the existence of such questions or will answer them negatively. He will say that one must do one's duty, that it is absolutely binding and that that is the end of it. For him or her moral questions stop here: there is no need or place for further questions; there is no theological frontier to ethics. For the person of faith there must be. Moral experience fits into a wider world-view, which has something to say about the source of the human person and of his or her moral experience and about its final meaning. The Christian cannot be a Christian finally without saying how he sees the whole world and everything in it, including ethics — particularly ethics. He has more to say about ethics than that it is autonomous.

It seems to me *pace* Schüller, that this is how our authors are to be interpreted. Despite the very ambiguous remarks already quoted, this appears to be the general thrust of their positions. Böckle says that he is unhappy about the refusal of so many of his contemporaries to raise the metaphysical question and tells us that in insisting on the theonomy of morality what he wants to establish is that the human person is not his own total explanation and must not set himself up as an absolute.[38] Auer says that one has to grant the autonomy of morality as one grants the autonomy of technology or of science but that neither science nor morality nor any other worldly order has an absolute autonomy: it stands in a relationship to something else which does not impair the nature and inner laws of the worldly order. To be a believer is to recognise the final grounding of all things in God. So Auer says that to insist on the autonomy of morality is

185

not to tell the whole story.[39] Korff sees the fundamental logic of the world and of history in the fact that the human being is the image of God and that his normative power to legislate for himself is only truly seen when it is acknowledged to be a share in the reason of God.[40]

If this is what the authors mean by saying that morality requires or needs or demands a final grounding or justification, this is a different sense of 'requires' from that advocated by the neo-Scholastics. The majority of the neo-Scholastics, as we saw, held that the obligation to do good and avoid evil arises or fully arises only from the imposition of the will of God: without that command there would be no moral obligation. What we have here is a different view of the relation of God to the world. It is such that it allows that the worldly orders have their own inherent consistency and logic — likewise, morality has its own autonomous structure and makes its own unconditional demand. Such a faith-view of the relation of God to the world says that to be a Christian is to recognise this autonomous order and accept responsibility for it but to acknowledge also that the final significance of the admittedly autonomous structure of morality is seen only when the total picture of the meaning of the human being is assembled.

It is in this sense also that an even more controversial remark of the authors is to be interpreted — that morality is the law of God. It is remarkable that they have had to resort to this term. One would have thought that, with their crusade against heteronomy, the description of morality as the law of God is the one they would have been most anxious to avoid. They might have remembered Maclagan's objection:

If we are not to use anthropomorphic concepts the theory cannot be stated, and if we are to use them it cannot be defended: and one or the other we must do. There is no escape from the dilemma.[14]

But perhaps there is a use of 'law of God' that does escape from the dilemma. When Böckle, Auer and Korff use the expression 'law of God', they all use it with reference to Aquinas's expression, 'the eternal law'. Aquinas has an analogical notion of law: there are varieties of law.[42] Through his wisdom, he says, God is the founder of the universe of things. As being the principle through which the universe is created, divine wisdom

186

means art, or exemplar or idea, and likewise it also means law, as moving all things to their due ends.[43] So he sees the eternal law as the divine intelligence by which each thing has its own nature, tendencies and end: things are subject to the eternal law in that the formative idea in them all is divine wisdom.[44] If there is a lawgiver it is the human person. The plan of the divine intelligence, he says, is that the human person is to provide for himself and others.[45] The person does this by recognising that he should act according to reason, according to his due end: this is the natural law in us. Aquinas does not see the eternal law as if it were the imposition of the divine will upon creation. He does not describe natural law as eternal law passively received in man. He describes the first principle of natural law, which is directive of human life, as a participation by us in the eternal law, in the wisdom of God.[46] Obligation for him was a derived concept: natural law imposed an obligation because it primarily imposed, with rational necessity, that an end must be pursued.

This is a different understanding of law from the anthropomorphic model of someone with a will imposing commands, which was envisaged by Maclagan. As I understand it, when the authors refer to morality as the law of God or as finding in God its source, end and justification, what they are proposing is more a view about the world — its source, its meaning, its end — than about morality. They appear to me to want to say some or all of the following.

(i) The Christian understanding of God is that he is the creator and cause of the human being. He is the explanation of our ability and our need to be rational, to recognise the good, to seek values, to respond to the rational appeal of principles.[47] It is, therefore, a reasonable use of language to refer to God as the source of our autonomous moral activity. Indeed, some such expression is necessary if the Christian is to communicate his view of the world. (ii) On the analogy of what is known to us — human beings who by acts of thinking, choosing and making bring states of affairs into existence in accordance with a prior plan in the human mind — the Christian refers to the totality of what exists, especially persons with their law of flourishing, development and well-being, as the creative plan or purpose or intention of God.[48] (iii) It is not easy for us to know just what moral living involves. But God knows it perfectly. He is supreme reason. He wills whatever is the demand of right reason. The

Christian can reasonably refer to one's rationality or power of understanding as a participation in or a reflection of the reason of God and can refer to God as the ultimate justification, guarantee and ground of the claim of human rationality.[49] (iv) If Christian and non-Christian alike recognise the way of morality as that of the recognition of the claim of the human person, the Christian knows that in God is found the perfect love of all human beings. So all true moral response is in the likeness of God.[50] (v) If moral growth is thought of as growth in perfection or flourishing, it can still be only a limited perfection without God. The Christian knows that union with God is the goal of all flourishing.[51] All moral response, therefore, all choice of the good which perfects, is some share in our final good, who is God.[52]

None of this compromises the autonomy position but it makes some sense of its language of relational or theonomous autonomy. It is still holding to its stance that the human being as created by God recognises that the distinction between good and evil makes a claim that is obligatory or over-riding or in-escapable for his intelligence. As Mackey says, nothing has to be proved or postulated about God or an after-life in order that the human moral enterprise get off the ground and move towards its goal.[53] Yes, but that is not enough. If the Christian is to give an adequate account of moral experience and obligation in his life he or she has to have recourse to some of the expressions which we have been considering.

It will be noted that some moral theories fit more easily with the considerations we have been discussing than others. The theory espoused by Auer and company is heavily dependent on Aquinas and on the closely interconnected notions of nature, perfection, good and end.[54] It is an approach that has always been prominent among Roman Catholics but it is not univer-sally accepted and may be on the way to becoming less popular.[55] It is certainly not a view to which an autonomy stance about morality is committed. But whatever moral theory the Christian espouses, he cannot do justice to his world-view by referring to naked moral experience: he will have to refer it to God in some way. To do so, to refer to moral obligation as the will of God, for example, is not simply a device to make 'clear and tangible' the connection between the moral order and God. It is a device, if it must be called such, which a Christian knows is not at all clear but which helps him to say something about his total understanding of morality.[56] The humanist may refer to the same moral demand simply as one's duty.[57] The Christian can agree that one can have an absolute duty. He can agree that moral duty would exist even if, *per impossibile*, God did not exist. The two have different views of the source and autonomy of life rather than different views of the source and autonomy of morality. They are expressing things in terms of these different world-views, using different language frames. Both descriptions of the moral demand are valid. But the Christian will want to say that, in his view, the Christian description is contextually more comprehensive than the other.

(There are not only presuppositions about morality but also about theology in the autonomy school's approach and they will not be shared by all. The possession of human reason and its possibilities are strongly emphasised: this is seen as a participation in the reason and wisdom of God and as our likeness to God. There are, of course, other interpretations of 'likeness'. Christians of all denominations might also ask if the fact of sin has been sufficiently taken account of. There is also a strong portrayal of God as *telos* or End and of the good life as the human being's orientation of himself or herself towards the End. That situates ethical life in a way with which some will have difficulty — again, some of all denominations. Some of the issues here relate more to the second major question which we raised — and dropped. That is the question of the relation of moral life and salvation. In spite of these reservations, many Christians will find points of contact with the attempt of the autonomy school to give its autonomous morality a Christian context.)

The position outlined here is not by any means new in Roman Catholicism. It is a position that reaches back beyond the renewal movement and the neo-Scholastics to Vasquez and Aquinas.[58] It has been a constant of the best of Roman Catholic philosophy.[59] To my way of thinking this movement for a 'morality from below' is not only right in its understanding of moral obligation but in its realisation of the importance of the emphasis on autonomy. Moral demand is epistemologically independent of knowledge of God or belief in a command of God. But it is not metaphysically independent. For the Christian there cannot be a split between morality and religion

189

and one must try to express this further dimension. This, it has rightly been said, is a baffling semantic task.[60]

Talk of morality at this level is a form of God-talk and is subject to the limitations of God-talk. It is one thing to have a particular conception of morality and to try to understand its relationship to God. But it is another to find a suitable metaphor or model or language-bridge to express one's vision. Theology is very impoverished here: the expressions which we have met so far are well worn and have not contributed to a solution. A measure of the problem is the extraordinary experience of the autonomy movement which set out to dispel the notion of the heteronomy of morals and found itself, in the end, reverting to the language of morality as the law of God. One may retort that it is only a model or an analogy. But models are chosen from everyday life for their aptness or adequacy in conveying our viewpoint. One could hardly imagine a model that was less calculated to dispel the notion of heteronomy. 'Law of God' language seems to me to be particularly ambiguous. The risk of assimilating God to the ruler who issues laws is enormous and nothing could be more antithetical to the whole autonomy position. Indeed, the whole forensic metaphor of laws, judgment, reward and punishment has, in my view, done damage in Roman Catholicism — both to the idea of God and to the idea of morality.[61] It shows little sign of abating. The favoured language of churchmen and of theologians is still that of the law of God. That is why the effort of the autonomy movement to recast the thinking about morality is important. That is also why one hopes that future discussion about the identity of Christian ethics will recognise the importance of this area and will issue in dialogue between moralists and systematic theologians.[62]

G. F. Wood once suggested that we are least unsuccessful when we interpret morality as the creative will of God.[63] Perhaps 'will' is better than 'law'. It does not necessarily have the same overtones of the issuing of a decree and may not carry the same threat to the notion of autonomy. One does not have to think of the imposition of a will. One can think rather of God as Creator, Lord and Father, whose will is supremely rational and loving. To seek to know the moral good is necessarily to seek his will. To do the moral good is necessarily to be aligned with his will. The love of God who is supremely good involves seeking to

190

share his will. One must settle for the inadequacy of language here but one can try to use it as carefully as possible. Anybody who tries will, no doubt, end by agreeing with Ramsey that the logic of religious discourse is 'bafflingly tortuous', 'with the logic of personality illuminating some parts of the discourse and the logic of impersonal phrases like "moral demand" illuminating other parts'.[64]

A notable absentee in this chapter so far has been Fuchs. I doubt if he would greatly disagree with anything that has been said. But the stress in his approach to the problem of the relation of morality to God has been somewhat different — although his approach also rests on Aquinas and on the traditional theory of morality outlined above. He does not use the language of 'law', 'will', 'ground', 'justification'. His interest is to overcome the idea that God is outside the world and that there is an external connection between God and morality — it is hard to avoid this in the language of law. He stresses that we must not think of the moral life 'as existing alongside the "theologal" life of relationship with God.'[65] They exist in one another. He says: 'True morality . . . contains within itself a "theologal" life and is that life's practical expression.'[66] In the very moral activity itself, in the choice of the good, he sees an implicit but real choice of God, an acceptance or rejection of God's gracious gift of himself so that there is an organic connection between moral life and God.[67] Fuchs calls this the transcendental or supernatural or Christian intentionality of morality.[68]

Let us pursue him a little further. When I do a single good act, he asks, is that all that I do? Or is it not the case that I am realising myself? He appears to mean that I am creating or developing myself as a particular kind of person and that my individual act is the expression of my stance as a person. He goes on to say that through this single act I 'realize my own human personality — and this indeed with reference to an Absolute'.[69] Or, as he puts it, moral experience is open to or implies an Absolute and this absolute is the personal Absolute of revelation, God.[70] His position is, it seems, that in choosing this particular moral good, I am chosing goodness, I am declaring and expressing my fundamental option for goodness and — if I only knew it — I am choosing the final good, who is God. This Fuchs holds to be true for everyone: this is the link between morality and union with God; and it is realised in the life of everyone.[71]

191

The approach offered by Fuchs, like that of the authors discussed a few pages back, depends on a particular theory of morality and on certain theological positions. Granted that, it has considerable attractions for one who wishes to uphold the autonomy of morality and the importance of dialogue with non-Christians. It allows considerable agreement with the humanist about the content of morality and about the source of moral obligation. It has no hint of a need to bolster moral obligation with appeal to an authority. But it interprets morality theologically as having a deep significance unknown to the humanist. The Christian is to be aware of this context. He is to live his life of union with God in the knowledge of the deep meaning of his daily moral choices. In them he meets God. In them he lives his life of love of God. In them he accepts or rejects the gift of union with God. Fuchs seems to be saying to us something like the following: When you think about the autonomous, inner-worldly reality of morality and you ask how it relates to God or God to it, do not have recourse to the language of law or will. Morality is the will of God and one is responding to his will in the sense that to choose the good is to choose God. Morality makes its own demand. But that is not the whole story about it. That is not the Christian interpretation of reality. For the Christian, God is the Good, the horizon or implication of all good choice.

Fuchs recognises that he is immediately dependent on Karl Rahner. Rahner has not concerned himself much with the problem of a Christian morality but some of his general theological writing has had implications for moral theology. It is significant that one area which has received some criticism from him is the forensic model of the relationship between morality and God. He agrees that we cannot give up the idea of God as the founder and guardian of the moral order: how to conceptualise this, of course, is our very problem. His complaint is that we have put forward a law-judgment-reward image of God in which 'the model of punishment in its secular and juridical uses always pushes itself too quickly and automatically into the foreground'.[72] So God's punishment is understood in the sense of the punishment imposed on offenders against the civil law of civil society. What he presses for is a more organic relationship between moral life and union with God: God must not be seen as one who makes laws and distributes rewards and punishments that have no intrinsic connection with good or bad moral life; the salvation or damnation that consists in the gain or loss of God 'must not be understood as a merely external reaction of a condemning or rewarding God but as itself seen to be already achieved in this freedom'.[73]

The idea of transcendence is the key concept for Rahner. The person is defined as absolute transcendence or absolute openness.[74] By transcendence he means a 'going-beyond', i.e. a going beyond what is immediately and explicitly known and chosen. The human being's transcendence is towards God. He is made for God and is fulfilled only in the possession of God. But how is he to attain God? If the person has or is this transcendental openness, he is also embodied spirit, spiritualised body. This limits him. He can grasp and choose only the limited realities appearing to him in space and time.[75] The essential of what Fuchs takes from Rahner is that in the knowing and choosing of these particular realities, to which the person is limited because he is bodily spirit, there is some kind of knowing and choosing of the Absolute, God. One can only choose to give alms, for example. But in this particular, limited choice there is some apprehension and choice of its enveloping reality, of the 'beyond' of it, the horizon of it, for which our intellect and will are made.[76] So, a stance towards God is involved in all of our choices. 'In this light freedom towards the encountered individual beings is always also a freedom towards the horizon.'[77]

The considerations sketched here run through all of Rahner's writings and are explicated at great length and in great depth. They do not occur specifically in the context of morality. But I think their relevance for the moralist can be seen:

But is is nevertheless part of the specifically Christian experience of freedom that this freedom is freedom not solely with respect to some object of categorial experience within the absolute context which is God, but that it is freedom, if always only mediated, with respect to God Himself and turned towards Him: a freedom to accept or to reject God Himself. . . .[78]

The 'categorial experiences' refer to the everyday choices: whether man likes it or not or is aware of it or not, they involve a *prise de position* with regard to God.

Since morality is summed up in love for the other, it is above all in the moral claim of our neighbour, Rahner says, that we meet God. But we must see an organic relationship between the two. Here there emerges clearly the question we have been urging all through this chapter of the particular contextual model we have for the relationship between God and morality. It is not the case, Rahner says, that one loves God and then, in accordance with the will of God, one is well disposed to the neighbour and does him good. It is not that we have been commanded to love the neighbour and do so out of love of God. It is not that love of God is the motive for love of neighbour.[79] No, the categorial explicit love of neighbour is the primary act of love of God. There is a radical unity between the two: 'One can love God whom one does not see only *by* loving one's visible brother lovingly.'[80] So that the whole incalculable mystery of the human person — that is, the whole mystery of his or her union with God or loss of God — is contained and exercised in this act of love of neighbour.[81]

Our question has been: what do the authors have to say about the relationship between an autonomous morality and God? What emerges in Rahner's philosophical and theological scheme and what Fuchs and others have adopted from him offers the most radical relationship between the two.[82] The last paragraph shows that Rahner is rejecting other models — even some of the more benign models that derive from neo-Scholasticism. It would seem that this is also what Fuchs intends when he stresses that moral and theologal life do not exist beside one another but in one another and that moral life contains within itself a theologal life. I understand him to say that it is not through the notion of obligation that an autonomous morality is integrated into Christian life but by understanding that God is the Good, the Value, the Ideal, the 'beyond' of and the condition of possibility of human choice. The openness to God, which is exercised through moral choice is the Christian meaning and context of man's freedom.[83] This is an approach that accommodates well a theory of an autonomous morality within a Christian context. Because of its understanding of the person as by nature open to transcendence and of human choice as involving the choice of the corresponding pole of that transcendence, the Absolute, God, it is able to endorse the autonomy of morality and, at the same time, to understand the total Christian context.

Many, both within and without Roman Catholicism, will have problems with the Fuchs-Rahner approach. There will be questions about how it understands love for God and whether it limits the breadth and scope of such love. There will be the recurring question about the interpretation of the human being's response to God: is the emphasis to be on his or her orientation to and choice of the End or Good, or is it to be on his or her trust in the forgiving mercy of God? There will be question about the weight and significance to be given to moral life. There will be doubt about the apparent playing down of explicit faith. This last question, in particular, has been hotly debated and has resulted in some modification of his views from Rahner: more recent writing stresses the importance of explicit response.[84] It should be recognised, however, that within the Roman Catholic community at least, what is being proposed is not entirely new. It is based on Aquinas.[85] We have already seen some elements of it among the other authors. We have seen a version of it in Gilleman. We meet it in Christian philosophy.[86] The reservations which I mention are important: many shade into the area which I have been trying to hive off from this work — that of morality and salvation, of merit and justification. (The fact that they do, points up, once again, the work that remains to be done by moralists and theologians in dialogue.) But having granted the reservations, it seems to me that the approach of Fuchs, while it is far from complete and while it will not be easy to communicate in popular language, goes some distance towards doing justice both to the autonomy of morality and to its integration into Christian life. It should be remembered that he is not only giving a metaphysical interpretation of human freedom but is urging also that the implications of it be recognised and made as explicit as possible in human life. That is the point of talking about context.

In this chapter I have tried to gather what are largely incidental thoughts (Fuchs, perhaps, excepted) of our authors. The content of Christian morality has received a lot of attention from them. But the problem of moral obligation and the general situating of morality within the total structure of the Christian scheme of things has not received much attention. There have been remarks about context. But the language of context is very vague and tends to cover over some major questions. I have isolated the question of moral obligation as one that should be particularly revealing. Anyone who looks at the neo-Scholastic model, or at the emphasis on the will of God as source of moral obligation in the renewal movement, or even at some recent works of moral theology, will realise how crucial it is to one's conception of morality.[87] To change this thinking, to give morality a different identity — essentially something discovered by human beings as making an overriding and undeniable claim on them — was the aim of the autonomy movement. The question for its advocates, however, is whether they can retain their concept of morality and do justice to the vision of Christianity. (As we saw, some have held that it is impossible.) One's concept of moral obligation will be a critical factor.

The autonomy movement has not advanced the God-talk of morality very much. But it seems to me that the general thrust of autonomy and of the wider 'morality from below' is right. One can take one's stand with Aquinas that God's providence is that the human being is to provide for himself within the moral area: by this I mean that the awareness of moral obligation is God's gift to us and part of God's governance of the world. It is, like much else in life, a relatively autonomous area which must be responsibly accepted: to do so is to honour God. Finding the right moral response is a further problem and one in which we have found the autonomy school somewhat inadequate. But the rejection of heteronomy, the situating of moral obligation in human intelligence and the stress on responsibility are all a welcome emphasis in Christian morality. A wider acceptance of them would do much both for the understanding of morality in Christian life and for the popular understanding of God.

Conclusion

The authors of the renewal of the forties and fifties were right in their basic insight: religion should make a difference to morality; Christian faith should affect Christian ethics. The early insights were simple and enthusiastic. Roman Catholic theology was entering a new experience when it left the security of neo-Scholastic natural law and opened up the question of an ethic of faith. The early insights raised deeper questions than perhaps their advocates were aware of. To talk of Christian ethics is to bring together two profound areas of human experience — religion and morality. They shade into one another and there is a great variety of complex relationships between them. It took time even to begin to see that complexity. It was only through a period of trial and error that Roman Catholics came to see the implications of what it means to do morality in full awareness of the Christian revelation. That period of trial and error is far from over: the history which we have surveyed shows that there is still, as Häring said recently, 'a burning question on the identity of Christian ethics'.[1] An appreciation of the different layers of the question, a realisation of the need to clarify concepts and define terms and a groping towards a method that would do justice both to the fullness of faith and to the need for rigorous argument must count as some kind of progress. There have been advances in the period: here I put together some final reflections on it.

I begin with what some would regard as the periphery of the question. At the most general level, the notion of a Christian ethic or of the Christian character of ethics should refer to how one situates ethics. By that I mean the significance which one attaches as a Christian to the whole ethical project or the relation which one sees between ethics and salvation. I have

197

made the point through this work that it is an area that is in need of greater interdisciplinary study. This is particularly important because there has been development in an area that is correlative. That is the area of merit and justification in Roman Catholic theology. I have not been able to go into that territory and, given the accepted division of Roman Catholic theology into dogmatic and moral theology, the moralists could not have been expected to explore it. But it is highly relevant to the overall identity of Christian ethics. Not long ago I asked a postgraduate student of theology what he thought of the Catholic doctrine of merit: he told me that he had never heard of it. I think that is more an indication of a changed emphasis in theology than a reflection on his training. I have not found any formal treatment of the subject among the moralists but there are indications of a change of understanding. It is a commonplace now to find Roman Catholic moralists placing the emphasis on faith, de-emphasising merit and reward and treating of morality as a response to the good news of Christ.[2] All of that affects identity. What is important to note is the radical change from what we found among the neo-Scholastics in the first chapter of this work. It is something to keep in mind when one discusses the identity of ethics among Roman Catholics today. It is also important for the ecumenist who is trying to plot convergences.

Closely related to this is the question of the overall religious model which the Christian gives to moral life. The renewal sought to find one theme which would unify all moral life and from which all principles could be derived. That proved more difficult than had been anticipated. However, the themes which were explored are still important although they play a different role: it is not easy to find a master theme and perhaps not even desirable. The point I make now is that to understand moral life as response to the love of God or as the following of Christ or as discipleship is to give one's moral life an identity that is quite distinctive. One may not be easily able to derive content from it in the way that those who participated in the early renewal thought possible. That is not the point at the moment: whatever the content, one is giving a shape to one's moral life that marks it off from secular morality or from the morality of other religions. Some such conception of morality as love of God or as following or discipleship seems to me to be an essential part of Christian life. For the early Christian, morality clearly was a lived relationship with the Father and with Christ. The nexus between faith and ethic was close. To be in the light was to believe in the Son of God and to love the brethren. To do justice to being not only moral but moral as a Christian one has to try to catch that spirit. Perhaps it is best caught by the notion of morality as discipleship. We need to stress the point: I have the suspicion that neither the *Glaubensethik* nor the autonomy school regards this contextual element as of great significance.

'Following', 'discipleship', 'response' are important but they need to be supplemented. The Christian must also situate morality in the overall scheme of the relation of God to the world. For him morality must, in some way, be referred to the lordship of God. He does not say how he sees things as a Christian unless he says something about the fact of creation and of the dependence of all things, including human beings and the whole moral order, on God. How he is going to state that is the problem. Here is a sensitive point which touches the nerve both of one's conception of God and of morality. The traditional law-of-God language, we have seen, presents problems. It carries a threat to the notions of the genesis of morality, of moral demand, and of the final significance of morality. The autonomy movement has done something to dispel the cruder notions of morality as law and it is a pity that its efforts in that direction have been labelled as an undermining of Christianity and even of religion. To some it will seem to be labouring the obvious but, in the light of the tradition, it is important that the autonomy school continue to insist that it is not necessary to know God or to postulate a command of God in order to subscribe to the institution of morality, to construct a moral theory or to have an intelligible notion of moral demand. But it has to be recorded that no significant contribution has been made to the development of a new language to express how the moral order is seen by the Christian as an element of the lordship of God: the moralist is limited by the inherent inadequacies of God-talk.

It is also part of the character of Christian ethics that the Christian world-view contains a wide complexus of beliefs and stories that enlighten, sustain and give a total significance to the whole enterprise of morality. Christianity can affect one's character and desires. It can open one's eyes to the truly good and enable one to desire it for its own sake. It helps one not only

199

to see and appreciate what is moral but to do what one knows to be morally good. Morality is so much a matter of the education of desires. Christianity should have an educative effect. It should be hard to escape this effect if one takes seriously what one professes and celebrates about the care, fidelity, love and forgiveness of God and the self-emptying of Christ: one should be enabled to come to see the value and beauty of such virtues. This is true not only of particular virtues. In the more general sense, Christianity makes for moral seriousness and encourages moral carefulness.

Not only does Christianity contribute to the education of moral character, but it also contributes a whole range of religious reasons to the moral effort. The Christian has religious as well as moral reasons for doing good. This dispositional power has been played down. Although the autonomy movement has said that what is specific about Christian morality is not content but motivation, one has the impression that neither side has valued motivation very much. The *Glaubensethik* has dismissed it as mere decoration. Among those of the autonomy movement, paraenesis has become a pejorative term. But paraenesis, once it is recognised for what it is, is important. The debate has been almost entirely about moral knowledge, but much of our trouble about morality is not in the knowing but in the doing. Paul knew the power of the example of Christ and of appealing to Christian beliefs as support for moral effort. This is true not only of particular choices but also of the whole enterprise of morality. There is a religious hope in doing things and a religious perseverance in well-doing. There is a belief in the purposiveness of things. There is a confidence that the best of our moral endeavours will not end in the grave but will be found again. These relationships between what is inherent to morality and what is inherent to Christian religious experience must find expression in any full consideration of the identity of Christian morality. What is important is not to diminish the range of the relationships. One cannot give an authentic account of Christian morality if one isolates it from this whole sustaining and enabling context.

It is probable that neither side in the debate would regard the considerations so far adduced as touching the heart of the matter. I have, right through this work, been deliberately trying to broaden the scope of the question, because I believe that the

200

issue of what it means to understand or do morality as a Christian suffers from being limited to content. When we do turn to what has been the core of the debate, what should we fasten on that will be important for future work in this area? The early renewal threw together a very undifferentiated assortment of Christian elements. But it was a worthy effort in the right direction. The *Glaubensethik* has also put forward a very undifferentiated collection of material in a desperate determination to prove specificity of content. It has sometimes been right for the wrong reasons. It is only after questions of definition have been raised that much of what it proposes can be even admitted to the domain of morality, still less to the area of content. Whatever refinements have come, have been mostly from the autonomy movement and from the confrontation — not yet sufficient but fruitful, nevertheless — of theologians and philosophers. What should be avoided is any feeling or fear that such confrontations must result in the diminishment of a religious ethic. It may well work in the opposite direction.

It will have emerged from our discussions that, for the future, it will be important for theologians to bear in mind the distinction between religion and morality and to remember that not all religion action-guides or value-systems are to be classified as moral action-guides. It will be necessary to keep clear the distinction of content and motivation, of the genesis of moral positions and their justification, of paraenesis and normative ethics. When one refers to the inter-dependence of morality and religion it will be essential to distinguish epistemological and ontological dependence, causal and psychological dependence. Roman Catholics will need to remember, too, that the moral theory they are espousing is pertinent: they cannot assume any more that all Roman Catholics operate with one moral theory; I have pointed out that some theories accommodate themselves more easily to the traditional relations between morality and Christianity than others. It is only if the theologian bears such distinctions in mind that he will know what he is doing and that others will know also. That said, the point must be acknowledged, that the concept of morality in religious morality may be richer and more complex than that found in the philosophical tradition, and may evade the precise usage and definition that philosophers often seek.

It was important that the 'naïve biblicism' of the renewal and of the *Glaubensethik* should be subjected to rigorous criticism. It is true that a more sophisticated approach to the Bible has become widely accepted since the early renewal days: the notion of revelation, for example, has been greatly refined. But even if Roman Catholics have gone beyond a very literal notion of revelation, it is still widely held, as we saw from the *Glaubensethik*, that through the moral insights of the early community God has made known to us precepts which are his will for human living.[3] The language of law and all its connotations dies hard. The problems about regarding the Bible as a source of moral precepts are considerable and it is difficult to get theologians to take them seriously.

Nevertheless I have disagreed with the bald statement that there is never a specific Christian content to ethics. That does not mean for me that one is dependent on the Bible for a revealed ethic. It means that in every age Christians must work out an ethic that is consonant with their world-view and that in any age they will occasionally arrive at moral judgments that are justified precisely in terms of the specific elements of that world-view. It is, of course, difficult to determine the extent to which a Christian today would opt for or expect from others or find intelligible stances about poverty, detachment, virginity or self-sacrificing love if we did not have suggestions about them in the Bible: would they appear as justifiable choices if we had no tradition about them? One may ask especially about self-sacrificing love. Although even love of enemies is found in non-Christian literature, the belief of the Christian community — that second-mile morality is to be expected and required from Christians generally — seems to depend on its religious memory and on its conviction that in the tradition of agape attaching to the teaching and life of Jesus, it has preserved the core of his moral teaching and the truth for living.

The logic of the autonomy position is that, as far as what they call content is concerned, one can simply ignore biblical morality. But it seems to me that the least that must be said is that there should be the closest dialogue between the community's discernment today and the general faith-orientations that lie behind and find expression in the biblical ethic. What one finds in the Bible is also faith trying to express itself, to prove itself in action, to do the truth. The faith of today and the faith of the Bible are in continuity: it seems unrealistic to say that faith now has nothing to learn about content from the efforts of that privileged community — whatever the exegetical and hermeneutical problems that have to be attended to even in relation to the most general moral attitudes of the Bible. It may be that the significance of biblical ethics lies not so much in what it says should be done — in explicit teaching — as in what it can reveal about the way in which the early Christian community dealt with certain types of situation. It is doubtful if one can be fully sensitive to Christian discernment without trying to catch that nexus of ethos and ethic, of faith and practice.

There are other problems. The autonomy school has never resolved the obscurity of its claim that morality is substantiallly the same for all but fully available to Christians, or that it is in principle and *per se* available to unbelievers, or that the Christian view of the human person (*Menschenbild*) performs a critical function. What does 'fully' mean? One must ask if a full moral vision does not mean a different moral vision and one that will sometimes lead to a clash with non-Christian vision. One also wants to ask how and why the non-Christian tends to go astray and what elements of the Christian view bring about the adjustment. Can the authors hold, in the end, that the Christian view does not sometimes make a difference to discernment? There is a certain unreality about the autonomy position: it is hard to escape the feeling that it is surrounded by escape clauses because it cannot quite accommodate Christian life as expereinced within its very rigid theory.

It is not surprising that we have found some confusion about the analysis of the moral act: it is a very difficult area. The bland distinction between content and motive has been crucial to the autonomy thesis. It needs to be re-examined. It is not just that it affects how one is to adjudicate the debate about specificity. What is more important is that it affects the whole business of what one means by human action and how it engages one's personality. I have stressed the importance of vision, disposition, reasons, intention, virtue, desires. The autonomy position plays down all of them. This seems to me to be a mistake and to under-estimate the meaning of human freedom and human choice. It also has the effect of making the thesis of the autonomy authors, even if it were true, not very interesting. They may come closer to identity of content with secular ethics. But they are leaving out of the moral act much of what is most important and interesting about it. Whether one agrees with my analysis of human action or not, the importance of definition and the way in which the whole debate has been crippled by lack of it have emerged. If the debate is to continue along the same lines, there will have to be agreement about basic terms or at least agreement to disagree.

Part of the struggle between the two schools is about whether God makes known authoritatively a morality that may not and need not be understood by us or whether it is God's purpose that we discover a morality that we see as inherently rational and demanded by the nature of things. The general position of the autonomy school here seems to me to be not only right but important. We are to discover our morality and we ought to be able to clarify how we do so and not simply appeal to the biblical text or to a vague 'light of revelation'. But I question the autonomy notion of 'the nature of things' and of 'inherently rational'.[4] It seems to operate as if one's understanding of 'the nature of things' remains untouched by religious considerations. I cannot see how Christian vision, values and meanings can be excluded. While the autonomy movement has, in my view, made Christian morality credible to a world come of age and exposed some very loose theological thinking — it would be hard to overestimate the contribution which Fuchs in particular has made to this — it seems that it fails to catch the whole of the Christian experience and that its total alignment of Christ and culture in the moral area (allowing only a clash with culture gone corrupt) sells Christianity short. The individual Christian or the Christian community cannot simply farm out or sub-contract morality to others and then re-insert it into faith. Moral discernment has to be done in fidelity to who one is as a Christian. One must do full justice to the moral agent.

The attempt to prove that there is or is not a Christian morality has sidetracked theologians somewhat, as if the whole future of Christianity or the whole future of dialogue with un-believers depended on the resolution of the issue — remember that the *Glaubensethik* said that the fate of Christianity was in the balance. It is not a necessary element of Christian faith or a necessary sign of credibility to prove specificity of content. On the other hand, one must ask if dialogue is everything or if total dialogue on moral matters can reasonably be expected between those who are deeply divided culturally, philosophically or

204

religiously: I have said something about how close religion goes to the deep things of the human spirit and how radically it shapes one's outlook. One can certainly find areas of agreement: that much has been stressed. It is often said that there is a basic rationality about Roman Catholicism: I take this to mean that it finds considerable coincidence in moral matters between itself and many who engage in morality seriously and scientifically but who do not subscribe to religious beliefs. The Christian should not feel any compulsion to prove a difference of moral stance. But neither is difference disreputable. What is important and justifiable is that the Christian go about his task in loyalty to and full awareness of the totality of his Christian experience.

'Rationality', however, as sociologists, philosophers and anthropologists have discovered, is a difficult concept. There is no pure rationality walking around that is uncontaminated by metaphysical presuppositions: the atheist or agnostic position is not 'pure'. Within the limited tradition and the short span studied by this work, we have found different understandings of 'rationality'. In the neo-Scholastics and in the renewal movement it referred to an absolute distinction between the order of nature and the order of grace. When theological development led to the recognition that there is but one order, it was allowed that the rational includes supernatural elements. This was later taken to refer to what is available to human beings without thematic revelation. Some of our authors have been arguing that the term must not be disallowed to the person of faith: otherwise, what is one to call him or her — irrational, non-rational? Perhaps one needs some qualification and should refer to Christian rationality. It is one with this quality who has to discern and I have been arguing that it is the fruit of such a one's discernment that is the concern of Christian ethics. The detachment from all background beliefs and world-views which some look for in the doing of morals is neither possible nor desirable. There is a Christian rationality that commits one to work intelligently and logically towards the elaboration of moral positions in fidelity to the total vision which forms the Christian consciousness.

This means that one must allow the whole Christian tradition of beliefs, stories, myths and symbols to play their part. It is here that the biblical tradition comes powerfully into play: it is what I mean by the (admittedly blurred) distinction of theological use and normative use of the Bible. I said that discipleship does not easily yield content in the facile way in which the renewal understood it when it was hoped that one could read off the demands of Christian life from the biblical account of the life of Jesus. But discipleship does lead to discernment in the sense that the disciple shares the faith of the Lord. This gives a new range of facts, values and meanings to the Christian. This is the source of what I have been referring to as Christian vision, attitudes, dispositions, intentions, behaviour. It is the source also of what the Christian has to say about ideals, even personal ideals. Again, one is not trying to cut across any other ethic. One is trying to explore the implications for morality of one's own world-view and value-system.

The autonomy movement has not taken sufficient account of this. Neither does any approach that insists on beginning with experience, unless this is understood as the total Christian experience: one cannot legitimately excise Christian morality from this. One wonders if even what appears to be an entirely laudable sentiment of Böckle is correct — one with which I have much sympathy. He says that while there can be dogmatic mysteries there can be no moral mysteries. I have argued for a morality from below, discovered by the Christian who is sensitive to the total Christian awareness. But such a person is one who is dealing with the love of God, with love faithful to death, love that believes in resurrection. Such love is part of the mystery of God. The call to us to love our fellow human beings in this way shares in the mystery. Auer speaks of the inherent rationality of moral positions. Is such love inherently rational? If it is, it is only within a very special sense of rational that embraces the mystery of how God has loved us.

To find a way of harnessing the full range of Christian consciousness and developing the authentic response to it is the task of Roman Catholic ethics for the future. What one is looking for, then, is the typical or characteristic or consistent Christian response to the Christian world-view. It may be more fruitful to think in such terms than in terms of 'specific'. Whether such responses are also required by secular ethics, i.e. by those who do not subscribe to a thematic revelation, is not unimportant. Issues of law, of public policy, of social and political programmes, of equality and educational opportunity, of war and peace, of medical policy, all have a moral background.

Fortunately, there is some shared vision of common values: some would say that Christian values are operative even where they are not subscribed to. It is also true that divergence of moral opinion may be something that has nothing to do with religion. On the other hand, it might well be argued that Christians have too limited a view of morality and do not allow their values to be operative in a sufficiently wide range of social and political choices.

Comparisons with the morality of unbelievers or with a secular ethic are not easy. I said earlier that the notion of a secular ethic is oversimplified. However, they were the terms of the question chosen by both the renewal-*Glaubensethik* school and the autonomy school. One can make broad statements of comparison but it should be remembered that the secular ethic is very varied. The overlap with Christian ethics, as we have seen especially in the chapter on agape, will depend on the particular secular ethic in question. The values in one society differ from another and the concerns of one ethical theory differ from another. There is no standard humanist who might serve as a clear term of comparison. The question of specificity is not easy, therefore. What one can try to do is to determine what is typical of or consonant with Christianity. How specific that will be will depend on the term of comparison and on the values espoused by that term of comparison.

This makes a point about the validity of the Christian ethical enterprise. World-views differ even in the secular realm. We have to live with differences about some of the most profound elements of human life. Christianity is one such world-view. It is entitled to put forward its story of reality and to draw conclusions about patterns of conduct. I have been arguing for as credible a presentation as possible, one which will take account of the methodological problems and distinctions which we have considered, which will value the insights of the tradition of moral philosophy, and which, one hopes, will be intelligible even to those who do not subscribe to the Christian faith or the Christian ethic. There are, of course, further problems about imposing one's moral views on others, about tolerance, about the institutionalising of morality. That I accept. But to put forward how one sees reality because of one's faith in Christ and how one arrives at a moral outlook as a result of it is not a chauvinist or disreputable position.

207

In the short period which we have studied, Roman Catholic moral theory has swung from a natural law ethic to one that sought to distance itself from philosophical reasoning and to stress revelation. In the autonomy movement it has reverted to natural law — a changed conception of it but, nevertheless, natural law. The *Glaubensethik* has seen this as virtually a betrayal of Christianity and has argued again for a faith-ethic. Plainly, Christian ethics has suffered a crisis of identity among Roman Catholics. But progress can be reported. The debate has sharpened out thinking, has uncovered the layers of the question, has exposed loose argument and has led to important distinctions and definitions. The attention to world-view, vision, attitudes, dispositions and intentions has opened up for theologians a wider range of ethical considerations, even if they have not yet been fully integrated into a clear method. A more complete and dynamic understanding of moral discernment and of moral action are emerging in the tradition. None of this absolves the theologian from hard work and rigorous argument. It does not, in any way, mean that moral positions are easily found, or that there is only one right moral response to every situation, or that it is either possible or necessary for the churches to have clear and certain views on every moral problem. That would take us into another whole range of problems that have also recently concerned Christian moralists. But before one gets to that, the moralist has to think about what it means to do morality as a Christian — an issue that has been a source of confusion for Roman Catholic moralists for the past forty years. My hope is that the analysis of the probings of the last few decades in this work will, in some way, contribute to a climate in which better debate is possible and better answers are likely to emerge.

Notes

Introduction
(pp. 1-8)

1. R. Simon et al., 'L'Éthique chrétienne à la recherehe de son identité', *La Vie Spirituelle* 23(1970).
2. Until recently the terms 'Christian ethics' and 'theological ethics' were used mainly in the Protestant tradition while Roman Catholics referred to 'moral theology'. Now Roman Catholics use all three terms interchangeably. They also use the terms 'ethics' and 'morality' interchangeably (although philosophers distinguish them in a variety of ways). I follow this practice.
3. Paul VI, Encyclical Letter *Populorum Progressio*, n. 22.
4. John Paul II, Encyclical Letter *Laborem Exercens* (trs. Vatican Polyglot Press), n. 4.
5. Paul VI, Encyclical Letter *Humanae Vitae* (trs. A.C. Clark and G. Crawford), Catholic Truth Society, London, n. 4.
6. *Declaration on Procured Abortion* issued by the Sacred Congregation for the Doctrine of the Faith (English trs. *Osservatore Romano*, 25/26 Nov. 1975), n. 4.
7. *Declaration on Certain Questions Concerning Sexual Ethics* issued by the Sacred Congregation for the Doctrine of the Faith (trs. Vatican Polyglot Press), nn. 4ff.
8. John Paul II, Apostolic Exhortation 'Familiaris Consortio', nn. 11ff.
9. *Conscience And Authority, A Doctrinal Statement of the Irish Episcopal Conference*, Irish Messenger Publications, Dublin, pp. 16, 9, 7.
10. G. J. Hughes, *Authority in Morals: An Essay in Christian Ethics*, Heythrop Monographs, London, 1978, p.v. Cf. E. D'Arcy, '"Worthy of Worship": A Catholic Contribution' in G. Outka and J.P. Reeder Jr., *Religion and Morality*, Doubleday, New York, 1973, pp. 173ff.; G.L. Hallett, *Christian Moral Reasoning: An Analytic Guide*, Univ. of Notre Dame Press, Notre Dame and London, 1983, passim.
11. W. Frankena, 'Love and Principle in Christian Ethics' in A. Plantinga (ed.) *Faith and Philosophy*, Erdman's, Grand Rapids, 1964, p. 203. Cf. H.D. Lewis, *Morals and Revelation*, Allen and Unwin, London, 1951, p. 14.
12. Thils's book *Tendances Actuelles en Théologie Morale*, one of the earliest books of the renewal movement, appeared in 1940.

Chapter 1,
(pp. 9-36)

1. Parallel to the manual tradition, there had been in nineteenth-century Germany an anti-Enlightenment flowering of moral theology. It is associated mainly with the names of Sailer, Hirscher, Jocham and Linsenmann. It was quite different in spirit from neo-Scholasticism. Its interest was in the great biblical themes and in a preachable, kerygmatic theology. It sought not to set out minimum demands but the fullness and attractiveness of Christian life. So it proposed a theology loosely organised about the great themes of the kingdom, grace and the freedom of the sons of God. But because of the dominance of Latin as the language of theology, the influence of this movement was limited to German-speaking areas and it declined towards the end of the century. At the beginning of this century the Latin neo-Scholastic manual was the staple diet of the Roman Catholic world. Cf. Bernard Häring, *The Law of Christ*, 3 vols., (English trans. Edwin Kaiser), Mercier, Cork, 1961, vol.1, pp. 22ff.

   It should be noted that there is little difference in Roman Catholic thought in this period between moral theologians and moral philosophers. The philosopher starts from the position that man can know God and he frames his morality accordingly. If he adverts to the morality of atheists it is to make the point that if men are ignorant of God it is through their own fault and he is not slow to attribute to such a depraved form of life. Cf. M. Nivard, *Ethica*, Beauchesne, Paris, 1938, p.125; Josef Donat, *Ethica Generalis*, Rauch, Innsbruck, 1920, p.135.

2. Leo XIII, Encyclical Letter, *Aeterni Patris*, 4 Aug. 1879, Henricus Denzinger, *Enchiridion Symbolorum Definitionum et Declarationum de rebus fidei et morum* (twenty-third edition, Adolfus Schönmetzer), Herder, Freiburg, 1965, n. 3135.

3. Cf. H. Noldin, *Summa Theologiae Moralis*, 3 vols., twenty-eight edition revised by A. Schmitt, Herder, Barcelona, 1951, vol.1, p.40.

4. Cf. F. Hürth and P.M. Abellan, *Notae ad Praelectiones Theologiae Moralis*, 2 vols., Gregorian University Press, Rome, 1948, vol.1, p.7.

5. Cf. Dominicus M. Prümmer, *Manuale Theologiae Moralis*, 3 vols., fifth edition, Herder, Freiburg, 1928, vol. 1, p.3. Cf. Marcellino Zalba, *Theologiae Moralis, Summa*, 3 vols., second edition, Biblioteca de Autores Cristianos, Madrid, 1957, vol.1, p.3.

6. Cf. Benedictus H. Merkelback, *Summa Theologiae Moralis*, 3 vols., fifth edition, Desclée, Paris, 1946, vol.1, p.108; Noldin, vol.1, p.43; Prümmer, vol.1, p.26.

7. Cf. Ed. Genicot, *Institutiones Theologiae Moralis*, 2 vols., sixteenth edition revised by J. Salmans, L'Edition Universelle, Brussels, 1946, vol.1, p.7; Noldin, vol.1, p.3.

8. Cf. Thomas A. Jorio, *Theologia Moralis*, 3 vols., fourth edition, D'Auria, Naples, 1953, vol.1, p.1; Noldin, vol.1, pp. 3,130; Prümmer, pp. 3,113; Hürth-Abellan, p.9; Merkelbach, pp. 11,12. One author who dissented from this common opinion was Vermeersch: even the title of his work is revealing. Cf. Arthurus Vermeersch, *Theologiae Moralis: Principia-Responsa-Consilia*, 4 vols., fourth edition, Gregorian University Press,

210

Rome, 1947-48, pp. 5-6. One of the criticisims of the moral theology of the period was that it had in mind only the determination of serious moral fault with a view to the confession of sins in the sacrament of penance.

9. Cf. *Summa Theologiae*, I-II, q.90, a.4.
10. Cf. Genicot, vol.1, p.31; Prümmer, vol.1, p.104; Merkelbach, vol.1, pp. 222-4.
11. Cf. Prümmer, vol.1, p.104; and Merkelbach, vol.1, p.223.
12. Prümmer, vol.1, p. 98. Cf Zalba, vol.1, p.41.
13. Cf. Noldin, vol.1, pp. 41, 43, 45, 109; Prümmer, p.93; Genicot, pp. 38-40; Merkelbach, pp. 179-81.
14. Cf. Merkelbach, vol.1, p.238; Noldin, vol.1, pp.116-117; Carolus Boyer, *Cursus Philosophiae*, 2 vols., Desclée, Louvain, vol.1, p.495; Victor Cathrein, *Philosophia moralis*, Herder, Freiburg, 1907, p.149.
15. Cf. Merkelbach, vol.1, pp. 108, 121.
16. Cf. Noldin, vol.1, p.125.
17. Prümmer, vol.1, p.112; Hürth-Abellan, vol.1, p.39; Noldin, vol.1, p.125.
18. Cf. Prümmer writes: 'Solent omnes theologi distinguere ordinem naturalem et ordinem supernaturalem. Ordo naturalis intelligitur ille, qui propriis viribus naturalibus observari potest, et in quo ratio naturalis est suprema regula et norma actuum humanorum. Ordo supernaturalis est ille ordo, qui excedit vires humanas naturales...', vol.1, p.26. Vermeersch writes: 'Ratio autem naturalis, per se, solum ordinem naturae humanae proportionatum cognoscere potest. Quare lex naturalis circumscribitur illa parte legis aeternae quae ordinem ponit congruentem cum natura non elevata, ordinem igitur hypothetice, i.e. supposita creatione, necessrium...', vol.1, pp. 126-7. Cf. Noldin, vol.1, p.120; Genicot, vol.1, p.72; Hürth-Abellan, vol.1, pp. 30,31.
19. Zalba writes: 'Lex naturalis est divina creaturae rationalis in finem ultimum naturalem ordinatio, necessaria, in ipsa natura expressa, naturali lumine rationis percepta...', vol.1, p.228. Cf. Noldin, vol.1, p.120; Merkelbach, vol.1, p.226; Jorio, vol.1, p.109; Henry Davis, *Moral and Pastoral Theology*, 4 vols., third edition, Sheed and Ward, London, 1941, vol.1, pp. 124, 125.
20. Cf. Merkelbach, vol.1, p.228.
21. '...Lex revelata supernaturalis legem naturae non aufert sed complet...', Noldin, vol.1, p.125. Cf. Prümmer, vol.1, p.112; Zalba, vol.1, p.243.
22. Cf. Noldin, vol.1, p.127.
23. Cf. Noldin, vol.1, p. 127; Jorio, vol.1, p. 110; Davis, vol.1, p. 133; Hürth-Abellan, vol.1, p.42; Vermeersch, vol.1, p.205. So too Genicot, vol.1, p.74. So also Prümmer, vol.1, p.113: he points out that the new commandment of love is contained at least *quoad substantiam* in the natural law.

It should be noted that while the authors were clear that one's end was now supernatural this did not mean for them that one had to live a new or different content of morality. On this point Zalba writes: 'Conditiones certo requisitae ad actum supernaturalem sunt: (a) ut sit moraliter honestus; (b) ut a principio supernaturali proveniat. .... Actus debet esse

211

naturaliter seu ethice bonus...', vol.1, p.199. Cf. Noldin, vol.1, p.106. Some authors required a supernatural motive but, in effect, this was regarded as present in one who was in grace. Cf. Jorio, vol.1, p.54; Prümmer, vol.1, p.95; Genicot, vol.1, p.40;

24. Cf. note 8 above.

25. Cf. Merkelbach, vol.1, pp. 126, 130, 230; Noldin, vol.1, p.76; Zalba, vol.1, p.229. This was especially true of the moral philosophers. Cf. Cathrein, p. 145; Michael Cronin, *The Science of Ethics*, Gill, Dublin, 1909, p.597.

26. Suarez defined law as, 'actus voluntatis iustae et rectae quo superior vult inferiorem obligare ad hoc vel illud faciendum': cf. *Francisci Suarez Opera Omnia*, (ed. Carolus Berton), Vivés, Paris, 1866, De Legibus, lib.1, Ch.5, n.24. He required the intervention of God's will as a condition of moral obligation, 'quia lex naturae non indicat Deum ut praecipientem sed indicat quid in se bonum vel malum sit...': cf. ibidem, lib.2, ch.6, n.2.

Vasquez takes the opposite point of view: sins are forbidden, he says, 'non quidem prohibente aut iudicante Deus sed hoc ipso quod Deus talis est': cf. Gabriel Vasquez, *Commentariorum ac Disputionum in Primam Secundae Sancti Thomae*, Cardon, Lugduni, 1631, t.1, Disp.97, nn. 6, 9.

27. Noldin, vol.1, p.74. Cf. Zalba, vol.1, p.229; Davis, vol.1, pp. 36,37. The position was supported by Pius IX and Leo XIII. Cf. Denzinger-Schönmetzer, nn. 2903, 3247.

One author who disagrees with this general position is Merkelbach, vol.1, pp. 227, 231.

28. Cf. especially Merkelbach, vol.1, pp. 111 ff.; Prümmer, vol.1, p.70; Hürth-Abellan, vol.1, pp. 30-31; Zalba, vol.1, p.139.

29. Cf. Davis, vol.1, p.134; Prümmer, vol.1, p.115; Noldin, vol.1, p.129; I. Aertnys and C. Damen, *Theologia Moralis*, 2 vols., seventeenth edition, J. Visser, Marietti, Rome, 1956, vol.1, p.145. Merkelbach does not seem to agree, vol.1, p.285.

30. Cf. Aquinas, S.Th., I-II, q.100, a.8, ad 3; II-III, q.154, a.2, ad 2; Noldin, vol.1, p.124; Prümmer, vol.1, p.109; Genicot, vol.1, p.74; Zalba, vol.1, p.235; Merkelbach, vol.1, p.240; Aertnys-Damen, vol.1, p.142.

31. Cf. Zalba, vol.1, p.234; Merkelbach, vol. 1, p.241; Aertnys-Damen, vol.1, p.142.

32. Merkellbach says that by a miracle God can change the order of things: cf. vol.1, p.240.

33. G. Thilis, *Tendances, Actuelles en Théologie Morale*, Gembloux, Paris, 1940; Jacques Leclercq, *L'Enseignement de la Morale Chrétienne*, les Editions du Vitrail, Paris, 1949; Odon Lottin, *Au Coeur de la Morale Chrétienne*, Desclée, Bruxelles, 1957; Gerard Gilleman, *The Primacy of Charity in Moral Theology*, (English trans. W.R. Ryan and A. Vachon), Burns and Oates, London, 1959 (original French, *Le Primat de la Charité en Théologie Morale*, Desclée, Paris, 1952); Bernard Häring, *The Law of Christ*; Josef Fuchs, *Theologia Moralis Generalis*, Gregorian Univ. Press, Rome, 1960; Otto Schilling, *Grundriss de Moraltheologie*, 2nd edition, Herder, Freiburg, 1949; Philip Delhaye, 'La Theologie Morale d'hier et d'aujourd'hui', *Revue des Sciences Religieuses* 27 (1953) 112-30; Fritz Tillmann, 'Um eine katholische Sittenlehre', in Heinen/Höffner (eds.), *Menschenkunde im*

Dienste der Seelsorge und Erziehung (Festschrift für Th. Müncker), Trier, 1948, pp. 9-19.

34. Cf. Leclercq, *L'Enseignement* . . ., p.226; Tillmann, 'Um eine . . .', pp. 9, 17.

35. Cf. Delhaye, 'La Théologie Morale . . .', p. 130.

36. Cf. Tillmann, 'Um eine . . .', p.11: '. . . die herkömmlich allgemeine Moral . . . ein Gemisch von Philosophie, Psychologie, Jurisprudenz u.a. ist.'

37. Cf. Johannes Stelzenberger, *Lehrbuch der Moraltheologie*, Schöningh, Paderborn, 1965, pp. 17, 24: 'Ihr Ausgangspunkt liegt in der Offenbarung ... Moraltheologie Ohne Dogmatik is nicht zu denken . . . Ihr spezielle Gegenstand sind die sittlichen Inhalte der Offenbarung'; Leclercq, *L'Enseignement* . . ., p.19; L. Alonso-Schokel, 'L'Argument d'Écriture et théologie biblique dans l'enseignement theologique', *Nouvelle Revue Theologique* 81 (1959) 337-54.

38. Cf. Servais Pinckaers, *Le Renouveau de la Morale*, Casterman, Paris, 1964: 'Une dimension nous est révelée qui boulverse nos conceptions.' Cf. Tillmann, 'Um eine . . .', p.10: 'Erstens ist diese Sittenlehre wesensmässig von jeder nur natürlich, auf Vernunft, Erfahrung und Geschichte aufbauenden verschieden . . .'.

39. J.P. Audet, 'La Morale de l'Évangile'. *La Vie Spirituelle: Supplement* 4(1951) 153-70; Delhaye, 'L'Obligation morale dans les évangiles', *L'Ami du Clergé* 72(1962) 324-6; idem, 'L'Exigence chrétienne chez S.Paul' ibid., p.403.

40. Cf. Häring, *The Law of Christ*, vol.1, pp. viiff.; Rudolf Schnackenburg, 'Die neutestamentliche Sittenlehre in ihrer Eigenart im Vergleich zu einer natürlichen Ethik', in Stelzenberger (ed.), *Moraltheologie und Bibel*, Schöningh, Paderborn, 1964, pp. 39-69; Fuchs, 'Theologia moralis perficienda: votum Concillii Vaticani II', *Periodica de re Morali, Canonica, Liturgica* 55(1966) 499-548 (English version, 'Moral Theology According to Vatican II' in J. Fuchs, *Human Values and Christian Morality*, Gill and Macmillan, Dublin, 1970, pp. 1-55); Ceslaus Spicq, *Vie Morale et Trinité Sainte selon Saint Paul*, Cerf, Paris, 1957; Enda McDonagh, 'Moral Theology: The need for Renewal', in *Idem* (ed.), *Moral Theology Renewed*, Gill, Dublin, 1965; Delhaye, 'Le recours a l'Écriture sait dans l'enseignement de la théologie morale', *Bulletin des Facultés catholiques de Lyon* 19(1955)5-19; 20(1956)5-26; AA.VV., *Morale Chrétienne et Requetes Contemporaines*, Casterman, Tournai, 1954, especially Albert Descamps, 'La Morale des Synoptiques', pp. 27-46, F.M. Braun, 'Morale et Mystique á l'école de saint Jean, pp. 71-84, Ceslaus Spicq, 'La Morale Paulinienne', pp. 47-70.

41. Cf. Fuchs, *Human Values and Christian Morality*, p.28.

42. Cf. J. Etienne, 'Théologie morale et renouveau biblique', *Ephemerides Theologicae Louvanienses*, 40(1964) 232-41.

43. Cf. P. Hadrossek, *Die Bedeutung des Systemsdenkens für die Moraltheologie in Deutschland seit der Thomas-Renaissance* (Münchener theologische Studien), Karl Zink, München, 1950, pp. 354ff.; Stelzenberger, 'Reich Gottes bei den deutschen Moraltheologen 1800-1850', in idem (ed.), *Moraltheologie und Bibel*, pp. 70-98; Häring, *The Law of Christ*, vol.1, pp. 23ff.

44. Cf. Enda McDonagh, *Invitation and Response*, Gill and Macmillan, Dublin, 1972, p.1.
45. Cf. Spicq, *Théologie Morale du Nouveau Testament*, Gabalda, Paris, 1965; Schnackenburg, *The Moral Teaching of the New Testament* (English trans. Holland-Smith/O'Hara, Burns and Oates, London, 1965, from the 2nd revised German edition (original *Die sittliche Botschaft des Neuen Testaments*, Hueber, München, 1954); Stanislaus Lyonnet, 'Liberté chrétienne et loi de l'Esprit selon S.Paul', *Christus* 4(1954) 6-27;idem, *De Peccato et Redemptione*, Gregorian Univ. Press, Rome, 1957; Lyonnet and Ignace de la Potterie, *La Vie selon l'Esprit, condition du chrétien*, Cerf, Paris, 1964; Cf also Marcel Reding, *Der aufbau der christlichen Existenz*, Hueber, München, 1952; Engelbert Neuhäusler, *Anspruch und Antwort Gottes*, Patmos, Düsseldorf, 1962; AA.VV., 'Grandes Lignes de la Morale du Nouveau Testament', *Lumière et vie* (special number) 21(1955).
46. Dogmatic Constitution on Divine Revelation, in Walter Abbott (ed.), *The Documents of Vatican II*, Chapman, London-Dublin, 1966, p.127.
47. Decree on Priestly Formation, *ibid.*, pp. 451-2.
48. Cf. Fuchs, 'Die Liebe als Aufbauprinzip der Moraltheologie', *Scholastik* 29(1954)79-87; Franz Böckle, 'Bestrebungen in der Moraltheologie', in J. Feiner et al. (eds.), *Fragen der Theologie Heute*, Benziger, Einsiedeln 1958, pp.425-45; Rudolf Hofmann, *Moraltheologische Erkenntnis und Methodenlehre*, Hueber, München, 1963; Ernst Hirschbirch, *Die Entwicklung der Moraltheologie im Deutschen Sprachgebiet seit der Jahrhundertwende*, Bernina, Klosterneuburg, 1959; Klaus Demmer, *Sein und Gebot*, Schöningh, München, 1971, pp. 168ff.
49. Cf. Émile Mersch, *Morale et Corps Mystique*, Desclée, Bruxelles, 1949;Fuchs, *De Baptismo et Confirmatione*, Gregorian University Press, Rome, 1959; Joseph Ratzinger, *Die sakramentale Begründung christlicher Existenz*, Kyrios Freising, 1967; Ambrogio Valsecchi, *La 'Legge Nuova' del Cristiano secondo San Tommaso D'Aquino*, no publisher given, Varese, 1963; Edouard Hamel, *Loi Naturelle et Loi du Christ*, Desclée, Bruges-Paris, 1964; Häring, 'Die Stellung des Gesetzes in der Moraltheologie', in Virgil Redlich (ed.), *Moralprobleme im Umbruch der Zeit*, Hueber, München, 1957, pp. 135-52; Gottleib Söhngen, *Gesetz und Evangelium*, Alber, Freiburg/München, 1957. Stelzenberger's *Lehrbuch der Moraltheologie* takes the kingdom as its central theme. He defines moral theology as 'die wissenschaftliche Darstellung der Sittlichkeitslehre der Königherrschaft Gottes', p.17.
50. Cf. Gustav Ermecke, 'Die Stufen der sakramentalen Christusbildlichkeit als Einteilungsprinzip der speziellen Moral' in T. Steinbüchel and T. Müncker (eds.), *Aus Theologie und Philosophie* (Festschrift für Fritz Tillmann), Patmos, Düsseldorf, 1950, p.36; cf. R. Hoffman, *Moraltheologische Erkenntnis und Methodenlehre*, pp. 81, 82, 89.
51. J. van der Meersch, art. 'Grace', *Dictionnaire de Théologie Catholique*, t.6, cols.1609-12. Journet puts it: 'There are, then, two universes. First of all the *universe of natures*: the nature of a mineral, of a plant, of an animal, of a man — animated body, incarnate soul. . . . But God does not leave us in that condition. . . . That is the mystery of the elevation of our nature by grace, and that is why we call this new life *super natural.*' Charles Journet,

The Meaning of Grace, (English trans. A.V. Littledale), Chapman, London, 1960, p.8.

52. 'A l'ontologie surnaturelle qui a le Christ comme centre, correspond done une vie morale christique...', *Tendances Actuelles en Théologie Morale*, p.18.

53. *Au Coeur de la Morale Chrétienne*, p.47.

54. Joseph Mausbach, *Katholische Moraltheologie*, ninth edition revised by Gustav Ermecke, Aschendorff, Münster, 1959, pp. 11, 14.

55. 'Die aus der Ontologie des christlichen Seins sich ergebenden Grundgesetze der Fundamentalmoral...', ibid., p.16.

56. Cf. ibid., p.71.

57. 'Die Heilige Schrift enthält die Grundgedanken der Sittlichkeit mit voller Klarheit', Ibid., p.44.

58. CF. *Human Values and Christian Morality*, p.5. Cf. pp. 4, 14, 43; cf. idem, *Theologia Moralis Generalis*, vol.1, pp. 68, 76, 102; idem, *Natural Law: A Theological Approach* (English trans. Reckter/Dowling), Gill, Dublin, 1965, pp. 43, 51, 54.

59. Cf. *Fundamental Concepts of Moral Theology* (English trans. William Jerman), Paulist Press, New York, 1968, pp.3, 4, 23. Cf. pp. 18, 20, 22.

60. Cf. *The Law of Christ,* vol.1, pp. 36, 229, 233-35, 257-58; vol.2, pp. 3, 354.

61. 'L'Obligation morale dans les évangiles', *L'Ami du Clergé* 72(1962), p.328.

62. Cf. L. B. Gillon, *Christ and the Moral Life* (English trs. Cornelius Williams), Alba, New York, 1967, p.95.
      Cf. also Spicq, *Théologie Morale du Nouveau Testament*, vol.2 especially pp. 756-61.

63. *Principes de Morale*, Editions de l'Abbaye du Mont Cesar, Louvain, 1947, vol.1, p.309.

64. Ibid., p.29. Karl Rahner wrote about the notion of grace with which these theologians were working at this time as follows: 'Supernatural grace is a reality which we know about from the teaching of the faith but which is completely outside our experience.... We make up from the elements of our natural powers, habits etc. those acts in which we intentionally direct ourselves towards God's revealed mysteries and which we know to be "essentially" (but only "essentially") supernaturally raised.' *Nature and Grace*, (English trans. Dinah Wharton), Sheed and Ward, London, 1963, pp.4, 6-7.

65. While the neo-Scholastic moralists recognised a sharp distinction between nature and grace they did not propose a new Christian morality: the content of morality for them was essentially natural law.

66. 'Die Stufen...', p.44.

67. Cf. Fuchs, *Human Values and Christian Morality*, p.43.

68. Cf. Ermeeke, 'Die Stufen...', p.38.

69. Cf. Stelzenberger, *Lehrbuch der Moraltheologie*, p.22. Cf. Tillmann: 'Eine christ-katholische Sittenlehre besitzt ein eigenes Ziel, eigene Aufgaben, und die zu ihrer Lösung notwendigen Kräfte, die einer nur natürlichen Sittenlehre grundsätzlich und für immer fremd sind', 'Um eine katholische Sittenlehre', p.10.

70. Cf. Lottin, *Au Coeur de la Morale Chrétienne*, p.54; Ermecke, 'Die Stufen...', pp. 43-4; Stelzenberger, *Lehrbuch der Moraltheologie*, p.70.
71. Cf. *Katholische Moraltheologie*, vol.1, pp. 32-3.
72. Cf. *Theologia Moralis Generalis*, vol.1, p.98.
73. Cf. *An Coeur de la Morale Chrétienne*, p.125, also pp. 49-51, 125-7.
74. Cf. Mausbach, *Katholische Moraltheologie*, p.32; Lottin, *Au Coeur de la Morale Chrétienne*, pp. 55, 125; Fuchs, *Human Values and Christian Morality*, p.3; Stelzenberger, *Lehrbuch der Moraltheologie*, pp.21; Häring, *The Law of Christ*, pp.35ff.
75. Cf. Lottin, *Au Coeur de la Morale Chrétienne*, pp. 55ff.; Fuchs, *Human Values and Christian Morality*, pp. 16ff., 62, 69; Thils, *Tendances Actuelles en Théologie Morale*, pp. 40ff., 87ff.; Spicq, *Vie Morale et Trinité Sainte*, pp. 23, 31, 37, 41; Häring, *The Law of Christ*, pp. 36ff.
76. Cf. Spicq, *Vie Morale et Trinité Sainte*, pp. 37, 41; Pinckaers, *Le Renouveau de la Morale*, p.39; Leclereq, *L'Enseignement de la Morale Chrétienne*, p.14; Fuchs, *Human Values and Christian Morality*, pp. 76ff.; Idem, *Theologia Moralis Generalis*, vol.1, pp. 29ff.; Böckle, *Fundamental Concepts of Moral Theology*, pp. 22-5.
77. *Katholische Moraltheologie*, p.5.
78. Cf. *Theologia Moralis Generalis*, vol.1, p. 38.
79. Cf. *The Law of Christ*, vol.1, pp. 35, 39, 47, 92; vol.2, p.123.
80. Cf. *Christ and the Moral Life*, p.51. Cf. also Stelzenberger, *Lehrbuch der Moraltheologie*, pp. 69, 129.
81. Cf. *Tendances Actuelles en Théologie Morale*, pp. 149-50.
82. Gilleman, *The Primacy of Charity in Moral Theology*; idem, 'Théologie morale et charité', *Nouvelle Revue Theologique* 84 (1952) 806-20; idem, 'Morale chrétienne en notre temps: psyche, penuma, agape', *Lumière et Vie* 50 (1960) 55-81; René Carpentier, 'Vers une morale de la charité', *Gregorianum* 34 (1953) 32-55; idem, Le primat de l'amour dans la vie morale', *Nouvelle Revue Theologique* 93 (1961) 3-24; idem, 'Le primat de la charité en morale surnaturelle', ibid., pp.255-70; idem, 'Le primat de l'amour-charité comme méthode de théologie morale, ibid., pp. 492-509.
83. Cf. McDonagh, 'The Primacy of Charity' in McDonagh (ed.), *Moral Theology Renewed*, pp. 130-50; Fuchs, *Theologia Moralis Generalis*, vol.1, pp. 106ff.; Hamel, *Loi Naturelle et Loi du Christ*, p.163.
84. Cf. *The Primacy of charity*, pp. xxi-xxxviii.
85. Ibid., p.xxiv.
86. Cf. Aquinas, S.Th., I-II, qq.1-3,26-7; II.II, qq.23-7.
87. '...moral life can be defined only by reference to charity' *The Primacy of Charity*, p.279. Cf. pp. 8, 101-2, 144, 148. Cf. Carpentier, 'Le primat de l'amour-charité...', pp. 492-3, 498.
88. *The Primacy of Charity*, p.9.
89. Ibid., p.35. Cf. p.178. Aquinas says: 'nulla vera virtus potest esse sine caritate', II-II, q.23, a.7.
90. '...charity-love, and thus the ultimate end, is already present in the essence and definition of the particular virtues which, nevertheless, preserve their proper nature',ibid., p.39.
   'The moral act is at once the exercise of the virtue of charity and the

exercise of particular virtues', ibid., p.181. Cf. pp. 11, 14, 34, 172, 174, 177. Cf. Gilleman, 'Morale chrétienne en notre temps...', p.73.

91. Cf. Gilleman, *The Primacy of Charity*, pp. 8. 11, 14. Carpentier shows here a sharp distinction of baptised and non-baptised: he says that such natural love of the end exists also in the pagan, 'là où la grâce n'existerait pas', 'Le Primat de la charité...', p.257.

92. 'Such is the range of our love of charity, which is "super-love"', Gilleman, *The Primacy of Charity*, p.157. Cf. pp. 16ff., 156ff. Note the significance of the titles of Carpentier's articles. He says of his article, 'Le primat de la charité...': 'Les pages qui suivent transposent ce primat de l'amour au plan surnaturel où la charité est notre volonté divinisé', p.255.

93. Cf. Gilleman, *The Primacy of Charity*, pp. 21, 156, 183; Carpentier, 'Le primat de la charité...', p.257.

94. S.Th., II-II, q.23, a.8, corpus, ad 2, ad 3; Gilleman, *The Primacy of Charity*, pp. 29ff.

95. *The Primacy of Charity*, pp. xxxvi, 204.

96. There is some obscurity in what Gilleman is proposing and in its significance for moral living. On the one hand he seems to be offering an ontological explanation of the moral action of the pagan and of the Christian — the finality which is present whether one adverts to it or not. Cf. *The Primacy of Charity*, pp. 21, 93, 156, 183. On the other hand he is suggesting that one's ontological tendency towards God should be made as conscious as possible in one's moral life:
'We find here an invitation to harmonise our psychology with our profound ontology.' Ibid., p.185.
'This theology is essentially personalising, for it transforms all moral life into an exchange between persons.' Ibid., p.96.
'It pre-exists ontologically, but becomes truly human only if we freely ratify it...', Ibid., p.148.
'Moral life...consists in ever preparing an act of perfect charity.' Ibid., p.279. Cf. Gilleman, 'La morale chrétienne en notre temps...', p.73.

97. *The Primacy of Charity*, p.186.

98. Ibid., p.xxxii.
Gilleman identifies moral obligation as the obligation to obey the inherent tendency to the ultimate end — making the transition from the ontological to the ethical order without comment. He says: 'It follows that the most authentic obligation is love, that nothing is more fundamentally obligatory than love, and that all moral obligation derives its absolute character from what we might call our built-in necessity for loving, which God constantly impresses in our being.' *The Primacy of Charity*, p. 255; Cf. 'Morale chrétienne en notre temps...', p.74; Cf. Carpentier, 'Le primat de l'amour-charité...', p.497. Gilleman does not make clear whether this obligation refers to the 'bonitas prima' — the ontological finality of the act — or to the active direction of one's moral life to God in charity.

99. Cf. *The Primacy of Charity*, pp. 221-2; Carpentier, 'Le primat de la charité...', p.255.

100. Gilleman, *The Primacy of Charity*, p.xxv; cf. pp. 195, 211; idem, 'Morale chrétienne en notre temps...', p.73.
101. *The Primacy of Charity*, p.176. Carpentier writes: 'Il y trouve un ordre des choses crée par Dieu et auquel il doit se soumettre...en pleine conformité avec la loi', 'Vers une morale de la charité', p.49. It is not clear to what law he is referring or what is the source of morality for him. Cf. Fuchs: 'Quod autem caritatem exprimere, ideoque per eam in finem ultimum dirigi possunt, hoc habent ex intrinseca sua conformitate cum recta ratione, resp. cum voluntate creatrice Dei', *Theologia Moralis Generalis*, p.107. Cf. McDonagh, *Moral Theology Renewed*, p.147.
102. Cf. *The Primacy of Charity*, pp. 198, 203-4; Carpentier, 'Le primat de la charité...', p.256; idem, 'Le primat de l'amour-charité...', p.505.
103. *The Primacy of Charity*, pp. 183-4.
104. Ibid., pp. 221-2.
105. Ibid., pp. 221-2
106. Cf. for example his treatment of Christian justice, ibid., pp. 337-8. Carpentier tells us that Christian justice gets beyond a static rational notion, beyond irreducible altereity and sees the other as a son of God, whereas the pagan notion is blind to the personal element, cf. 'Le primat de la charité...', p.506. Cf. also Gillon, *Christ and the Moral Life*, p.129.
107. Note Carpentier's remark: '[St. Thomas] suppose une vue pratique audacieuse, dont la foi chrétienne nous certifiera la verité: l'identification de la vie morale et de la vie religieuse', 'Le primat de l'amour...', p.23.
108. Cf. Gilleman, *The Primacy of Charity*, pp. xxx, xxxii.
109. Fritz Tillmann, *Handbuch der katholischen Sittenlehre*, vol. III, *Die Katholische Sittenlehre, Die Idee der Nachfolge Christi*; vol. IV, *Die Verwirklichung der Nachfolge Christi*, fourth edition, Patmos. Düsseldorf, 1953. Much of Tillmann's writings was done in the thirties. But it was in the forties and fifties that his influence began to be felt and new editions of his work appeared. A shorter work of his, first published in 1937 with a new edition in 1948 has been translated into English, *The Master Calls*, (English trans. Gregory J. Roettger), Helicon, Baltimore, 1960. Cf. also the 1948 article by Tillmann, 'Um eine katholische Sittenlehre' already cited.
110. 'Eine katholische Sittenlehre kann ihrem Wesen nach nichts anderes sein als eine wissenschaftliche Erarbeitung und Darstellung des christlich-sittlichen Lebens, seiner Aufgaben und Pflichten, wie sie in der übernatürlichen Offenbarung, näherhin in der Lehrverkündigung des Herrn enthalten sind...die einer nur natürlichen Sittenlehre grundsätzlich und für immer fremd sind.' 'Um eine katholische Sittenlehre', p.10.
111. *Die Idee der Nachfolge Christi*, Foreword.
112. *Die Idee der Nachfloge Christi*, p.9. Note the title of chapter 2: 'Die übernatürliche Grundlegung und die übernatürliche Kräfte der Nachfolge Christi.' Cf. 'Um eine katholische Sittenlehre' where the expression 'Glaubenswissenschaft' occurs several times.
113. *Die Idee der Nachfolge Christi*, p.20.
114. 'Um eine katholische Sittenlehre', pp. 12, 13.
115. *Die Idee der Nachfolge Christi*, p.9.
116. Ibid., p.49.

117. Ibid., pp. 46ff.
118. 'Die Idee der christlichen, an der Person Jesu normierten Persönlichkeit ist jedoch nicht nur der Inhalt der katholischen Sittenlehre, sie ist zugleich auch das was man theologisch das Moralprinzip zu nennen pflegt...', ibid., p.12. He says that Christ is 'Vorbild und Nachbild, Norm und Wert, Sollen und Sein, Idee und Leben', ibid., p.9. Man has a new being (*Daseinsform*) 'eine neue Seins-und Lebensordnung', ibid., p.95.
119. Cf. ibid., pp. 46ff.; idem, 'Um eine katholische Sittenlehre', pp. 10, 13.
120. *die Idee der Nachfolge Christi*, p.48. Cf. p.49.
121. 'Sie offenbart sofort ihren urtümlichen christlichen Inhalt und deckt damit ihren wesensmässigen Unterschied von jeder anderen Sittenlehre auf...', 'Um cine katholische Sittenlehre', p.13. Cf. *Die Idee der Nachfolge Christi*, p.22.
122. It should be noted that, in contrast to the neo-Scholastics, Tillmann proposes the highest perfection for every Christian: he regards moral, ascetical and mystical theology as one. Cf. *Die Idee der Nachfolge Christi*, pp.323, 326, 327.
123. Ibid., p.143; Cf. pp. 14ff.
124. Cf. ibid., p.152.
125. Ibid., p.18. Cf. pp. 138ff.
126. Tillmann says: 'Was die Entfaltung der christlichen Persönlichkeit gemäss ihren Vorbild fördert ist gut, was sie hemmt oder gar zerstört ist bös', ibid., p.12.
127. Cf. 'Um eine katholische Sittenlehre', p. 10. Cf. note 79 above.
128. *Moraltheologische Erkenntnis-und Methodenlehre*, pp. 236ff., 246ff.
129. Ibid., p.252.
130. Cf. ibid., p.251.
131. Cf. ibid., pp. 82, 89, 165, 166.
132. Cf. ibid., p.102:'Ihren eigenlichen Gegenstand empfangt die Moraltheologie wie jede Theologie aus dem Glauben....'
133. Scripture is the *Erkenntnisquelle*. There must be 'eine umfassende biblische Grundlegung der gesamten moraltheologischen Arbeit', ibid., p.134. The New Testament is the immediately available source of moral knowledge — 'die unmittelbarste und vorzüglichste Quellenschrift der moraltheologischen Erkenntnis', ibid., p.139.
134. Cf.ibid., p.227.
135. Cf. ibid., pp. 80, 159-60, 229.
136. Cf. ibid., p.141.
137. Cf. ibid., pp. 90, 159, 246.
138. Cf. ibid., p.159.
139. Cf. 'The Natural Law and the Law of Christ' in A. Scheuermann and G. May (eds.), *Ius Sacrum: Klaus Morsdorf zum 60 Geburtstag*, Schöningh, München, 1968.
140. Cf. 'The Law of Christ' in McDonagh (ed.), *Moral Theology Renewed*, pp. 72ff. Cf. idem, *Human Values and Christian Morality*, pp. 6, 7, 15.
141. Cf. Fuchs, 'The Law of Christ', in *Moral Theology Renewed*, pp. 72-5; McDonagh, 'The Natural Law and the Law of Christ' in *Ius Sacrum*, p.73.

142. Fuchs, 'The Law of Christ', p.74.
143. Cf. McDonagh, 'The Natural Law and the Law of Christ', p.71.
144. McDonagh, 'The Natural Law and the Law of Christ', p.75.
145. Fuchs, 'The Law of Christ', pp. 76-7; Cf. Idem, *Human Values and Christian Morality*, p.5.
146. Cf. McDonagh, 'The Natural Law and the Law of Christ', p.75; Fuchs, 'The Law of Christ', p.79.
147. Cf. McDonagh, 'The Natural Law and the Law of Christ', p.69.
148. Cf. Spicq, *Vie Morale et Trinité Sainte*, pp. 21ff., 33ff.
149. Cf. Spicq, *Théologie Morale du Nouveau Testament*, vol.2, pp. 761ff.
150. Cf. Spicq, *Vie Morale et Trinité Sainte*, pp. 41ff.
151. Cf Tillmann, *Die Idee der Nachfolge Christi*, p.49.
152. *The Law of Christ*, vol.2, p.xxi.
153. Ibid., vol.3, p.414.
154. Ibid., vol.3, p.548.
155. Ibid., vol.3, p.563.   156. Ibid., vol.3, p.315.   157. Ibid., vol.3, p.316.
158. Ibid., vol.3, p.316.   159. Ibid., vol.1, p.viii.   160. Ibid., vol.3, p.7.
161. James P. Mackey, *Life and Grace*, Gill, Dublin, 1966, p.87.
162. McDonagh wrote in 1979: 'After some twenty years of intensive activity by the professionals, the quest for a renewed moral theology remains unfinished and confused.' Cf. *Doing the Truth: The Quest for Moral Theology*, Gill and Macmillan, Dublin, 1979, p.14.

Chapter 2
(pp. 37-66)

1. Josef Fuchs, *Human Values and Christian Morality*, Gill and Macmillan, Dublin, 1970 (trs. Heelan/McRedmond/Young/Watson).
2. Bruno Schüller, 'Die Bedeutung des natürlichen Sittengesetzes für den Christen' in Georg Teichtweier and Wilhelm Dreier (eds.), *Herausforderung und Kritik der Moraltheologie*, Echter Verlag, Würzburg, 1971, p.191.
3. Alfons Auer, *Autonome Moral und christlicher Glaube*, Patmos, Düsseldorf, 1971, p.27.
4. Gerard J. Hughes, 'A Christian Basis for Ethics', *The Heythrop Journal* 13 (1972), P.43.
5. Cf. Tillmann, ch.1, note 79.
6. Cf. Fuchs, 'The Law of Christ' in McDonagh (ed.), *Moral Theology Renewed*, pp. 76ff.
7. Auer says: 'Neben der Glaubensethik haben wir die Position einer "autonomen Moral im christlichen Kontext".' Cf. Alfons Auer, 'Die Bedeutung des Christlichen bei der Normfindung' in Joseph Sauer (ed.), *Normen im Konflikt*, Herder, Freiburg, 1977, p.33.
8. Franz Böckle, *Fundamentalmoral*, Kösel, München, 1977, p.16. English

translation *Fundamental Moral Theology*, (trans. N.D. Smith), Gill and Macmillan, Dublin (hereafter *Fundamental...*).

9. Cf. Auer, 'Die Bedeutung des Christlichen...' in Sauer (ed.), *Normen im Konflikt*, p.34; Fuchs, 'Autonome Moral und Glaubensethik' in Dietmar Mieth and Francesco Compagnoni (eds.), *Ethik im Kontext des Glaubens*, Herder, Freiburg, 1978, pp. 47ff., 68; Sergio Bastianel, *Il Carattere Specifico della Morale Cristiana*, Cittadella Editrice, Assisi, 1975, p.45; Francesco Compagnoni, *La Specificità della Morale Cristiana*, Dehoniane, Bologna, 1972, pp.21-3; Theo Beemer, 'The Interpretation of Moral Theology', *Concilium* 5(1969), p.62.

10. Auer says that the obligation of moral norms must be seen to come from their inner rationality ('von der inneren Vernünftigkeit'): cf. 'Die Bedeutung...', p.34. Böckle says that they must be understandable ('aud der sittlichen Vernunft auch selbstverständlich'): cf. 'Möglichkeiten einer dynamischen Sexualmoral' in idem (ed.), *Menschliche Sexualität und kirchliche Sexualmoral*, Patmos Düsseldorf, 1977, p.128. Cf. also Böckle, *Fundamentalmoral*, p.292; Wilhelm Korff, *Theologische Ethik: Eine Einführung*, Herder, Freiburg, 1975, pp. 32-9.

11. Abbot (ed.), *The Documents of Vatican II*, pp. 233-4.

12. Cf. Karl rahner. *Mission and Grace*, (trans. Cecily Hastings), Sheed and Ward, London, vol.1, pp. 110-11.

13. Cf. Yves Congar, *Lay People in the Church*, (trans. Donald Attwater), Chapman, London, 1957, pp. 18-19.

14 Cf. M.D. Chenu, *The Theology of Work* (trans. L. Soiron), Gill, Dublin, 1963, p.20. Cf. also Edward Schillebeeckx, *Vatican II: Struggle of Minds*, Gill, Dublin, 1963, pp. 46ff.; P. Teilhard de Chardin, *Le Milieu Divin* (trans. Bernard Wall et al.), Collins, London, 1960, pp. 49ff.

15. Cf. Schillebeeckx, *World and Church* (trans. N.D. Smith), Sheed and Ward, New York, 1971, p.105; idem, *God the Future of Man* (trans. Smith), Sheed and Ward, London and New York, 1969, pp. 146ff.

16. Cf. especially Johannes B. Metz, *Theology of the World* (trans. William Glen-Doepel), Burns and Oates, London, 1969, pp. 41ff., 65ff.; Rahner, 'The Man of To-day and Religion', *Theological Investigations*, v.6 (trans. Karl-H. and Boniface Kruger), Darton, Longman and Todd, London, 1969, pp 3ff. Cf. also Fuchs, *Human Values and Christian Morality*, p.164.

17. 'Gibt es eine spezifisch christliche Moral?' *Stimmen der Zeit* 95 (1970), p.103. Cf. the sharp reply by Philip Delhaye, 'La mise en cause de la spécificité de la morale chrétienne', *Revue Théologique de Louvain* 4(1975), pp. 308-39. The originals of Fuchs's articles have appeared in different languages. My references are generally to the original. Apart from *Human Values and Christian Morality* two other collections have appeared in English translation, *Personal Responsibility and Christian Morality* (1983) and *Christian Ethics in a Secular Arena* (1984) both published by Georgetown Univ. Press, Washington, D.C. and Gill and Macmillan, Dublin. There is also a useful collection in Italian, *Sussidi per lo studio della Teologia Morale Fondamentale* (no publisher, n.d.).

18. *Human Values and Christian Morality*, pp. 121-2.

19. Ibidem, p.122, footnote 4.

20. 'Esiste Una Morale Non-Cristiana?' *Sussidi*, p.336.

21. 'Autonome Moral und Glaubensethik' in Mieth-Compagnoni (eds.), p.65.

22. He says that he excludes from the term 'human morality' or 'morality of man as man' everything that we know only from God's revelation about man as he is. Cf. *Human Values and Christian Morality*, p.114. We shall see that Fuchs was vague about this term in the following years but that he finally clarified it. Cf. note 107, below.

23. Cf. ibidem, pp. 50, 60; 'Esiste Una Morale Non-Cristiana?', p.331.

24. Cf. 'Esiste Una Morale Non-Cristiana?', *Sussidi*, p.332.

25. Cf. ibidem, p.332; 'Gibt es eine spezifisch christliche Moral?', p.107.

26. Cf. *Human Values and Christian Morality*, p.125.

27. Cf. 'Autonome Moral...' in Mieth-Compagnoni, p.47. The issue is of considerable practical importance: Fuchs says that his article was occasioned by *Humanae Vitae*. Cf. 'Gibt es...', p.99.

28. Cf. ibid., p.65; 'Formule Morali Male Intese', *Sussidi*, p.369.

29. Cf. *Human Values and Christian Morality*, pp. 123ff.

30. Ibid., p.160. Cf. p.124: 'This Christian intentionality is what makes the moral behaviour of the Christian truly and specifically Christian.''

31. Cf. 'Autonome Moral...' in Mieth-Compagnoni, p.67: 'im strengen Sinne ein Mehr *nicht primär* sittlicher, sondern religiösder Art.....'

32. Cf. 'Gibt es...', p.110; 'Autonome Moral...' in Mieth-Compagnoni, p.66.

33. Cf. *Human Values and Christian Morality*, p.168; 'Esiste Una Morale Non-Cristiana?', *Sussidi*, p. 333.

34. *Human Values and Christian Morality*, p.125.

35. Cf. ibid., p.126: '... the ideal of Christian virginity can only be understood and accepted by someone who conceives the human situation in accordance with a complete Christian anthropology.'

36. Cf. ibid., pp. 119, 123, 164-6.

37. Cf. 'Autonome Moral...' in Mieth-Compagnoni, p.51; *Human Values and Christian Morality*, pp. 129, 131; *Christian Ethics in a Secular Arena*, pp. 12ff.

38. *Human Values and Christian Morality*, p.154.

39. 'Esiste Una Morale Non-Cristiana?', *Sussidi*, p.334.

40. Ibid., p.331.

41. Cf. *Autonome Moral und christlicher Glaube*, Patmos, Düsseldorf, 1971, p.160 (hereafter *Autonome Moral...*); 'Tendenzen heutiger theologischer Ethik' in Bitter/Müller (eds.), *Konturen heutiger Theologie*, p.314 (hereafter 'Tendenzen...').

42. Cf. 'Die Bedeutung des Christlichen bei der Normfindung' in Joseph Sauer (ed.), *Normen im Konflikt* (hereafter 'Die Bedeutung...'), pp. 37-8.

43. Cf. 'Tendenzen...', p.321;*Autonome Moral...*, p.27; 'Ein Modell theologischethischer Argumentation: "Autonome Moral"' in Auer/Biesinger/Gutschera (eds.), *Moralerziehung im Religionsunterricht*, Herder, Freiburg, 1975, p.42 (hereafter 'Ein Modell...'); 'Autonome Moral und christlicher Glaube', *Katechetische Blätter* 102(1977), p.60 (hereafter 'Autonome Moral...').

44. Cf. *Autonome Moral...*, p.161: 'Der Inhalt der christlichen Moral ist menschlich und nicht unterscheidend christlich....' Cf. 'Die

Bedeutung...', p.38: 'Der Christ ist Mensch wie jeder andere auch, er hat kein eigenes Einmalsein.... Das Menschliche ist menschlich für die Heiden wie für die Christen.'

45. Cf. *Autonome Moral*..., p.30; 'Autonome Moral...', p.61.

46. Cf. 'Ein Modell...', p.50.

47. Cf. *Autonome Moral*..., p.188; 'Ein Modell...', p.43.

48. Cf. 'Die Bedeutung...', pp. 39-42; 'Tendenzen...', pp. 320-321 and especially Auer's article, 'Die Autonomie des Sittlichen nach Thomas von Aquin' in Demmer/Schüller (eds.), *Christlich Glauben and Handeln*, Patmos, Düsseldorf, 1977, pp. 31-54.

49. Cf. 'Tendenzen...', p.321: also *Autonome Moral*..., pp. 177ff.; 'Autonome Moral...', p.61; 'Ein Modell...', p.46; 'Die Bedeutung...', pp. 42-9.

50. Cf. *Autonome Moral*..., pp. 177ff.; 'Tendenzen...', p.323: 'Ein Modell...', pp. 46ff.; 'Autonome Moral...', pp. 62ff.; 'Die Bedeutung...', pp. 45-6; 'Die Ethische Relevanz der Botschaft Jesu' in Auer/Biesinger/Gutschera (eds.), op.cit., pp. 75ff.

51. Cf. 'Tendenzen...', p.323: 'Es geht immer nur um "relationale Autonomie"'.

52. Cf. *Autonome Moral*..., p.177: 'Der Christ muss sich in den Bereichen der Welt genau so verhalten wie der Heide....'

53. Cf. 'Ein Modell...', p.48; 'Autonome Moral...', p.63; 'Tendenzen...', p.323; 'Die Bedeutung ...', pp. 45-6.

54. Cf. *Autonome Moral*..., p.178. Auer understands by natural or human morality what is available to the non-believer, to reason without faith. He distinguishes sharply between reason and faith. In 'Die Bedeutung...' having made the point that the discovery of norms is a matter of reason ('in einer vernünftigen Prozedur') he asks rhetorically: who then is competent for the determination of such norms, faith or reason, the church or the human community ('der Glaube oder die Vernunft, die Kirche oder die Gesellschaft')? Cf. p.38.

55. Cf. 'Die Ethische...', pp. 67ff.

56. Cf. 'Ein Modell...', p.51; *Autonome Moral*..., p.193.

57. Cf. *Autonome Moral*..., p.178: 'eine neue Kraft der Motivation'.

58. Cf. *Autonome Moral*..., pp. 173ff.; 'Tendenzen...', p.321; 'Autonome Moral...', p.61; 'Ein Modell...', p.42; 'Die Bedeutung...', pp. 45-9.

59. Cf. *Autonome Moral*..., p.194.

60. Cf. 'Tendenzen...', p.321; 'Ein Modell...', p.31; 'Autonome Moral...', p.69.

61. Cf. 'Tendenzen...', p.321.

62. Cf. 'Ein Modell...', p.52; *Autonome Moral*..., p.197.

63. Cf. 'Tendenzen..., p.321; 'Die Bedeutung...', p.42; *Autonome Moral*..., p.102.

64. Cf. Dietmar Mieth, 'Autonome Moral im Christlichen Kontext', *Orientierung* 40(1976) 31-34; idem, 'Norma Morale e Autonomia dell'Uomo: Problema della Legge Morale Naturale e sua Relazione con la legge Nuova' in Tullo Goffi (ed.), *Problemi e Prospettive di Teologia Morale*, Queriniana, Brescia, 1976, pp. 173-97; Franz Furger, 'Zur Begründung eines christlichen Ethos:Forschungstendenzen in der

katholischen Moraltheologie' in idem (ed.), *Theologische Berichte* IV, Benziger, Einsiedeln, 1974, pp. 11-48; Wilhelm Korff, *Theologische Ethik: Eine Einführung*, Herder, Freiburg, 1975.

65. Bruno Schüller, 'Typen ethischer Argumentation in der katholischen Moraltheologie', *Theologie und Philosophie* 45(1970), p.526 (hereafter *TuP*).

66. Cf. 'Zur theologischen Diskussion uber die lex naturalis', *TuP* 41(1966), p.500 (hereafter 'Zur theologischen Diskussion...'); 'Die Bedeutung des natürlichen Sittengesetzes für den Christen' in Teichtweier/Dreier (eds.), *Herausforderung und Kritik der Moraltheologie*, Echter, Würzburg, 1971, p.105 (hereafter 'Die Bedeutung...'). Cf. 'Wieweit kann die Moraltheologie das Naturrecht entbehren?', *Lebendiges Zeugnis* 20 (1965), p.42.

67. Cf. 'Wieweit...', pp. 52, 65; 'Zur theologischen Diskussion...', p.493; Mieth, 'Autonome Moral...', p.31.

68. Cf. 'Wieweit...', p.50; 'Die Bedeutung...', pp. 110-12; cf. Korff, *Op.cit.*, pp.13, 33; Furger, *Op.cit.*, pp. 15, 24ff.

69. Cf. 'Zur Diskussion um das Problem einer christlichen Ethik', *TuP* 51 (1976), pp. 331-2 (hereafter 'Zur Diskussion um das Problem...'). (An English translation is given in C. Curran and R. McCormick (eds.), *Readings in Moral Theology no. 2*, Paulist, New York, 1980, pp. 207-33.)

70. *Ibidem*, p.338; 'Die Bedeutung...', pp. 117-18. Cf. Mieth, 'Norma Morale...', p.195.

71. Cf. 'Die Bedeutung...', p.106; Mieth, 'Autonome Moral..., p.31; Korff, *Op.cit.*, pp. 34-9.

72. Cf. 'Die Bedeutung...', p.115; 'Wieweit...', p.51; Mieth, 'Norma Morale...', pp. 192-3.

73. Cf. 'Die Bedeutung...', pp. 115-17; 'Zur theologischen Diskussion...', p.493.

74. The papers were published as a special number of *La Vie Spirituelle: Le Supplement* 92(1970) entitled 'L'Éthique Chrétienne à la recherche de son Identité.'

75. Cf. J. Jullien, 'Nouvelles Orientations en théologie morale. Reflexions sur la méthode', pp. 113-14, ibidem, pp. 113-14.

76. Cf. the contribution of Manaranche as reported by Simon, 'Panorama de questions et de reponses,' ibidem, pp. 47-54.

77. Cf. J.M. Aubert, 'La spécificité de la morale chrétienne selon saint Thomas', *Ibidem*, pp. 69-70: 'Donc l'agir moral du chrétien (en dehors de la sphère cultuelle et sacramentelle) ne se manifeste pas essentiellement par des actes qui lui seraient propres: "materialiter" ils lui sont communs avec les autres hommes. ... Le spécifique chrétien est ailleurs.' Cf. also p. 72.

78. Cf. R. Simon, 'Spécificité de l'Éthique Chrétienne', ibidem, p.86.

79. Cf. idem, 'Théologie Morale et Atheisme', *Recherches de Science Religieuse* 59(1971); idem, *Fonder la Morale*, Editions du Seuil, Paris, 1974, p.187: '...les Eglises se placent sur un terrain qui leur est commun avec l'ensemble de l'humanité. ...'

80. Cf. Edward Schillebeeckx, *God and Man* (English trans. N.D. Smith), Sheed and Ward, London, 1969, pp. 272-3; idem, *God the Future of Man*

(English trans. N.D. Smith), Sheed and Ward, London, 1969, p.196.
81. Cf. *God and Man*, pp. 272-3.
82. Cf. Conrad van Ouwerkerk, 'Gospel Morality and Human Compromise', *Concilium* 1(1965)5-12; idem, 'Secularism and Christian Ethics: Some Types and Symptoms', ibid., 3(1967)47-67; Theo Beemer, 'The Interpretation of Moral Theology', ibid., 5(1969)62-72; Josef Blank, 'New Testament Morality and Modern Moral Theology', ibid., 3(1967)6-12; idem,'Evangelium und Gesetz', *Diakonia* 5(1974)363-375; William van der Marck, *Toward a Christian Ethic*, (English trans. D.J. Barrett), Newman, New York, 1967.
83. Cf. Francesco Compagnoni, *La Specificitá della Moral Cristiana*, p.169: 'Il contenuto materiale della vita etica cristiana non si distingue di guello humano'; Cf. idem, 'L'Ermeneutica nella Teologia Morale', *La Rivista di Teologia Morale* 2(1970) 105-129; idem, 'Dalla Specificitá formale all Specificitá d'insieme della Morale Cristiane', ibid, 6(1974) 221-39; Ambrogio Valsecchi, *Nuove vie dell'Etica Sessuale*, Queriniana, Brescia, 1972; Enrico Chiavacci, *Proposte Morali tra l'Antico e il Nouvo*, Cittadella Editrice, Assisi, 1975.
84 Cf. Tadaeusz Styczen, 'Autonome und christliche Ethik als method-ologisches Problem', *Theologie und Glaube* 66(1976) 212: 'Die Zeit sei reif für die Emanzipation der Ethik heute, so wie sie reif geworden war für die Physik zur Zeit der Renaissance, als sie sich von der Natur-philosophie emanzipierte. Diese Meinung ist in Polen... auf vielfache Weise unterbreitet'; Cf. T. Styczen/Helmut Juras, 'Methodologische Ansätze ethischen Denkens und ihre Folgen für die theologische Ethik' in Furger, *Theologische Berichte IV*, pp. 89-108.
85. Charles Curran, *Catholic Moral Theology in Dialogue*, Fides, New York, 1976, p.62; Cf. pp. 20-21, 60, 63. Cf. also 'Is There a Catholic and/or Christian Ethic?' in Curran and McCormick, *Readings in Moral Theology No. 2*, pp. 60-89.
86. Richard McCormick, 'Current Theology: Notes on Moral Theology', *Theological Studies* 38(1977), pp. 69-70. Cf. also 'Does Religious Faith Add to Ethical Perception' in Curran and McCormick, *Readings....No. 2*, pp. 156-173.
87. Cf. Enda McDonagh, 'Towards a Christian Theology of Morality: Morality and Christian Theology', *Irish Theological Quarterly* 37 (1970): 'The order of the words in the title "Morality and Theology" is therefore important. One begins with morality as a human phenomenon and sub-sequently seeks to understand or illuminate it theologically. The human phenomenon has to be given its full value before any attempt is made to interpret it in Christian fashion.' However, in *The Making of Disciples* McDonagh has developed his position. There he says that the starting point, goal and subject of theological reflection must be the disciple of Jesus Christ in the community of disciples: 'the *disciplina* of the *discipuli* forms the original starting point for reflecting disciples and should issue in a richer, more self-conscious grasp of Christian meaning as well as a greater commitment to Christian living'. Cf. *The Making of Disciples*, Gill and Macmillan, Dublin, 1982.
88. Cf. James P. Mackey's review in *The Tablet* (3/5/1975). Cf. Mackey, *The*

Problems of Religious Faith, Helicon, Dublin, 1972, p.265: 'These are reciprocal relationships, mutual influences, between two internal autonomies.'

89. Gerard J. Hughes, *Authority in Morals*, Heythrop Monographs, London, 1978, p.24.

90. Ibidem, p.25.

91. Idem, 'A Christain Basis for Ethics', *Heythrop Journal* 13(1972), p.43.

92. Cf. Böckle, 'Theonome Autonomie: zur Aufgabenstellung einer fundamentalen Moraltheologie' in Grundel/Rauh/Eid (eds.), *Humanum*, Patmos, Düsseldorf, 1972, pp. 21-2 (hereafter 'Theonome Autonomie...'); idem, 'Was ist das Proprium einer christlichen Ethik?' *Zeitschrift für Evangelische Ethik* 11(1967), pp. 148-9 (hereafter 'Was ist das Proprium...'); idem 'Möglichkeiten...', p.128; idem, *Fundamental...*, p.227.

93. *Fundamental...*, p.223.

94. Cf. 'Was ist das Proprium...', p.159.

95. Cf. Piet Fransen, *The New Life of Grace* (trans. G. Dupont), Chapman, London, 1973, pp. 98ff; Cornelius Ernst, *The Theology of Grace*, Mercier, Dublin and Cork, 1974, pp. 62ff., James P. Mackey, *Life and Grace*, Gill, Dublin, pp. 25ff.; idem, 'Grace', *The Furrow* 24 (1973), pp.338ff., Karl Rahner, 'Reflections on the Experience of Grace', in *Theological Investigations*, vo.3, pp. 86ff.

96. Fuchs, *Human Values and Christian Morality*, p.128; Cf. idem, Sussidi, p.212; Auer, *Autonome ...*, pp. 79, 90-94.

97. Cf. Rahner, 'Anonymous Christians', *Theol. Invest.*, vol.6, p.391; Anita Röper, *The Anonymous Christian*, trans Joseph Donceel, Sheed and Ward, New York, 1966.

98. Nobody had a greater influence on this than Rahner. In 1957 he wrote: 'It may well be that there are many... who think that they are not believers, who do not know that in the ultimate, honest depths of their hearts they do believe in the message of freedom in the love of God.... The necessity for '*fides ex auditu*' makes no difference to the fact that the faith thus preached is addressed to a person who, by grace already given in advance of this preaching, already really possesses that which he now hears', *Mission and Grace* (trans. Cecily Hastings), Sheed and Ward, London, 1964, vol.1, pp. 140, 128. Cf. *Theol. Invest.*, vol.4, pp. 200ff.; vol.5, pp. 123ff.; Cf. also Charles Davis, *The Study of Theology*, Sheed and Ward, London, 1962, pp. 127ff.; idem, *God's Grace in History*, Collins (Fontana), London, 1966, pp. 70ff.: Schillebeeckx, *World and Church*, pp. 91ff., Fransen, 'How Can Non-Christians find Salvation in their own Religions' in J. Neuner (ed.), *Christian Revelation and World Religions*, Burns and Oates, London, 1967, pp. 67ff.

99. Fuchs, *Human Values and Christian Morality*, pp. 14-15.

100. *Ibid.*, p.14. Cf. McDonagh, 'The Natural law and the Law of Christ', p.77ff.

101. Cf. 'Esiste una morale non-cristiana?', *Sussidi*, p.336.

102. *Fundamental Concepts of Moral Theology* (trans. W. Jerman), Paulist Press, New York, 1968, p.4, (original German, *Grundbegriffe der Moral*, 1966). Although published in 1966, this appears to contain some of his earliest

thinking — there is no reference to the issues raised by Rahner.

103. Cf. 'Bestrebungen in der Moraltheologie', in J. Feiner et al. *Fragen der Theologie heute*, Benziger, Einsiedeln, 1960, pp. 425ff. Cf. also *Law and Conscience* (trans. M.J. Donnelly), Sheed and Ward, New York, 1966, pp. 81ff.; 'Was ist das Proprium...', pp. 153, 155, 159.

104. *Fundamental...*, p.223.

105. Cf. 'Was ist das Proprium...', p.148: '... wir sind zum Dialog mit dem innerweltlichen Humanismus und den Weltreligionen gefordert.'

106. On the issue of content it is not easy to discover what Böckle holds. He says that such values as love for others may be found outside Christianity but that where it is found it is a share in Christian faith ('Was ist das Proprium...', p.159). He says that some values receive a special grounding and security in revelation, that they only become a compelling demand for the Christian. This is true, he says, of respect for others and of the moral norm against divorce: they only receive their stringency in Christianity ('Was ist das Proprium', p.156; Thenonome Autonomie...', p.34: *Fundamental...*, p.230). He says that faith in Christ's death and resurrection leads one to a way of life that is not 'normal' by ordinary standards (*Fundamentalmoral*, p.228). He says that morality must be rational and that 'the morality of revelation is the true morality of reason' (*Fundamental...*, pp. 5, 225). He also says that faith plays a corrective and selective role and that judgment must be made by reason enlightened by faith ('Theonome Autonomie...', pp. 30, 43-45; *Fundamental...*, pp. 176-179): faith modifies our insight into goods and values (*Fundamental...*, p.231). He refers to specifically Christian values and directives and acknowledges that Christian radicalism may lead one to a life without recourse to reason and calculation. (*Fundamental...*, pp. 179, 231). He regards the communication of moral norms to non-Christians as the major problem.

One suspects that he may be giving a new meaning to 'rational', i.e. that he may be understanding it as reason enlightened by faith. It is not clear what he means by the corrective role of faith. That is, it is not clear whether he regards moral norms as available to and understandable by reason without faith — is he saying that Christian rationality is the only true rationality or is he saying that Christian insights are an additional (but not indispensable) help in moral discernment?

107. Cf. Fuchs, 'Autonome Moral...', in Mieth-Compagnoni, p.59.

108. 'The Church in the Modern World', in Abbott, *The Documents of Vatican II*, pp. 199-201, 214.

109. Cf. Gustav Ermecke, 'Christlichkeit und Geschichtlichkeit der Moraltheologie', *Catholica* 26 (1972).

110. Cf. Schüller, 'Typen ethischer Argumentation in der katholischen Moraltheologie', *TuP* 45 (1970), p.526.

111. Cf. Bernard Häring, *Moralverkündigung nach dem Konzil*, Kaffke, Bergen-Enkheim, 1966, p.72: 'Immer noch spukt in manchen Köpfer (auch katholischer Theologen) die unglaubliche Idee, die Sittenlehre des Neuen Testamentes füge inhaltlich nichts Neues zum blossen Naturrecht hinzu; sie bringe lediglich eine neue Motivierung.'

112. Cf. Philip Delhaye, 'La mise en cause de la specificité de la morale chrétienne', *Revue Theologique de Louvain* 4(1973) 308-39.
113. 'Christlichkeit...', pp. 193, 195, 199,211.
114. Cf. Bernhard Stoeckle, 'Flucht in das Humane?: Erwägungen zur Diskussion über die Frage nach dem Proprium christlicher Ethik', *Internationale Katholische Zeitschrift* 6 (1972), p.312.
115. Cf. Stoeckle, 'Flucht...', pp. 315-18; *Idem, Grenzen der autonomen Moral*, Kösel, München, 1974, pp. 34-8 (hereafter *Grenzen...*); idem, *Handeln aus dem Glauben*, Herder, Freiburg, 1977, pp. 9-12, 25 (hereafter *Handeln...*).
116. Cf. Konrad Hilpert, 'Die Theologische Ethik und der Autonomie-Anspruch', *Münchener Theologische Zeitschrift* 28 (1977), p.336. (hereafter 'Die Theologische Ethik...'). For a much milder statement see Hilpert, 'The Theological Critique of "Autonomy"', *Concilium* 172(2/1984), pp. 9-15.
117. Cf. ibidem, especially pp. 333-42; Cf. idem, art. 'Autonomie' in Stoeckle (ed.), *Wörterbuch Christlicher Ethik*, Herder, Freiburg, 1975, pp. 24-34.
118. Cf. Joseph Ratzinger, 'Kirchliches Lehramt — Glaube — Moral' in idem (ed.), *Prinzipien Christlicher Moral*, Johannes, Einsiedeln, 1975, pp. 44,46 (hereafter Ratzinger's essay as 'Kirchliches Lehramt' and the book as *Prinzipien* ...). For an English translation see Curran and McCormick, *Readings...no. 2*, pp. 174-89. Note also Hans Ratter's article, 'Kann das Naturrecht die Moraltheologic entbehren?' (Can natural law do without moral theology?), *Zeitschrift für Katholische Theologie* 96 (1974), 76-95 in reply to Schüller's earlier article, 'Wie weit Kann die Moraltheologie das Natturrecht entbehren?' (How far can moral theology do without natural law?).
119. Cf. Dietmar Mieth, 'Autonome Moral im christlichen Kontext. Zu einem Grundlagenstreit der christlichen Ethik', *Orientierung* 40 (1976), p.31; Schüller's review of Ratzinger's *Prinzipien...*, *Theologische Revue* 73 (1977), col. 143; idem, 'Zur Diskussion um das Problem einer christlichen Ethik', *TuP* 51 (1976), passim; Alfons Auer, 'Die Bedeutung des Christlichen bei der Normfindung' in J. Sauer (ed.), *Normen im Konflikt*, p.33.
120. Stoeckle refers to the autonomous position as mere decoration: cf. 'Flucht...', p.314.
121. Cf. Ratzinger, 'Kirchliches Lehramt, p.63: '...die christliche Praxis aus der Mitte des christlichen Glaubens gespeist wird....'
122. Cf. Ratzinger,ibidem, pp. 43ff.
123. Cf.ibidem, p.61: 'er legt den inneren Anspruch der Gnade aus....'
124. Cf. ibidem, p.59: '...die apostolische Paraklese ‘nicht ein moralisierender Anhang ist, dessen Inhalte auch ausgetauscht werden könnten, sondern konkrete Benennung dessen, was Glauben heisst und daher mit dem Zentrum unlöslich verbunden.'
125. Cf. ibidem, p.61:'...nicht variable Zutat zum Evangelium, sondern gedeckt von der Autorität des Herrn....'
127. Cf. Heinz Schürmann, 'Die Frage nach der Verbindlichkeit der neutestamentlichen Wertungen and Weisungen' in Ratzinger (ed.), founded on a divine revelation of will...only the will of God can establish the boundary between good and evil....'

127. Cf. Heinz Schürmann, 'Die FRage nach der Verbindlichkeit der neutestamentlichen Wertungen und Weisunge' in Ratzinger (ed.), *Prinzipien...*, pp. 11ff.; idem, 'Haben die paulinischen Wertungen und Weisungen Modellcharakter?', *Gregorianum* 56 (1975) 234-71.

128. Cf. 'Die Frage...', p.38; 'Haben...', p.270.

129. About the word 'value', which is used by Schürmann and others, note that Roman Catholic authors use it in two different senses, (a) as referring to goods or objects of desire, (b) in the expression 'moral values' as referring to general or *prima facie* moral principles.

130. Cf. Delhaye, 'La mise en cause...', pp. 328ff.; Josef Ziegler, 'Moraltheologie nach dem Konzil', *Theologie und Glaube* 59 (1969), especially pp. 170-175. Cf. the contributions of Hamel, Galbiati, di Pinto and Penna in *Fondamenti Biblici della Teologia Morale: Atti della XXII Settimana Biblica* (Associazione Biblica Italiana), Paideia, Brescia, 1973.

131. Cf. Häring, *Free and Faithful in Christ*, St. Paul, Slough, 1978, p.332. Cf. Hans Rotter, *Grundlagen der Moral*, Benziger, Zurich, 1975, p. 169.

132. Cf. Rotter, Grundlagen..., p.165; idem, 'Kann das Naturrecht...', especially pp. 86ff.; Stoeckle, 'Flucht...', pp. 319ff.; idem, *Grenzen...*, pp. 131ff.; idem,*Handeln...*, pp. 27ff.

133. Johannes Gründel, 'Ethik ohne Normen?: Zur Begründung und Struktur christlicher Ethik' in Gründel/H. van Oyen, *Ethik ohne Normen?*, Herder Freiburg, 1970, pp. 72-3 (hereafter 'Ethik ohne Normen?').

134. Cf. Häring, *Free and Faithful*, pp. 333ff.; Gründel, 'Ethik ohne Normen?', pp. 73ff.; Stoeckle, 'Flucht...' especially pp. 318-19; idem, *Handeln...*, p.44; Rotter, *Christliches Handeln*, Styria, Graz, 1977, pp. 40ff.

135. Rotter, *Grundlagen...*, p.169. Cf. a similar statement by Hamel. 'La Legge Morale e I Problemi che pone al Biblista' in *Fondamenti Biblici*, p.43.

136. Cf. Klaus Demmer, 'Elementi Base di Un'Anthropolgia Cristiana' in Goffi, *Problemi e Prospettive di Teologia Morale*, pp. 31-47; idem, 'Hermeneutische Probleme der Fundamentalmoral' in Mieth/Compagnoni, *Ethik im Kontext des Glaubens*, especially pp. 110ff.; idem, Moralische Norm und theologische Anthropologie, *Gregorianum* 54 (1973), especially pp. 267ff.

137. Michael Simpson 'A Christian Basis for Ethics?', *The Heythrop Journal* 13 (1972) 285-97.

138. Cf. Ermecke, 'Christlichkeit und...', pp. 199, 205, 207; Delhaye, 'La mise en cause...', p.334; Ziegler, 'Moraltheologie nach dem Konzil', p.180; Norbert Rigali, 'Dialogue with Richard McCormick', *Chicago Studies* 16 (1977), p.304 (hereafter 'Dialogue...').

139. Hans Urs von Balthasar, 'Neun Sätze zur christlichen Ethik', in Ratzinger (ed.), *Prinzipien...*, pp. 71, 73. (For an English trans. see Curran and McCormick, *Readings...No. 2*, pp. 190-206).

140. It is mentioned by Ratzinger, Schürmann, Delhaye, Stoeckle, Rigali, Ermecke, Gründel, Guzzetti and Penna. Cf. p. 146 above.

141. Rigali, 'On Christian Ethics', *Chicago Studies* 10 (1971), pp. 239ff. McCormick seems to recognise this. Cf. *Readings...No.2*, p.171

142. Rigali, 'Dialogue...', pp. 300ff.; idem 'The Historical Meaning of the Humanae Vitae Controversy', *Chicago Studies* 15(1976), pp. 134ff.

143. Häring, *Free and Faithful*..., p.23. This seems to be particularly unfair to Fuchs: cf. his *Human Values*..., especially pp. 114ff, 178ff.

144. Cf. Stoeckle, *Grenzen*..., pp. 139ff.; Gründel, 'Ethik ohne Normen?', pp. 72ff.; Rotter, *Grundlagen*, p.163.

145. McDonagh, *Doing the Truth*, p.14.

146. Schüller challenges the *Glaubensethik* to give even one example of how truths of faith lead to concrete behaviour that is specific to Christians: cf. his review of Ratzinger's *Prinzipien*... in *Theologische Revue* 73 (1977), col. 143.

147. Cf. Fuchs, *Sussidi*, p.328. Cf. Denzinger-Schönmetzer, nn.3875, 3876.

148. Vallery maintains that the autonomy thesis of the identity of human and Christian morality is valid only when the term of comparison is a theist conception of the world. Cf. J. Vallery, *L'Identité de la Morale Chrétienne. Points de vue de quelques théologiens contemporains de langue allemande*, Centre Cerfaux-Lefort, Louvain-la-Neuve, 1976, pp. 190ff.

Chapter 3
(pp. 69-94)

1. The expression (*'ein naiver Biblizimus'*) is Furger's; cf. 'Aur Begründung eines christlichen Ethos' in *idem* (ed.), *Theologische Berichte IV*, p.41. Cf. Josef Endres, 'Genügt eine rein biblische Moraltheologie?' in *Studia Moralia 2* (1965) 72. Cf. Beemer, 'The Interpretation of Moral Theology', *Concilium* 5 (1969) 62-71; Blank, 'New Testament Morality and Modern Moral Theology', *Concilium* 3 (1967) 6-12.

2. Abbott, *The Documents of Vatican II*, pp. 112ff.

3. A good example of this kind of appeal is the 1975 'Declaration on Certain Questions Concerning Sexual Ethics' (Vatican Press) which refers to 'the revealed positive law' and to the teachings of Jesus and of Paul as proof of its moral stance on several issues: cf. pp. 6, 8, 11, 12 (hereafter *Sexual Ethics*).

4. It should be noted that this corresponds to a second and more indirect approach to morality found in Vatican II. The document *Gaudium et Spes* recommends that Christians should scrutinise the 'signs of the times' and study them 'in the light of the gospel': cf. Abbott (ed.), *The Documents of Vatican II*, p.248. For comment on this cf. Fuchs, 'Vocazione e Speranza: indicazioni conciliari per una morale cristiana', *Seminarium* 23 (1971) 492-512; Helmut Weber, 'Um das Proprium christlicher Ethik', *Trierer theologische Zeitschrift* 81 (1972) 257-75.

5. Jack T. Sanders wonders whether moralists can solve the problems of biblical ethics or whether they will be obliged to 'throw out the New Testament as an aid to ethics once and for all'; cf. his *Ethics in the New Testament*, S.C.M., London, 1975, p.248. For interesting accounts of the problem in recent Protestant ethics cf. Bruce Birch and Larry Rasmussen. *Bible and Ethics in the Christian Life*, Augsburg, Minneapolis, 1976 and Brevard Childs, *Biblical Theology in Crisis*, Westminster, Philadelphia, 1970.

6. Schüller, 'Zur Diskussion um das Problem einer christlichen Ethik', *TuP* 51 (1976), p.332 refers to Christ-positivism (*Christ-positivismus*);

Juros/Styczen, 'Methodologische Ansätze ethischen Denkens und ihre Folgen für die theologische Ethik' in Furger (ed.), *Theologische Berichte IV*, p.105 to revelation-positivism (*Offenbarungspositivismus*); Böckle, *Fundamentalmoral*, p.292 to theological-positivism (theologischer Positivismus); Furger, 'Zur Begründung...', p.27 to obedience-morality (*Gehorsamsmoral*). Cf. Fuchs, 'Autonome Moral und Glaubensethik' in Mieth/Compagnoni, pp. 61-2.

7. Cf. Hughes, *Authority in Morals*, p.2 (hereafter *Authority*...); Schüller, 'Zur Diskussion...', p.338.

8. Cf. Hughes, *Authority*..., pp. 4ff.; William K. Frankena, 'Is Morality Logically Dependent on Religion?' in G. Outka/J.P. Reeder Jnr., *Religion and Morality*, Anchor/Doubleday, New York, 1973, pp.295-317; P.H. Nowell-Smith, 'Morality: Religious and Secular' in Ian T. Ramsey (ed.), *Christian Ethics and Contemporary Philosophy*, S.C.M., London, 1966, pp. 95-112; Kai Nielsen, 'Some Remarks on the Independence of Morality from Religion', *Ibidem*, pp. 140-51; Nielsen, *Ethics Without God*, Pemberton, London, especially pp.1-47; A.C. Ewing, 'The Autonomy of Ethics', in Ian T. Ramsey (ed.), *Prospect for Metaphysics*, Allen and Unwin, London, 1961, pp. 33-49; Anthony Flew, *God and Philosophy*, Hutchinson, London, 1966, pp. 107ff.

9. It is a key tenet of the autonomy movement that moral norms must be understandable. Cf. Fuchs, 'Autonome Moral...', p.61 and ch.2, note 10, above.

10. Eric D'Arcy, ' "Worthy of Worship": A Catholic Contribution', in Outka/Reeder, *Religion and Morality*, p.192. Cf. John Finnis, "Reflections on an Essay in Christian Ethics, Part One: Authority in Morals', *The Clergy Review* 66 (1980), p.51; Hugo Meynell. 'The Euthyphro Dilemma', *The Aristotelian Society* 46 (1972) suppl. vol., pp. 228ff.

Since this is the traditional Roman Catholic position, I have not considered whether divine command theories that tend to a more voluntarist stance can be justified. Cf. also the debate between Hughes and Finnis, *The Clergy Review* 66 (1980), nn.2, 3, 5, particularly on the issue of 'ultimate justification'. Hughes is right to say that the Bible cannot be the ultimate justification but the position which he attacks is not one that is widely held, if held at all, in Roman Catholicism.

11. Cf. ch.2, note 139, above.

12. Cf. ibidem; Rigali, 'The Historical Meaning of the *Humanae Vitae* Controversy', *Chicago Studies* 15 (1976), p.135.

13. C. Henry Peschke, *Christian Ethics*, Goodliffe Neale, Alcester and Dublin, 1977, vol.1, pp. 111ff. takes the same position on dispensation from the natural law as the neo-Scholastics.

14. Cf. *Authority*..., pp. 5, 6, 10.

15. Cf. *Nichomachean Ethics*, Bk.10, chs.5,6.

16. Cf. Basil Mitchell, *Morality: Religious and Secular*, Clarendon, Oxford, 1980, pp.148-55.

17. Cf. Fuchs, 'Esiste una morale non-cristiana?' in *Sussidi*, p.332; idem, 'Formule Morali Male Intese', ibid., p.372; 'Autonome Moral...', p.65; Auer, 'Autonome Moral und christlicher Glaube', p.64; idem,

'Tendenzen heutiger theologischer Ethik', p.323; idem, 'Ein Modell theologischethischer Argumentation: "Autonome Moral"', pp. 46, 59.

18. Abbott, *The Documents of Vatican II*, pp. 119-20.
19. Hughes, 'Christian Ethics: The Real Issues', *Clergy Review* 66 (1980), p.215.
20. Cf. ch.2, nn.123-5, above.
21. Cf. Edward Lohse, *Colossians and Philemon* (English trans. Poehlmann and Karris) Hermeneia, Philadelphia, 1971, p.156;, Wolfgang Schrage, 'Zur Ethik der Neutestamentlichen Haustafeln', *New Testament Studies* 21 (1975), p.7.
22. Cf. Lohse, op.cit., p.155, note 4: 'These rules for the household are not, in so far as their content is considered a "genuinely Christian creation" and thus they cannot without further ado be considered to be "applied kerygma"'. Cf. Francis W. Beare, *The Epistle to the Colossians,* in *The Interpreter's Bible* (ed. G.A. Buttrick), Abingdon, New York and Nashville, 1955, vol. 11, p.226: 'We cannot fail to be struck ... by the entire lack of appeal to any specifically Christian motive in the exhortations to husbands and to fathers. ...' Cf. Herbert Preisker, *Das Ethos des Urchristentums*, Bertelsmann, Gütersloh, 1949, p.213: 'Die gesunde Natürlichkeit erhält volles Recht. Eph.5.29 gibt den Ton an, 'Es pflegt doch niemand sein eigenes Fleisch zu hassen, sondern hegt und pflegt es''. So empfindet der antike Mensch, der Heide wie der Jude. ... Hier ist noch kein neues Eheideal im einzelnen gezeichnet. ...' Schrage, however, is of the opinion that the expression 'in the Lord' gives a new standard of conduct, cf. art. cit., pp. 19-22.
23. Cf. Auer, 'Ein Modell...', p.50; Fuchs, 'Vocazione e Speranza...', p.498.
24. Cf. Blank, 'Evangelium und Gesetz', *Diakonia* 5 (1974), pp. 372ff.; Mieth, 'Norma Morale e Autonomia dell'Uomo' in Goffi, *Problemi e Prospettive di Teologia Morale*, pp. 192ff.
25. Ratzinger, 'Kirchliches Lehramt-Glaube-Moral', in idem (ed.), *Prinzipien christlicher Moral*, p.58.
26. Karl Weidinger, *Die Haustafeln: Ein Stück urchristlicher Paränese,* p.64, quoted by Sanders, *Ethics...*, p.85.
27. Cf. Sanders, op.cit., pp. 84-5.
28. Cf. Schnackenburg, *The Moral Teaching of the New Testament*, p.270.
29. Cf. Ibidem, p.273.
30. This point is made against the *Glaubensethik* by Furger in his review of Stoeckle's *Handeln aus dem Glauben, Theologische Revue* 73 (1977), col.412. Cf. Blank, 'Evangelium und Gesetz', p.371; Fuchs, 'Formule Morali...' in *Sussidi*, p.371.
31. Cf. Schüller, 'Zur Diskussion um das Problem einer christlichen Ethik', *TuP* 51 (1976), pp. 327ff.
32. Cf. Schüller, review of Ratzinger's *Rinzipien...*, *Theologische Revue* 73 (1977), col.143. Cf. Mieth, "Autonome Moral im christlichen Kontext', *Orientierung* 40 (1976), p.34.
33. Cf. art. 'Marriage' by Waldemar Molinski, *Sacramentum Mundi* (ed. Rahner et al.), Herder and Herder, New York/Burns and Oates, London, 1969, vol.3, pp. 395, 397; The Document, 'Sexual Ethics...',

p.8. Cf. Denis O'Callaghan's conclusion to a survey of the history of indissolubility, 'How Far is Christian Marriage Indissoluble?', *Irish Theological Quarterly*, 40 (1973), pp. 169-70: 'All this leads to the important conclusion that in Christian tradition signification, i.e. the symbolism of the union of Christ and the Church, is the basis of the indissolubility of Christian marriage.'

34. Cf. de la Potterie, 'I Precetti Morali e Cristo secondo S. Giovanni', in *Fondamenti Biblici della Teologia Morale*, p.340. Cf. Blank, 'New Testament Morality...', p.7.

35. Cf. the remark of Hans Conzelmann, *The Theology of St. Luke* (English trans. Geoffrey Buswell), Faber and Faber, London, 1960, p.232: 'The shift of emphasis in eschatology brings about of its own accord a change of structure in ethical thinking.'

36. Cf. Bertrand Russell, 'Why I am not a Christian', in *The Basic Writings of Bertrand Russell* (ed. Egner and Denonn), Allen and Unwin, London, 1963, p.594 (original lecture 3 March 1927); Richard Robinson, *An Atheist's Values*, Clarendon, Oxford, 1964, pp. 143, 150, 151.

37. Cf. Ziegler, 'Moraltheologie nach dem Konzil', *Theologie und Glaube* 59 (1969), pp. 127ff.; Schürmann, 'Die Frage nach der Verbindlichkeit der neutestamentlichen Wertungen und Weisungen', in Ratzinger (ed.), *Prinzipien...*, pp. 21ff.

38. Gustafson describes a disposition as 'a lasting or persisting tendency, a bearing towards one another and the world, a readiness to act in a certain way' and an intention as 'a basic direction of activity, an articulation of what that direction is and ought to be, a purposive orientation for one's life'. Cf. J.M. Gustafson, *Christ and the Moral Life*, pp. 248, 256. For 'attitude', cf. R. Scruton, 'Attitudes, Beliefs and Reasons', in J. Casey, *Morality and Moral Reasoning*, Methuen, London, 1971, pp. 29ff.

39. Hughes, *Authority...*, p.13.

40. Cf. *Sexual Ethics*, pp. 8-12. Cf. criticism in McCormick, 'Current Theology: Notes on Moral Theology 1976', *Theological Studies* 38 (1977), pp. 101ff. and O'Callaghan, *The Furrow* 27 (1976), pp. 126ff.

41. Hughes, *Authority...*, p.13.

42. Schillebeeckx, 'Die christliche Ehe und die menschliche Realität völliger Ehezerrüttung, in P.J.M. Huizing (ed.), *Für eine neue kirchliche Eheordnung*, Patmos, Düsseldorf, 1975, pp. 41ff. Cf. Walter Kerber, 'Hermeneutik in der Moraltheologie', *TuP* 44 (1969), p.55.

43. *Sexual Ethics* says that 'divine Revelation... manifests the existence of immutable laws', p.6; cf. pp. 8, 9.

44. Cf. the suggestions of Schürmann, Häring, Gründel, Rotter, Stoeckle pp. 59-60 above.

45. Cf. Blank, 'New Testament Morality...', pp. 11-12.

46. Cf. Kerber, 'Hermeneutik...', pp. 57,60; idem, 'Grenzen der biblischen Moral', in Demmer/Schüller (eds.), *Christlich Glauben und Handeln*. Patmos, Düsseldorf, 1977, pp. 112ff. Cf. Tullo Goffi, 'L'uso della parola di Dio in teologia morale', *Rivista di Teologia Morale* 3 (1971) 13-23; F. Compagnoni, 'L'Ermeneutica nella teologia morale', ibid. 2 (1970) 105-29; idem, 'Della specificita formale alla specificità d'insieme della morale cristiana', ibid., 6 (1974) 221-39.

47. Cf. Fuchs, 'The Absoluteness of Moral Terms', *Gregorianum* 52 (1971), pp. 420-21; Schüller, 'Wieweit kann die Moraltheologie das naturrecht entbehren?', *Lebendiges Zeugnis* 20 (1965) pp. 57-8.
48. Cf. Hughes, *Authority* ..., p.16.
49. Cf. ibidem, p.19.
50. Cf. J. Jeremias, *The Sermon on the Mount / The Lord's Prayer / The Problem of the Historical Jesus* (English trans. N. Perrin), Theological Publications, Bangalore, n.d., pp. 42ff.
51. Hughes, *Authority* ..., p.24.
52. Cf. Denzinger-Schönmetzer, nn.3004-3020.
53. Cf. A. Dulles, *Models of Revelation*, Gill and Macmillan, Dublin, 1983, passim.
54. Cf. K. Rahner, *Foundations of Christian Faith; An Introduction to the Idea of Christianity* (English trans. W.V. Dych), Darton, Longman and Todd, London, 1978, pp. 158ff. Cf. E. Schillebeeckx, *Revelation and Theology*, Sheed and Ward, New York, 1967, vol.1, pp. 6ff.
55. *Sexual Ethics*, p.9. Cf. the report of the U.S. Bishops' Doctrinal Committee on the book, *Human Sexuality: New Directions in American Catholic Thought* in *Pastoral Letters of the United States Catholic Bishops*, vol.4, (ed. H.J. Nolan), U.S. Catholic Conference, Washington, 1983, p.229.
56. Cf. Dogmatic Constitution on Divine Revelation, n.12. It stresses the importance of critical method but concludes by saying that 'all that has been said about the way of interpreting Scripture is subject finally to the judgment of the Church'; Cf. Abbott, *The Documents of Vatican II*, pp. 120-21. The U.S. Bishops' Doctrinal Committee says that critical exegesis cannot be considered the ultimate source of the meaning of the sacred texts; cf. *Pastoral Letters*, vol.4, p.229.
57. Cf. Ratzinger, 'Kirchliches Lehramt ...', p.58.

Chapter 4
(pp. 95-114)
1. Keck says:' ... if one studies only the explicit moral exhortations, one misses a good deal of what NT ethics is all about'; cf. Leander E. Keck, 'Ethos and Ethics in the New Testament' in James Gaffney (ed.), *Essays in Morality and Ethics*, Paulist, New York, 1980, p.29. Cf. David H. Kelsey, *The Uses of Scripture in Recent Theology*, S.C.M., London, 1975, p.140: 'A theologian's decision to bring Scripture to bear on his proposal indirectly, say, rather than directly, brings with it a different sense in which Scripture is authority for that purpose.' Cf. James M. Gustafson, 'The Place of Scripture in Christian Ethics: A Methodological Study' in idem, *Theology and Christian Ethics*, Pilgrim Press, Philadelphia, 1974, pp. 121-45.
2. Cf. Stoeckle, *Handeln aus dem Glauben*, p.45; Gründel, 'Ethik ohne Normen?' in Gründel/van Oyen, *Ethik ohne Normen?*, pp. 69ff.
3. Cf. Rigali, 'On Christian Ethics', *Chicago Studies* 10 (1971), p.240.
4. Cf. Häring, *Free and Faithful in Christ*, vol.1, pp. 6ff.; Penna, 'Riflessioni sulle Relazioni' in *Fondamenti Biblici*, p.403.
5. Cf. Schürmann, 'Die Frage ...' in Ratzinger (ed.), *Prinzipien* ..., p. 33.

6. Cf. Ratzinger in idem (ed.), *Prinzipien* . . . , pp. 48ff.
7. Cf. Ermecke, 'Christlichkeit und Geschichtlichkeit der Moraltheologie', *Catholica* 28 (1972), pp. 198, 207.
8. Cf. Häring, *Free and and Faithful* . . . , pp. 82, 87-93: idem, review of Böckle's *Fundamentalmoral, Theologisch-Praktische Quartalschrift* 126 (1978), pp. 198-9.
9. Cf. R. W. Hepburn and Iris Murdoch, 'Vision and Choice in Morality' in I. Ramsey (ed.), *Christian Ethics and Contemporary Philosophy*, pp. 181-218, originally *Arist.Soc. Suppl.Vol.* 30 (1956).
10. Cf. J.L. Mackie, *Ethics: Inventing Right and Wrong*, Penguin, Harmondsworth, 2977, p.169.
11. Iris Murdoch, loc.cit., p.204.
12 Häring, *Free and Faithful* . . . , vol.1, p.334.
13. Ratzinger, 'Kirchliches Lehramt . . .', *Prinzipien* . . . , p.49.
14. Cf. G.E.M. Anscombe, 'Modern Moral Philosophy', *Philosophy* 33 (1958) 1-19; P. Foot, 'Moral Beliefs', *Arist.Soc. Proc.*, 59 (1958-59) 83-104; idem, *Virtues and Vices*, Blackwell, Oxford, 1978; Frankena, 'Prichard and the Ethics of Virtue', The Monist, 54 (1970); idem, *Ethics*, pp. 52ff.; Mary Warnock, *Ethics since 1900*, O.U.P., London.1960; G.H. von Wright, *The Varieties of Goodness*, Routledge and Kegan Paul, London, 1963, pp. 136ff.; Stanley Hauerwas, *Vision and Virtue*, Fides, Notre Dame, 1974; idem, *Character and the Christian Life: A Study in Theological Ethics*, Trinity Univ. Press, San Antonio, 1975; A. MacIntyre, After Virtue, Duckworth, London, 1981.
15. *Nichomachean Ethics*, Bk.2, ch.4 (trans. J.A.K. Thomson), Penguin, Harmondsworth, 1955, p.62.
16. Cf. P. Foot: 'It is primarily by his intentions that a man's moral dispositions are judged. . . . The disposition of the heart is part of virtue. . . . A man's virtue may be judged by his innermost desires as well as by his intentions; and this fits with our idea that a virtue such as generosity lies as much in someone's attitudes as in his actions. . . . Charity is a virtue of attachment as well as action, and the sympathy that makes it easier to act with charity is part of the virtue. The man who acts charitably out of a sense of duty is not to be undervalued but it is the other who shows most virtue and therefore to the other that most moral worth is attributed.' *Virtues and Vices*, pp. 4-5, 14. Cf. A. Donegan, *The Theory of Morality*, Chicago Univ. Press, Chicago, 1977, p.54.
17. Cf. M. Mandelbaum, *The Phenomenology of Moral Experience*, The John Hopkins Press, Baltimore, 1969, p.160.
18. Cf. G. Wallace and A.D.M. Walker, *The Definition of Morality*, Methuen, London, 1970.
19. Cf. Auer, 'Tendenzen heutiger theologischer Ethik' in Bitter/Müller (eds.), *Konturen heutiger Theologie*, p.319.
20. Jacques Maritain, *Moral Philosophy*, Bles, London, 1964, p.79.
21. Cf. Noldin-Schmitt, *Summa Theologiae Moralis*, vol.2, p.53.
22. Cf. *Summa Theologiae*, I-II, q.81, a.2, a.4.
23. Cf. Häring, *The Law of Christ*, vol.2, pp. 126-128. Cf. his remarks in *Free and Faithful*, vol.1, p.94: 'The foundation of a Christian morality is life in Christ Jesus. . . . The value-response in faith, hope, love, all that can be

synthesised in praise, thanksgiving and adoration, and human relationships marked by the same direct value-response, all this is what makes the tree good...'

24. Cf. Anders Nygren, *Agape and Eros* (English trans. Philip S. Watson), S.P.C.K., London, 1957, p.127; Emil Brunner, *The Divine Imperative* (English trans. Olive Wyon), The Westminster Press, Philadelphia, 1947, p.3311.

25. Karl Barth, *Church Dogmatics* (English trans. H.T. Mackay et al.), edited Bromley/Torrance, T. and T. Clark, Edinburgh, 1961, III/4, p.49.

26. Soren Kierkegaard, *Fear and Trembling* (English trans. Walter Lowrie), Anchor/Doubleday, New York, 1954, p.64.

27. Cf. Frankena, 'The Concept of Morality' in Wallace/Walker, *The Definition of Morality*, pp. 146-73; Foot, 'Moral Arguments', *Mind* 67 (1958) 502-13; G.J. Warnock, *The Object of Morality*, Methuen, London, 1971, especially ch.2; Bernard Williams, *Morality*, Penguin, Harmondworth, 1973, pp. 87ff.

28. Cf. Fuchs, ' The Absoluteness of Moral Terms', *Gregorianum* 52 (1971), p.417. Some philosophers acknowledge that Christians have additional moral obligations but they refer to them as derivative obligations, i.e. as extensions of a widely accepted moral principle. An example given is the obligation of gratitude to God which is derived from an accepted moral principle plus a theological truth. Cf. on this R.B. Brandt, *Ethical Theory*, Prentice-Hall, Englewood Cliffs, N.J., 1959, p.64; Frankena, 'Is Morality Logically Dependent on Religion?' in Outka/Reeder, *Religion and Morality*, pp. 305-9. It is doubtful, however if all acts directed to God, e.g. prayer, could be accommodated in this way — if they are to be regarded as part of morality.

29. Cf. Fuchs, 'Esiste una morale non-cristiana?' in *Sussidi*, pp. 332-3; 'Formule Morali Male Intese', *Sussidi*, pp. 369-70.

30. Cf. Böckle, *Fundamentalmoral*, p.291.

31. Cf. Gustafson, 'Religion and Morality from the Perspective of Theology' in Outka/Reeder, *Religion and Morality*, p.130. Cf. Ninian Smart, 'Gods, Bliss and Morality' in I. Ramsey (ed.) *Christian Ethics...*, pp. 15ff.

32. Cf. Anscombe, 'Modern Moral Philosophy', p.5.

33. Cf. Anthony Kenny, *Action, Emotion and Will*, Routledge and Kegan Paul, London, 1963, p.238.

34. Cf. Frankena, 'Obligation and Motivation in Recent Moral Philosophy' in A.I. Melden (ed.), *Essays in Moral Philosophy*, Univ. of Washington Press, Seattle and London, 1958, pp. 40ff.; W.D. Falk, '"Ought" and Motivation', *Arist.Soc.Proc.*, 48 (1947-48) 111-38.

35. Amscombe, *Intention*, p.21.

36. Cf. F. Hutcheson, 'Illustrations on the Moral Sense' (3rd ed. 1742): 'The Qualities moving to Election, or exciting to Action, are different from those moving to Approbation. We often do Actions which we do not approve and approve Actions which we omit' in L.A. Selby-Bigge, *British Moralists*, Clarendon, Oxford, 1897, vol.1, p.403. Hallett, *Christian Moral Reasoning*, p.38.

37. Fuchs, *Human Values and Christian Morality*, p.126.

38. Cf. 'Esiste una morale non-cristiana?', in *Sussidi*, p.333.

39. Cf. 'Formule Morali Male Intese', in *Sussidi*, p.370.
40. Cf. Auer, *Autonome Moral und Christlicher Glaube*, pp. 98ff. Auer sees the new Christian view of man (*Menschenbild*) as performing a critical function: does this not imply a function in the discernment of content? Cf. Auer, 'Tendenzen...', p.321; 'Ein Modell theologisch-ethischer Argumentation: "Autonome Moral"' in Auer/Biesinger/Gutschera (eds.), *Moralerziehung im Religionsunterricht*, p.31; 'Autonome Moral und christlicher Glaube', *Katechetische Blätter*, p.69.
41. Cf. Anscombe, *Intention*, p.12; cf. idem, 'The Two Kinds of Error in Action', *Journal of Philosophy* 60 (1963), 383-401.
42. Cf. William and Martha Kneale, *The Development of Logic*, Clarendon, Oxford, 1962, p.609: 'Our troubles arise from the fact that there are intensional functions and that some of them cannot be satisfied by an object as such but only by an object considered as falling under a certain description.'.
43. Cf. Auer, *Autonome Moral...*, p.193.
44. Cf. ibidem, p.88; cf. 'Ein Modell...', p.51.
45. Cf. Fuchs, 'Autonome Moral und Glaubensethik' in Mieth/Compagnoni, *Ethik im Kontext des Glaubens*, pp. 66-67; cf. *Human Values*, p.125.
46. Auer, *Autonome Moral...*, p.102.
47. Cf. Böckle, *Fundamentalmoral*, pp. 228,211ff.
48. Cf. Fuchs, *Human Values*, pp. 125ff.; Auer, *Autonome Moral...*, pp. 177ff.
49. Henri Bergson, *The Two Sources of Religion and Morality* (English trans. Audra/Brereton), Doubleday, New York, 1935, p.34.
50. Iris Murdoch, *The Sovereignty of Good*, Routledge and Kegan Paul, London, 1970, pp. 67, 54.
51. Cf. Auer, 'Autonome...', p.63; 'Ein Modell...', p.48; 'Tendenzen...', p.323.
52. D'Arcy, *Human Acts*, p.158.
53. Cf. P.H. Nowell-Smith, 'Morality: Religious and Secular' in I. Ramsey, *Christian Ethics...*, p.95. Cf. K. Nielsen, 'Some Remarks on the Independence of Morality from Religion', ibidem, 140; idem, *Ethics without God*, pp. 4ff.; J.P. Mackey, *The Problems of Religious Faith*, Helicon, Dublin, pp.215ff.
54. Cf. D'Arcy, *Human Acts*, p.163.
55. Cf. Rotter, 'Erneuerung der Moral aus christlicher Spiritualität, *Geist und Leben* 50 (1977) 278-87.

Chapter 5
(pp. 115-45)
1. This is the title of a book by Stoeckle. Cf. ch.2, note 115 above.
2. J. Wach, *The Comparative Study of Religion*, Columbia Univ. Press, New York, 1958, p.66. Cf. p.76.
3. Cf. Smart, 'Gods, Bliss and Morality', in I. Ramsey (ed.), *Christian Ethics...*, pp. 15ff.; R. Stark/C.Y. Glock, 'Dimensions of Religious Commitment', in R. Robertson (ed.), *Sociology of Religion*, Penguin

Books, Harmondsworth, 1969, pp. 256ff.; W. Alston, art. 'Religion', in *Encyclopedia of Philosophy*, vol.7-8, Collier-Macmillan, London-New York, 1968, p. 141; F. Heiler, 'The History of Religions as a Preparation for the Co-operation of Religions', in Eliade/Kitagawa (eds.), *The History of Religions*, Univ. of Chicago Press, Chicago, 1959, p.132.

Cf. my 'Religion and Morality', *Irish Theological Quarterly* 44 (1977), pp. 105-16, 175-91.

4. Cf. R. Scruton, 'Attitudes, Beliefs and Reasons', in J. Casey, *Morality and Moral Reasoning*, Methuen, London, 1971, pp. 29ff. Auer, on the other hand, says that the Bible gives new values but no new norms and he persists in his position that there is no new content. Will new values not lead to new norms or judgments? Cf. Auer, 'Tendenzen...', p.319; 'Autonome Moral...', p.64.

5. Paul Ricoeur, 'The Tasks of the Political Educator', *Philosophy Today* 17 (1973), p.146.

6. Cf. Peter Berger, *The Social Reality of Religion*, Faber and Faber, London, 1969, pp. 12ff., 29ff.

7. Cf. Böckle, *Fundamentalmoral*, pp. 296ff.; McDonagh, *Gift and Call*, chs.1,2; Schüller, 'Die Bedeutung der Erfahrung für die Rechtfertigung sittlicher Verhaltensregeln' in Demmer/Schüller, *Christlich Glauben...*, pp. 261ff.; Gründel, 'Die Erfahrung als konstitutives Element der Begründung sittlicher Normen', in Sauer (ed.), *Normen im Konflikt*, pp. 55ff.; Furger, *Begründung des Sittlichen: ethische Strömungen der Gegenwart*, Imba, Freiburg (Schweiz), 1975, pp. 17ff.

8. Cf. Demmer, 'Elementi Base di un' Antropologia Cristiana' in Goffi, *Problemi e Prospettive...*, p.49: 'La successiva riflessione non ha la forza coercitiva di un sillogismo. Anzi *si rappresenta* una concreta verità moral come giacente nel pendio della compresione interpretativa più originaria.'

9. Cf. Simpson, 'A Christian Basis for Ethics', *The Heythrop Journal* 13 (1972), p.286.

10. Cf. J.P. Mackey, *The Problems of Religious Faith*, pp. 275ff.

11. Rahner, 'The Problem of Genetic Manipulation', *Theol. Invest.*, vol.9, p.238.

12. Cf. D.M. McKinnon, 'The Euthyphro Dilemma', *Arist. Soc. Suppl.*, vol.46 (1972), p.218: 'The way in which men and women who believe find their faith changing the sense and direction of their moral action is often highly complex and elusive.'

13. It should be recognised that Mackey is not so much interested in contrasting Christian and secular morality as in pointing out the morality that is consonant with the Christian world-view.

14. Cf. Williams, *Morality*, p.90.

15. G.H. Warnock, *Contemporary Moral Philosophy*, Macmillan, London and Basingstoke, 1967, p.79, note 27. Cf. Williams, *Morality*, p.91: 'Moralities with a transcendent dimension have a greater logical freedom with respect to their content than moralities which have no such dimension; their transcendental picture speaks of men's general condition and role in terms which make partially intelligible as a moral outlook attitudes which could be utterly opaque if offered in a purely

secular framework.' Cf. Finnis, *Natural Law and Natural Rights*, Clarendon, Oxford, 1980, p.89:'... one of the basic human values is the establishment and maintenance of the proper relationship between oneself (and the orders one can create and maintain) and the divine.' Cf. also Peter Geach, *The Virtues*, C.U.P. Cambridge, 1977, p.81. Cf. B. Lonergan, *Method in Theology*, Darton, Longman and Todd, London, 1971, pp. 31ff.

16. Cf. Demmer, 'Elementi Base...', p.63. Cf. G.J. Warnock, *The Object of Morality*, Methuen, London, 1971, p.139: 'If persuaded that some course of action will lead to death and misery, perhaps for very many people, I may regard this, on the strength of my religious beliefs, as in fact not a specially important circumstance.'

17. Cf. Barth, *Church Dogmatics*, IV/2, p.816.

18. Cf. *In Search of a Theology of Development*, A Sodepax Report, published by The Ecumenical Centre, Geneva, 1969. The letter of Pope Paul VI, 'Evangelii Nuntiandi' (1975) is a useful reference point: it attempts, after years of debate among Roman Catholics, to find a balance between the two elements; cf. English trans. *Evangelisation in the Modern World*, Catholic Truth Society, London, 1975.

19. Cf. Rahner, 'History of the World and Salvation-History' and 'Christianity and non-Christian Religions', *Theol. Invest.*, vol.5, pp. 97ff. and 115ff.; Schillebeeckx, *Christ*, pp. 744ff.; Yves Congar, *Un Peuple Messianique, salut et liberation*, Cerf. Paris, 1975. Cf. also the literature on liberation theology, notes 32, 34 below.

20. D.H. Lawrence, *Apropos of Lady Chatterley's Lover*, quoted by Herbert McCabe, *Law, Love and Language*, Sheed and Ward, London and Sydney, 1968, p.62.

21. Cf. Schillebeeckx, *Christ*, p.829: 'It is the resurrection which gives the lie to the failure of the message and the life of Jesus, and at the same time to merely human conceptions of what "real success" must and can mean. The Christian conception is not so much concerned with coming to terms with the fact that human life is a mixture of partial success and partial failure: it goes deeper; it is another assessment of real success and human failure, and, therefore, in the last resort, another experience.'

22. Kierkegaard, *Works of Love* (English trans. Edna and Howard Hong), London, Collins, 1962, p.113. Cf. Gene Outka, *Agape: An Ethical Analysis*, Yale Univ. Press, New Haven and London, 1972, p.53: 'On the level of basic attachments to others, the agent must avoid any transfer from equal regard to unqualified obedience or adoration. And this may often be a relevant consideration in situations of moral choice. In personal relations, my affection for my spouse or friend may grow too ardent or too embittered; hence the God-relationship sometimes cools and sometimes soothes.'

23. Cf. J.P. Mackey, *Jesus, The Man and the Myth*, S.C.M., London, 1979, p.169: 'The opposite to the faith of Jesus is the practice of grasping at finite things and finite achievements in a futile effort to sustain our spirits. This is original sin, idolatry. It is the very contrary to the experience of grace.'

24. Cf. Simpson, 'A Christian Basis for Ethics?', pp. 289-91.

25. *De Sacra Virginitate*, nn.8,11.
26. Gustafson, 'Religion and Morality from the Perspective of Theology' in Outka/Reeder (eds.), *Religion and Morality*, pp. 130, 148.
27. Cf. Brandt, *Ethical Theory*, pp. 64, 69; Frankena, 'Is Morality...' in Outka/Reeder (eds.), op.cit., p.309.
28. Gustafson, *Can Ethics Be Christian?*, p.144.
29. Paul Ramsey, *Fabricated Man*, Yale Univ. Press, New Haven and London, 1970, pp. 23, 31; cf. Carney, 'On Frankena and Religious Ethics', *JRE* 3 (1975), p.21.
30. Gustavo Gutierrez, *A Theology of Liberation* (English trans. Inda/Eagleson), Orbis, Maryknoll, N.Y., 1973, p.ix.
31. Ibidem, p.143.
32. Cf. Ignacio Ellacuria, *Freedom Made Flesh* (English trans. John Drury), Orbis, Maryknoll, 1976; J.L. Segundo, *A Theory for Artisans of the New Humanity*, (English trans. Drury), Orbis, Maryknoll, 1973-74; idem, *The Liberation of Theology* (English trans, Drury), Orbis, Maryknoll, 1976; *Between Honesty and Hope* (Peruvian Bishops' Commission for Social Action), Orbis, Maryknoll, 1970; R. Gibellini (ed.), *Frontiers of Theology in Latin America*, (English trans. Drury), Orbis, Maryknoll, 1979; Leonardo Boff, *Jesus Christ Liberator*, (English trans. Patrick Hughes), Orbis, Maryknoll, 1978; *Concilium*, vol.6, no.10 (1974).
33. Ellacuria, op.cit., pp. 187ff.
34. Cf. Segundo, 'Capitalism versus Socialism: *Crux Theologica*', in Gibellini, op.cit., pp. 240ff.; 'I Have Heard the Cry of My People' (Statement by the Bishops of Northeast Brazil), *Doctrine and Life* 23 (1973), 506-24, 558-71; 'Justice in the World' (Statement of the Peruvian Hierarchy), ibidem, 22 (1972) 260-64.
35. Cf. Gustafson, *Can Ethics be Christian?*, pp. 133ff.
36. Frankena, 'Is Morality Logically Dependent on Religion?' in Outka/Reeder, *Religion and Morality*, p.295.
37. David Little and Sumner Twiss Jr., 'Basic Terms in the Study of Religious Ethics', ibidem, pp. 35-77.
38. Cf. Ronald Dworkin, 'Lord Devlin and the Enforcement of Morals' in R.A. Wasserstrom (ed.), *Morality and the Law*, Wadsworth, Belmont, Calif., 1971, pp. 63-4.
39. Cf. Murdoch, 'Vision and Choice in Morality' in I. Ramsey, *Christian Ethics...*, p.216.
40. Cf. Mitchell, 'Ideals, Roles, and Rules' in Outka/Ramsey, *Norm and Context in Christian Ethics*, S.C.M., London, 1969, p.357.
41. Hampshire, 'Morality and Pessimism' in idem (ed.), *Public and Private Morality*, C.U.P., Cambridge, 1978, p.10.
42. Cf. Hare, *The Language of Morals*, O.U.P., Oxford, 1962, p.69.

Chapter 6
(pp. 146-76)
1. Cf. Stoeckle, *Handeln aus dem Glauben*, pp. 42ff.; von Balthasar, 'Neun Sätze zur christlichen Ethik', in Ratzinger, *Prinzipien...*, p.76.

2. Cf. de la Potterie, 'I precetti Morali e Cristo secondo S. Giovanni', in *Fondamenti Biblici della Teologia Morale*, p.336; Giavini, 'Il Discorso sulla Montagna', ibidem, p. 264; Rémy, *Foi Chrétienne et Morale*, Centurion, Paris, 1973, p.186.

3. Gründel, *Ethik ohne Normen?*, p.79; Delhaye, 'La mise en cause de la specificité de la morale chrétienne, *Rev. Theol. Louv.* 4 (1973), pp. 308-9.

4. Cf. Rigali, 'The Historical Meaning of the *Humanae Vitae* Controversy', *Chicago Studies* 15 (1976), p.136; von Balthasar, 'Neun Sätze...', pp. 71ff.

5. Cf. Mausbach-Ermecke, *Katholische Moraltheologie*, vol.2, pp. 124ff.

6. Cf. Gilleman, *The Primacy of Charity in Moral Theology*, p. 183.

7. Cf. 'Esiste una morale cristiana?', *La Civiltà Cattolica*, 1972, n.3, 449-55.

8. Fuchs, *Human Values...*, p.134.

9. Cf. Auer, *Autonome Moral...*, pp. 85, 90.

10. Cf. Schüller, 'Zur theologischen Diskussion über die lex naturalis', *TuP* 41 (1966), p.497; idem, 'Die Bedeutung des natürlichen Sittengesetzes für den Christen' in Teichweier/Dreier (eds.), *Herausforderung und Kritik der Moraltheologie*, p.111.

11. Cf. Delhaye, 'La mise en cause...', p.330.

12. Cf. Frankena, *Ethics*, pp. 42-3; idem, 'The Ethics of Love Conceived as an Ethics of Virtue', *JRE* 1 (1973), p.22; idem, 'Love and Principle in Christian Ethics', in Alvin Plantinga (ed.), *Faith and Philosophy*, Erdmans, Grand Rapids, 1964, pp. 203ff.; Alan Donegan, *The Theory of Morality*, Univ. of Chicago Press, Chicago, p.62; D.J. Hoitinga, 'Love, Law and Liberty', *Calvin Theological Journal* 5 (1970), pp. 5ff.; J. Burnaby, art. 'Love' in John Macquarrie (ed.), *A Dictionary of Christian Ethics*, S.C.M., London, 1967, pp. 197ff.

13. Oscar Cullmann, *Christ and Time*, Westminster Press, Philadelphia, 1952, p.230. Cf. J. Piper, *Love Your Enemies: Jesus' Love Command in the Synoptic Gospels and The Early Christian Paraenesis*, C.U.P., 1979, pp. 100ff., 173.

14. As such statements stand, they do not provide justification, i.e. there is not immediate conclusion to the ethical position from the religious belief. But they may be understood as concealed divine commands. In the context of religious ethics one may also take Mill's point that 'there is a larger meaning of the word "proof" ' which does not involve strict entailment but in which the acceptance or rejection of a principle does not depend on 'blind impulse or arbitrary choice'. The Christian believes that the Creator and Father of all is love: must he not take it that love should be his guiding principle, without introducing the premiss that God does what is independently good? It seems to be the case that, as Frankena puts it, religious belief does suffice to justify the ethical principle of love — in the wider sense of 'justify' — for those who subscribe to it. Cf. J.S. Mill, *Utilitarianism*, Collins (Fontana), London, 1962, p.255; Frankena, 'Is Morality Logically Dependent on Religion?' in Outka/Reeder, *Religion and Morality*, p.299; R.M. Adams, 'A Modified Divine Command Theory of Ethical Wrongness', ibidem. pp. 318-47; Patterson Brown, 'Religious Morality', *Mind* 77 (1963) 235-44.

15. Cf. Paul Ramsey, 'The Biblical Norm of Righteousness', *Interpretation* 24 (1970), pp. 420-1: 'Expressly excluded from the heart and soul of biblical

241

ethics is the notion that we should deal with people only according to their merits, earned or unearned; or that we are simply to treat all men as their manhood intrinsically deserves.'

Cf. Brunner, *Justice and the Social Order* (English trans. Hottinger), Lutterworth, London, 1945, p.114: 'It is always love all-the-same, never love because. It is love born simply of the will to love, not of the nature of the beloved. It is not a love which judges worth but a love which bestows worth. Neither Aristotle nor any other pagan knew this love.'

Cf. H. Richard Niebuhr, *Christ and Culture*, Faber and Faber, London, 1952, p.32; Nygren, *Agape and Eros*, p.78.

16. Cf. Austin Farrer, 'A Starting-Point for the Philosophical Examination of Theological Belief' in B. Mitchell (ed.), *Faith and Logic*, Allen and Unwin, London, p.23.
Cf. Kierkegaard, *Works of Love* (trans. H. and E. Hong), p.72: 'He is your neighbour on the basis of equality with you before God, but this equality absolutely every man has and he has it absolutely.'

17. Cf. Stoeckle, *Handeln aus dem Glauben*, pp. 42ff.

18. Cf. Von Balthasar, 'Neun Sätze...', pp. 71ff.

19. Cf. Rigali, 'The Historical...', *Chicago Studies*, 15 (1978); idem 'Dialogue with Richard McCormick', ibidem, 16 (1977), pp. 303ff.

20. Cf. Gründel, *Ethik ohne Normen?*, p.79; Stoeckle, *Grenzen der Autonomen Moral*, pp. 138-9.

21. A further question which must be asked is whether an agapist is proposing a morality of pure agapism. If he is, he will have considerable difficulty in sustaining the position: there are problems about how agape knows and calculates and how other principles are derived from it. If he is not, but is using a combination of agape and other principles not derived from agape, e.g. natural law principles, one must ask how this affects the issue of specificity.
Since the renewal movement in the fifties it has become common for Roman Catholics to urge the primacy or centrality of charity or agape (cf. ch.2, note 51 above). But it has never been clear what this means. Does it mean that morality is to be built out of agape as a central principle — pure agapism? If not, what role is agape to play and how, in particular, does it relate to natural law, if that is the preferred system?

22. Cf. Schüller, *Die Begründung sittlicher Urteile*, Patmos, Düsseldorf, 1973, pp. 46ff. Caird and Scott regard the positive formulation by Jesus as a distinctive feature. Cf. G.B. Caird, *The Gospel of St Luke* (Pelican Gospel Commentaries), Black, London, 1963, p.104; Ernest F. Scott, *The Ethical Teaching of Jesus*, Macmillan, New York, 1924, p.20. Dihle disagrees: 'Es gibt seit frühster Zeit zahllose rein christlicher Belege für die negative und daneben eind Anzahl nichtchristlicher Belege für die positive Fassung'. Cf. Albrecht Dihle, *Die Goldene Regel. Eine Einführung in die Geschichte der antiken und frühchristlichen Vulgärethik*, Vandenhoeck and Ruprecht, Göttingen, 1962, p.10. Cf. Victor P. Furnish, *The Love Command in the New Testament*, S.C.M., London, 1973, p.57.

23. Bultmann says: '... whether it be given positive or negative formulation, the saying, as an individual utterance, gives moral expression to a naive egoism'. Cf. Rudolf Bultmann, *History of the Synoptic Tradition*, (English

trans. Marsh), Blackwell, Oxford, 1963, p.103. Tillich describes it as 'calculating justice' which needs love to be transformed into creative justice and thus to be truly great. Cf. Paul Tillich, *The New Being*, Scribner's, New York, 1955, p.32.

24. Cf. Marcus Singer, 'The Golden Rule', *Philosophy* 38 (1963) 293-313; R.M. Hare, *Freedom and Reason*, O.U.P. Oxford, 1963, passim.

25. Cf. W.G. Maclagan, 'Respect for Persons as a Moral Principle', *Philosophy* 35 (1960), especially pp. 207ff., 289ff.

26. R.S. Downie/E. Telfer, *Respect for Persons*, Allen and Unwin, London, 1969, p.37.

27. Cf. the definition of agape given by Outka: 'The normative content most often accorded to agape as neighbour-love may be stated in summary fashion as follows. Agape is a regard for the neighbour which in crucial respects is independent and unalterable. To these features there is a corollary: the regard is for every person qua human existent, to be distinguished from those special traits, actions etc. which distinguished particular personalities from each other.... One ought to be committed to the other's well-being independently and unalterably; and to view the other as irreducibly valuable prior to his doing anything in particular.' Cf. G. Outka, *Agape: An Ethical Analysis*, Yale Univ. Press, New Haven and London, 1972, p.9.

28. A. Donegan, *The Theory of Morality*, Chicago Univ. Press, Chicago, 1977, pp. 63ff. Cf. Immanuel Kant, *Foundations of the Metaphysics of Morals* (English trans. Beck), Bobbs-Merrill, Indianapolis/New York/Kansas City, p.47.

29. Cf. Kant, *Foundations...*, pp. 48-9.

30. Cf. Stoeckle, *Handeln aus dem Glauben*, pp. 113, 159; Rotter, *Grundlagen der Moral*, p.166; idem, 'Kann das Naturrecht die Moraltheologie entbehren?', *Zeitschr. für katholische Theologie*, 96 (1974), p.87.

31. Cf. Gründel, *Ethik ohne Normen?* pp. 72, 77; Stoeckle, *Grenzen der autonomen Moral*, pp. 137-9. Stoeckle seems to waver between saying that a true regard for the other is impossible without faith and saying that without faith there is no compelling reason for it. Cf. also Rahner, 'The Dignity and Freedom of Man', *Theol. Invest.*, vol.2, p.246; Böckle, *Fundamentalmoral*, p.299.

32. Gründel, *Ethik ohne Normen?*, p.74.

33. Gründel, ibidem, p.73; Stoeckle, *Handeln aus dem Glauben*, p.44.

34. Mill, *Utilitarianism*, p.268. Cf. Frankena, *Ethics*, pp. 42ff.; Mackie, *Ethics*, p.130. Donegan says: 'Utilitarianism has enough in common with traditional morality to be considered a rival to it on something like its own terms' — by 'traditional morality' he means the Christian tradition of love. Cf. Donegan, *The Theory of Morality*, p.27.

35. Timothy O'Connell, *Principles for a Catholic Morality*, Seabury, New York, 1978, p.162. Cf. J. Philip Wogaman, *A Christian Method of Moral Judgment*, S.C.M., London, 1976, p.82.

36. J. Connery, 'Morality of Consequences: A Critical Appraisal', *Theological Studies*, 34 (1973), p.396. For examples of this cf. Fuchs, 'The Absoluteness of Moral Terms', *Gregorianum* 52 (1971), p.444. Cf. P. Knauer, 'The Hermeneutic Function of the Principle of the Double

Effect', *Natural Law Forum* 12 (1967) 132-62; N. Crotty, 'Conscience and Conflict', *Theological Studies* 32 (1971) 203-32; J.G. Milhaven, 'Objective Moral Evaluation of Consequences', *Theological Studies* 32 (1971) 407-30; Schüller, 'Zur Problematik allgemein verbindlicher ethischer Grundsätze, *TuP* 45 (1970) 1-23.

37. Cf. Häring, *Free and Faithful in Christ*, vol.1, pp. 83, 341-2.
38. Cf. Finnis, *The Rational Strength of Christian Morality*, a lecture given at Netherhall House, London, published by Netherhall House. Cf. idem, 'Reflections on an Essay in Christian Ethics, Part Two: Morals and Method', *The Clergy Review* 65 (1980), p.90.
39. Cf. Ramsey, *Deeds and Rules...*, p.97; *War and the Christian Conscience*, Duke Univ. Press, Durham, N.C., 1961, p.14; *The Just War: Force and Political Responsibility*, Scribner's, New York, 1968, p.163; *Basic Christian Ethics*, S.C.M., London, 1950, pp. 116, 148.
40. Finnis, *The Rational Strength...*, p.15-16.
41. Frankena, *Ethics*, p.44. Cf. Downie and Telfer, *op.cit.*, p.39.
42. Cf. Carney, 'On Frankena and Religious Ethics', *JRE* 3 (1975), p.18: '... it may be that the principle of non-transgression takes priority over the other two in almost all instances, if not all....'
43. Cf. Mackie, *Ethics*, especially pp. 170ff., 190; D.A.J. Richards, *A Theory of Reasons for Action*, especially pp. 80ff.
44. Carney maintains that agape requires, at least, a conjoining of virtue and obligation notions, in order to make the full range of its claims and programmes clear. Cf. Carney, 'The Virtue-Obligation Controversy', *JRE* 1 (1973), p.1. Frankena says that we should think of love as a disposition to have certain feelings and thoughts and to do or intend to do certain actions in relation to one's neighbour. Cf. Frankena, 'The Ethics of Love...', p.29. Cf. ch.4, note 16. Cf. Donegan, *The Theory of Morality*, p.54: 'For both Judaism and Christianity, as religions, pay far more attention to the spirit in which a man acts than to whether objectively considered he does as he ought.'
45. Curran, *Catholic Moral Theology in Dialogue*, p.62, cf. pp. 20-21.
46. Cf. P.F. Strawson, 'Social Morality and Individual Ideal', *Philosophy* 20 (1961) 1-17.
47. Cf. R.M. Hare, *Freedom and Reason*, O.U.P., Oxford, 1963, pp. 137ff.
48. Cf. H.L.A. Hart, *The Concept of Law*, Clarendon, Oxford, 1961, pp. 165ff.
49. Cf. J.O. Urmson, 'Saints and Heroes', in A.I. Melden (ed.), *Essays in Moral Philosophy*, Univ. of Washington Press, Seattle and London, pp. 198ff.
50. W. Frankena, 'Conversations with Carney and Hauerwas', *JRE* 3 (1975), pp. 55-6.
51. Cf. Fuchs, *Human Values and Christian Morality*, pp. 127. 128; idem, 'Esiste una morale non-cristiana?' in *Sussidi*, p.331; Auer, *Autonome Moral und cristlicher Glaube*, pp. 92ff.; idem, 'Die ethische Relevanz der Botschaft Jesu', in Auer/Biesinger/Gutschera (eds.), *Moralerziehung im Religionsunterricht*, pp. 69ff.
52. Noldin-Schmitt, *Summa Theologiae Moralis*, vol.2, p.72.
53. One finds at least the following positions. (i) Self-love is wholly nefarious and contrary to agape (Nygren, *Agape and Eros*, p.131). (ii) It is not wrong

in principle. But, in practice, one needs to forget oneself, because man is *incurvatus in seipsum* (H.R. Niebuhr, *Faith and History*, Scribner's, New York, 1955, p.185). (iii) Man naturally loves himself but agape does not mean that one is commanded to love oneself: 'it is a mistake to admit self-love onto the ground-floor of Christian ethics as a basic part of Christian obligation' (Ramsey, *Basic Christian Ethics*, p.101). (iv) One's own good and the neighbour's good are equally important: the commandment of love is a rule ordering impartiality (R. Johann, *The Meaning of Love*, Paulist, New Jersey, pp. 30ff.; Martin D'Arcy, *The Mind and Heart of Love*, Faber and Faber, London, 1946, pp. 92ff.).

54. Noldin-Schmitt, pp. 129-32. Cf. ch.1, note 8 above.
55. Cf. ibidem, vol.1, p.132.
56. G. Kelly and J. Ford, *Contemporary Moral Theology*, Mercier, Cork, 1958, vol.1, pp. 82-92.
57. Cf. Carpentier, 'Vers une morale de la charité', *Gregorianum* 34 (1953), pp. 40ff.
58. Cf. Fuchs, 'Die Liebe als Aufbauprinzip der Moraltheologie', *Scholastik* 29 (1954) 79-87.
59. Cf. McDonagh, *Doing the Truth*, Gill and MacMillan, Dublin, 1979, p.16.
60. Cf. Gustafson, *Can Ethics Be Christian?*, p.153: 'In a sense it is fair to say, then, that there is a special ethics for Christians in addition to theologically grounded ethics that apply to all. These obligations are not merely "religious" obligations; they are also moral obligations within a "way of life" that Christians have been called to for more than moral reasons. On these grounds the "Christian" cannot be converted into the "natural" or the "human" without remainder....' Cf. Outka, *Agape*, p.307: 'It may make sense for those who locate themselves in a discernible community founded on such belief and authority to exhort and reproach one another concerning the requirements which transcend one's fundamental duties from every point of view.'
Cf. H. Oppenheimer, *The Character of Christian Morality*, Faith Press, London, 1965, p.68: 'Christian perfection is a harvest, the harvest of the Spirit. It is the consummation of Christian morality to which all God's people are called not just a special few.'
Paul Ramsey refers to 'Christian self-severity'. Cf. *Basic Christian Ethics*, p.79.
61. Cf. Auer, *Autonome Moral...*, pp. 98ff.
62. Cf. Ch.2, note 73 above.
63. Cf. Ch.4, note 39 above.
64. Cf. Rigali, 'On Christian Ethics', *Chicago Studies* 10 (1971), pp. 239ff.; idem, 'New Epistemology and the Moralist', ibidem 11 (1972), pp. 243ff.
65. Cf. Fuchs, 'Autonome Moral...', p.67.
66. Rahner, *Nature and Grace* (English trans. Dinah Wharton), Sheed and Ward, London and New York, 1963, pp. 63, 72, 97.
67. 'On the question of a Formal Existential Ethics', *Th. Invest.*, vol.2, pp. 217ff.; Cf. Schillebeeckx, *God and Man*, pp. 292ff.; Hughes, *Authority in Morals*, p.22; D.J. Dorr, 'Karl Rahner's "Formal Existential Ethics"', *Irish Theological Quarterly* 36 (1969), pp. 211ff.

68. Dorothy Emmet remarks: 'The notion of the "will of God" is most characteristically invoked in difficult, critical decisions... naturally linked with notions of vocation.... A person finds a way of working which is his way, and which strengthens his powers of responsible action.... [Decisions] can be made gropingly beyond what he clearly sees as right and wrong, and yet appear as risks he must take. Such decisions... may extend our moral notions in non-obvious ways... a wider context of creative activity which does not issue specific directions but which can draw us into ways of living through which moral powers and moral insights can be heightened.' Cf. Dorothy Emmet, 'On "Doing What is Right" and "Doing the Will of God"', *Religious Studies* 3 (1967), p.299. Cf Hallett, *Christian...*, p.51.

69. Cf. Hare, *The Language of Morals*, p.145.

70. Cf. Alisdair MacIntyre, 'What Morality is not', in Wallace/Walker (eds.), *The Definition of Morality*, p.30; Mitchell, 'Ideals, Roles and Rules', in Outka/Ramsey, *Norm and Context...*, p.355; Mackie, *Ethics*, p.87.

71. Cf. Peter Winch, 'The Universalisability of Moral Judgments', *The Monist* 49 (1965), pp. 205-6.

72. Mackie says: 'We can understand as moral the view of the ascetic that something that he does not condemn in others would be wrong for him, even though he does not claim that there is any relevant qualitative difference between himself and others... morality, it seems, forbids one to demand more from others than from oneself but not vice versa'. Cf. *Ethics*, p.187. Singer agrees: 'The sort of case condemned by the Golden Rule is one in which one claims a privilege for himself that he is not willing to grant to others, and not one in which one imposes a burden on himself that he is not willing to impose on others. Such cases are fairly common. There are people who, at least in certain lines of endeavour, are harder on themselves than they are on others. It would clearly be ludicrous to condemn this as immoral.' Cf. Marcus Singer, 'The Golden Rule', *Philosophy* 38 (1963), p.303.

73. Richards, *A Theory of Reasons for Action*, p.95.

Chapter 7
(pp. 177-96)

1. Cf. Auer, *Autonome Moral und christlicher Glaube*, p.177.

2. Cf. Fuchs, *Human Values and Christian Morality*, p.124.

3. Cf. Schillebeeckx, *God and Man*, pp. 267-275.

4. Cf. Auer, 'Die Bedeutung des Christlichen bei der Normfindung', in Sauer (ed.), *Normen im Konflikt*, pp. 51ff.; McDonagh, *Gift and Call*, pp. 172ff.; Mackey, *The Problems of Religious Faith*, pp. 259ff., 294ff.; idem, *The Tablet*, 3/5/1975.

5. Cf. Stoeckle, 'Flucht in das Humane?': Erwägungen zur Diskussion über die Frage nach dem Proprium christlicher Ethik', *Internationale Katholische Zeitschrift* 6 (1972), p.314.

6. Noldin-Schmitt, *Summa Theologiae Moralie*, vol.1, pp. 38, 40.

7. Cf. Häring, *The Law of Christ*, vol.1, pp. 228-9: '[The norm of morality] becomes binding as a law only in so far as it derives from a legislator who has the power to bind the will of men absolutely.... The commandments are imposed on us as decrees of the divine will....' Cf. Ziegler, 'Moraltheolgie nach dem Konzil', *Theologie und Glaube* 59 (1969), pp. 171ff.; C.H. Peschke, *Christian Ethics*, Goodliffe Neale, Alcester and Dublin, 1973, vol.1, pp. 94, 95, 100, 136.

8. Cf. ch. 1. pp. 13ff. and notes 26, 27 above. Joseph Rickaby said that God, having created man with a certain nature, issued a second decree ordering him to live according to that nature. Cf. his *Moral Philosophy*, Longmans, London, 1892, p.121. About moral obligation Boyer said: 'Obligatio ex suo conceptu dicit subiectionem eius qui obligatur ei qui obligat.' Cf. his *Cursus Philosophiae*, vol.1, pp. 476-7. Noldin said that the eternal law is the act of the divine will by which man is bound to observe the moral order. Cf. ch.1, note 27.

9. Simpson, 'A Christian Basis for Ethics?', p.289.

10. Cf. Auer, *Autonome* . . . , p.160; idem, 'Die Bedeutung . . .', p.29.

11. Cf. Böckle, *Fundamental* . . . , pp. 58, 6, 30ff.

12. Cf. Mieth, 'Norma Morale e Autonomia dell'Uomo', in Goffi (ed.), *Problemi e Prospettive di Teologia Morale*, p.174.

13. Cf. Schüller, 'Sittliche Forderung und Erkenntnis Gottes', *Gregorianum* 59 (1978), p.18.

14. Cf. Ch. 3, note 6 above.

15. John A.T. Robinson, *Honest to God*, S.C.M., London, 1963, p.113.

16. Ibidem, p.121.

17. Paul Ricoeur, 'Demythiser l'accusation', in *Demythisation et Morale*, (Actes du Colloque, Rome 7-12 January 1965), Aubier, Paris, 1965, pp. 48-65, especially pp. 55ff.

18. Cf. van Ouwerkerk, 'Christus en de ethiek', *Tijdschrift vor Theologie* 6 (1966), pp. 307-17, quoted by T. Beemer, 'The Interpretation of Moral Theology', *Concilium* 5 (1969), vol.5, p.65.

19. Van Ouwerkerk, 'Gospel Morality and Human Compromise', *Concilium* 1 (1965), vol.5, p.8.

20. Cf. van Ouwerkerk, 'Secularism and Christian Ethics: Some Types and Symptoms', *Concilium* 3 (1967), vol.5, p.51. He says that Roman Catholic morality is being asked to answer three questions to-day: what is meant by basing ethics on the will of God; what role does the evangelical kerygma play with regard to morality; what is the meaning of Christ as the ground, strength and norm of human actions. Ibidem, p.64. Cf. references ch.2, note 82 above.

21. Cf. Robinson, *Honest to God*, p.105. Cf. G. de Graaff, 'God and Morality' in I. Ramsey (ed.), *Christian Ethics and Contemporary Philosophy*, p.31: 'What has God to do with morality? A great deal, it would seem if one gives ear to common belief. The presumption that there is some sort of connection between morality and God seems to be shared by those who, for one reason or another, want to secularise morality. And of course it is obvious that those who want God back in morality presume that there is a place there for him. The nature of the supposed connection between God and morality is not nearly so obvious.'

22. The accusation has been made especially by Stoeckle and Hilpert. Cf. ch.2, notes 115,116,117 above.

23. Mackie, *Ethics*, p.230.
   Ayer argues that it is inconsistent to hold both that 'ethical values are absolute' and that they are 'validated by authority', even if the authority be that of God. (In a letter to *The Observer*, 13/10/57, quoted by I. Ramsey, *Freedom and Immortality*, S.C.M., London, 1960, pp. 45-6).
   Böckle recognises that certain forms of Church teaching on morals can only with difficulty be reconciled with the notion of autonomy. Cf. *Fundamental* ... pp. 5, 47.
   Maclagan asks whether 'a theological interpretation of the fact of duty' is 'either necessary or even possible'. Cf. W.G. MacLagan, *The Theological Frontier of Ethics*, Allen and Unwin, London and Macmillan, New York, 1961, p.55.

24. Cf. Schüller, 'Sittliche Forderung...', p.32, note 22.

25. Cf. Böckle, 'Theonome Autonomie...', in Gründel/Rauh/Eid (eds.), *Humanum*, passim; Fuchs, 'Autonome Moral und Glaubensethik' in Mieth/Compagnoni (eds.), *Ethik im Kontext des Glaubens*, p.70; Korff, *Theologische Ethik*, p.31.

26. Auer, 'Tendenzen heutiger theologischer Ethik' in Bitter/Müller (eds.), *Konturen heutiger Theologie*, p.323; Mieth, 'Norma Morale...', p.174. Cf. Fuchs, *Christian Ethics in a Secular Arena*, p.13.

27. Auer, 'Die Bedeutung...', p.50.

28. Cf. Auer, 'Tendenzen...', p.321, also *Autonome Moral*..., p.62.

29. Cf. Böckle, *Fundamental*..., p.63, also 'Theonome Autonomie...', pp. 26-7.

30. Cf. *Fundamental*..., pp. 63, 6.

31. Cf. Korff, *Theologische Ethik*, pp. 73, 76, also 38-9.

32. Böckle, *Fundamental*..., p.5.

33. Ibidem, p.6.

34. Ibidem, p.199.

35. Ibidem, pp. 62-3. He also says that an unconditional claim of the kind that is made in morality calls for an absolute point of reference as a ground (*verlangt als Grund einen absoluten Bezugspunkt*), Cf. ibidem, p.15.

36. Cf. Auer, 'Die Bedeutung...', p.34.

37. Cf. ibidem, p.52. Cf. Korff, op.cit., pp. 38-9.

38. Cf. Böckle, 'Theonome Autonomie...', pp. 25-6.

39. Cf. Auer, 'Autonome Moral und christlicher Glaube', *Katechetische Blätter* 102 (1977), pp. 62-3; idem, Autonome Moral..., p.173.

40. Cf. Korff, op.cit., p.73.

41. Maclagan, *The Theological Frontier of Ethics*, pp. 68-9.

42. Cf. *Summa Theologiae*, I-II, q.91.

43. Ibidem, q.93, a.1.

44. Ibidem, q.93, a.4, ad 1.

45. Ibidem, q.91, a.2.

46. Ibidem, q.94, a.2; q.91, a.2; q.21, a.1.

47. Cf. Korff, op.cit., pp. 73, 80; Auer, 'Autonome Moral...', pp. 62-64; idem, 'Ein Modell theologisch-ethischer Argumentation: "Autonome Moral"' in Auer/Biesinger/Gutschera (eds.), *Moralerziehung im Religionsunterricht*, pp. 46ff.

48. Cf. Korff, op.cit., pp. 34, 78, 80; Auer, *Autonome Moral . . .* , p. 189.
49. Böckle, *Fundamental . . .* , pp. 62, 63, 192; Korff, op.cit., p.81.
50. Auer, 'Die ethische Relevanz der Botschaft Jesu' in Auer/Biesinger/Gutschera (eds.), p.89; Schüller, 'Sittliche Forderung . . .', pp. 18, 19, 26; Böckle, *Fundamental . . .* , p.206.
51. Cf. Auer, 'Ein Modell . . .', p.47; idem, 'Die ethische Relevanz . . .', pp. 75, 79, 83, 90.
52. Cf. Finnis, *Natural Law and Natural Rights*, Clarendon, Oxford, 1980, pp. 388, 410 for some of the issues raised here. Cf. Mac Intyre, *After Virtue*, pp. 51ff.
53. Cf. Mackey, *The Problems of Religious Faith*, p.262.
54. Cf. *Summa Theol.*, I-II, q.I, aa.4-5; q.2, a.8; q.91, a.3; q.94, a.2, a.6. Cf. I, q.44, a.4, ad 3. Cf. Auer, 'Die Bedeutung . . .'; idem, *Autonome Moral . . .* , p.25; idem, 'Autonome Moral . . .', p.61; Korff, op.cit., pp. 21-2, 83, 122; Böckle, *Fundamental . . .* , pp. 61, 184, 204, 221, 233-5; Schüller, 'Sittliche Forderung . . .', p.18; idem, 'Dezisionismus, Moralität, Glaube an Gott', *Gregorianum* 59 (1978), p.493.
55. Some prominent Roman Catholics adopt quite different approaches to this nature-end-perfection approach. Cf. G.J. Hughes, *Authority in Morals* and E. McDonagh, *Gift and Call*. As already noted, Connery has pointed out that several Roman Catholics have, whether consciously or not, adopted a form of utilitarianism. Cf. ch.6, note 36 above.
56. Cf. D.A. Rees, 'The Ethics of Divine Commands', *Arist. Soc. Proc.* 57 (1956-7), pp. 90, 91; A.C. Ewing, 'the Autonomy of Ethics' in I. Ramsey (ed.), *Prospect for Metaphysics*, Allen and Unwin, London, 1961, pp. 43-4; I. Ramsey, *Freedom and Immortality*, pp. 39ff.; H.D. Lewis, 'The Voice of Conscience and the Voice of God', in I. Ramsey (ed.), *Christian Ethics and Contemporary Philosophy*, pp. 178ff.; Peter R. Baelz, *Christian Theology and Metaphysics*, Epworth, London, pp. 128ff.; Keith Ward, *Ethics and Christianity*, Allen and Unwin, London, 1970; idem, *The Divine Image*, S.P.C.K., London, 1976.
57. Cf. Maclagan, *The Theological Frontier . . .* , p.53: 'This duty is moral duty, of course, only inasmuch as a man regards himself as categorically required to act in a certain way . . . he will be trying to explain why the particular thing in question is what he "absolutely must" do.' Cf. however the important remarks of Anscombe on 'obligation' in 'Modern Moral Philosophy', *Philosophy* 33 (1958), pp. 1ff.
58. Cf. Auer, 'Die Autonomie des Sittlichen nach Thomas von Aquin' in Demmer/Schüller (eds.), *Christlich Glauben und Handeln*, pp. 31-54; Böckle, 'Theonome Rationalität als Prinzip der Normbegründung bei Thomas von Aquin und Gabriel Vazquez' in *L'Agire Morale: Tommaso d'Aquino nel suo settimo centenario* (Atti del Congresso Internazionale V), Edizioni Domenicane Italiane, Napoli, 1974, pp. 213-27; Schüller, 'Die Sittliche Forderung . . .', pp. 5-37.
59. Cf. J. de Finance, *Ethica Generalis*, Gregorian Univ. Press, 3rd edn., Rome, 1966, p.159: 'Concludamus ergo necessitatem faciendi bonum fluere ex ipsa ratione boni sicut necessitas vitandi contradictionem ex ipsa ratione entis fluit.' He goes on to say: 'obligatio. . . . Deum requirit ut fundamentum ultimum ac rationem sufficientem propriam.' ibidem, p.167. De

Finance discusses the different positions on the relation of moral obligation and God, ibidem, pp. 155ff. Cf. idem, 'Morale e Religione', *Rassengna di Teologia* 15 (1974) 161-173; idem, 'Ricerca del Fondamento della Moralità, *Sapienza* 28 (1975) 288-311; Etienne Gilson, *The Spirit of Mediaeval Philosophy* (English trans. Downes), Sheed and Ward, London, 1950, pp. 362ff.; John C. Murray, *We Hold These Truths*, Sheed and Ward, London, 1960, p.329; A.D. Sertillanges, *Foundations of Thomistic Philosophy* (English trans. Anstruther), Templegate, Illinois, n.d., especially pp. 232ff.; A.P. D'Entrèves, *Natural Law*, Hutchinson, London, 1951, pp. 38ff.

60. Cf. Bernard Williams, *Morality*, p.85: 'The religious moralist, now, can see the general requirements as stemming from a particular relation, that to God, and this relation can be represented as one of love, or awe, or respect, or whatever words are found appropriate for this baffling semantic task.'

61. Cf. Rahner, 'Guilt — Responsibility — Punishment Within the View of Catholic Theology', *Theol. Invest.*, vol.6, pp. 203, 215.

62. Cf. I. Ramsey's review of Maclagan's *The Theological Frontier of Ethics*, *Mind* 77(1963), p.298: 'Maclagan's frontier incidents will only end when theology has a better understanding of its metaphysical language and also a better grip on and criterion for the use of its models. . . . On this frontier with ethics theology for the most part has not even begun to realise its complex logic.'

63. Cf. G.F. Wood, *A Defence of Theological Ethics*, C.U.P., Cambridge, 1966, p.101.

64. I. Ramsey, review of Maclagan, *Mind*, p.297.

65. Fuchs, *Human Values* . . . , p.161.

66. Ibidem, p.160.

67. Cf. ibidem, pp. 153-60.

68. Cf. ibidem, pp. 126, 130, 132.

69. Ibidem, p.123.

70. Cf. Fuchs, 'Autonome Moral und Glaubensethik', in Mieth/Compagnoni (eds.), pp. 58-9.

71. Cf. Fuchs, *Human Values*, p.132.

72. Rahner, 'Guilt — Responsibility — Punishment . . .', in *Theol. Invest.*, vol.6, p.215.

73. Ibidem, p.203.

74. Rahner, 'Theology of Freedom', ibidem, p.179. Cf. 'The Concept of Mystery in Catholic Theology', ibidem, vol.4, pp. 49ff.; 'The Experience of God Today', ibidem, vol.11, pp. 156, 158, 160.

75. 'Guilt and its Remission: The Borderland Between Theology and Psychotherapy', ibidem, vol.2, pp.269-73.

76. Cf. 'Theology of Freedom', ibidem, vol.6, p.181.

77. Ibidem, p.182.

78. Rahner, 'On the Theology of Freedom', in J.C. Murray (ed.), *Freedom and Man*, Kennedy, New York, 1965, p.204.

79. Cf. Rahner, 'Reflections on the Unity of the Love of Neighbour and the Love of God', in *Theol. Invest.*, vol.6, p.247.

80. Ibidem.

81. Cf. Ibidem, p.242.

82. Böckle, at times, adopts this pattern also. Cf. *Funadmental* . . . , p.228 where he approves Fuchs's approach.
83. Cf. Fuchs, *Human Values*, p.153: '[Morality] is the experience of an inner tendency and direction towards an absolute which expresses itself as the *dictamen conscientiae*. For confrontation with an absolute, in conscience, is a confrontation with God.'
84. Cf. Rahner, 'Anonymous Christianity and the Missionary Task of the Church', *Theol. Invest.*, vol.12, pp. 161-78.
85. Cf. *Summa Theol.* I-II, q.2, a.8, c. and ad 3; ibid., q.4, a.7, ad 2.
86. Cf. J. de Finance, *Ethica Generalis*, pp.163ff.
87. Cf. a recent book on moral theology which has become popular in seminaries, C.H. Peschke, *Christian Ethics*. In many respects it is almost indistinguishable from the neo-Scholastic manual: 'Moral theology deals with those laws which result from man's obligation to orient all his activity toward the ultimate goal'. Cf. p.94. It refers to 'God's positively revealed commandments' (p.100) and says that 'The source of moral sanctions is God alone' (p.136). Cf. Kevin McNamara, *Sacrament of Salvation: Studies in the Mystery of Christ and the Church*, The Talbot Press, Dublin, 1977, p.59: he refers to God as giving external precepts, to the church as the teacher of the external precepts of Christ, and to the Spirit as lending his authority to a system of external precepts.

Conclusion
(pp. 197-208)
1. Häring, *Free and Faithful in Christ*, vol.1, p.26, note 12.
2. Cf. McDonagh, *Invitation and Response*, p.25; Häring, *Free and Faithful*, p.391; Böckle, *Fundamental* . . . , p.156; Auer, *Autonome Moral und christlicher Glaube*, pp. 92, 99; J. Burtchaell, *Living With Grace*, Sheed and Ward, London, 1973, pp. 53ff.
3. Cf. Peschke, ch.7, note 87 above.
4. Cf. Auer, 'Die Bedeutung des Christlichen bei der Normfindung', in J. Sauer, *Normen im Konflikt*, p.34.

Index

reward, merit, in neo-Scholastic thought,
11,14
Richards, D.A.J., 162, 175
Ricoeur, Paul, 118, 181
Rigali, Norbert, 62, 146, 153, 173
Robinson, John, 181, 182
Rotter, Hans, 60, 63, 156

sanctions, in neo-Scholastic thought, 11
Schillebeeckx, E., 48
Schnackenburg, Rudolf, 16, 78
Schüller, Bruno, 47, 54, 56, 79-81, 110, 172
on agape, 147, 154, 168
on moral theology, 181-3
Schürmann, Heinz, 57-9, 100
Scriptures see Bible
Scruton, R., 118
Second Vatican Council, 17, 39, 55, 69-70,
74
self-awareness, 61, 122, 129-31
self-sacrifice, 167
Sermon on the Mount, 52, 88, 106, 141,
167, 168
Simon, R., 48,
Simpson, Michael, 61, 121, 125, 130, 180
specificity see christian morality
Spicq, C., 16
Stoeckle, Bernard, 56, 100, 123, 146, 152,
156, 159
Strawson, P.F., 166
Suarez, F., 180
suffering, philosophy of, 130

suicide, 156
supernatural morality, 12, 19, 20, 52-3
and natural morality, 21, 25, 26-7, 31

theology, manuals of, 9, 10, 14, 16
Thils, G., 19, 23
Tillman, Fritz, 28-30
transcendence, 193
Twiss, S., 142

universalisation of moral rules, 144-5,
167, 173-4
Urmson, J.O., 167, 170
utilitarianism and agape, 160-1

values, 60, 70, 83, 118, 127, 132, 207
Van der Marck, W., 48
Van Ouwerkerk, Conrad, 48, 181, 247
Vatican I see First Vatican Council
Vatican II see Second Vatican Council
virginity, in Christian morality, 106, 130,
167
virtues, morality of, 25, 99, 101, 133
Von Balthasar, Hans, see Balthasar, Hans
von

Wach, J., 116
Warnock, G.H., 124
welfare in moral systems, 123-4, 142, 148,
155
will of God see morality
Williams, Bernard, 124
Wood, G.F., 190